ALL QUIET ON THE HOOLIGAN FRONT

TO: Andrew
Have a great birthday
Lots of Love
from: Mum & Dad.
x x x x

ALL QUIET ON THE HOOLIGAN FRONT

Eight Years that Shook Football

COLIN WARD
Author of the best-selling
Steaming In

MAINSTREAM
PUBLISHING

EDINBURGH AND LONDON

First published in Great Britain in 1996 by
MAINSTREAM PUBLISHING COMPANY (EDINBURGH) LTD
7 Albany Street
Edinburgh EH1 3UG

ISBN 1 85158 914 7

A catalogue record for this book is available from the British Library

Typeset in Times New Roman
Printed and bound in Great Britain by Butler and Tanner Ltd, Frome

CONTENTS

INTRODUCTION

In the beginning it was the people's game and through the years it became known as the beautiful game. It was still the game *of* the people *for* the people. Despite life changing, the game of football didn't change for those who watched from their concrete terrace. The same terrace that was there when young men marched away for King and country in 1914 and 1939 was intact and waiting for the lucky ones who returned.

Football looked at change with wary eyes. Even TV, which had revolutionised American sport, was held at arm's length as British football refused to embrace it. Prime Ministers, along with stadium disasters, came and went but football soldiered on and, after brief outpourings of angst, the sport declared itself clean and ready to go on.

Then came the ubiquitous hooligan and his desire to confront his tribalistic issues on the concrete terrace which he claimed as his own. Suddenly the pimply hooligan forced football to look inward for the first time. After the Hillsborough disaster, caused not by hooliganism but by football's political desire to react to hooliganism by erecting unforgiving steel cages which became coffins, the politicians stepped in and forced change on football: a change so great that it would touch the heart and soul of the game.

At the same time, one man saw the power of football to project his vision of a nation of armchair satellite viewers. Football needed the money to create the new era, so got into bed with Rupert Murdoch. The greedy fiddling directors of yesteryear with large back pockets were replaced by the big bang marketing ethos of corporate America.

The beautiful game became the corporate raider's 90 minutes and this *force majeure* swept away the collective history of over a century. Somewhere amongst this roller-coaster ride the hooligan went out of fashion, to be replaced by the sniper in the press-box. Stand-up fisticuffs were usurped by boardroom pugilism where the only rule was that there were no rules. As the love of money became all embracing, football's march became relentless. In this climate the spirit of what went before was forgotten as profit became the only motivation for loving the game.

At the time of Hillsborough, Arsenal were enjoying a great renaissance under the watchful eye of George Graham, who swept away the caveats at Highbury in much the same way as Murdoch did the arrogant posturing of the BBC who, for decades, had paid peanuts for the greatest spectacle on earth. The journey of Arsenal fans mirrored the pilgrimage of football with its twists and turns and myriad adventures. While football seemed to have licence to print money it started to look closely at cash exchanges which were ingrained in the football psyche, the only reason many unscrupulous businessmen entered the game in the first place, but the only guilty party they could find was the saviour of Arsenal, George Graham.

The story of terrace to seat, of passion to plastic, happened so fast that many fans never realised the enormity of the consequences. It happened so fast that nobody had a chance to mourn the passing of the beautiful game or got the chance to man the ramparts to ensure someone was left to defend football from itself. Who would defend it when the money men moved on to the next fast buck and the fans who had enjoyed standing getting wet for years were priced out of their love affair?

1

FAREWELL MY LOVELY

There is a picture of a packed Northbank at Highbury celebrating a goal hanging on the wall of a record company executive. It's an old picture, not in years, but in terms of the era it represents. When he gets a real bastard recording artist on the telephone he stares at the picture while agreeing with the pig at the end of the line. He looks into the eyes of the people and he sees the joy and spontaneity that the big terrace family used to evoke, everybody as one, laughing, hugging, arms aloft as one person. This is ours, this is real, this will never go away. The moment of joy when that goal goes in lasts for a second. In reality the emotional ties for those who stood on their own particular lump of concrete terrace will last them for ever. This picture looks as old as the pictures of the young men of northern France of 1916 because he got one of his friends to do it in a sepia style. That picture is old, he tells people who enter his office. It represents a time gone by. He tells everybody who listens about what feelings we had and how it will never come back. He uses terms of affection and the word 'we' to describe people in the picture as if he knew them all personally, because he did. He knew their fears, thoughts and aspirations because they were the same as his and he could really empathise with that.

Not that he can any more, now that the money men have turned football into a glitzy merry-go-round. And he talks about the moment the cheering died and how grown men stood and sang together for the last time – the day the music died. It was a scene repeated all over the country as the Kop, Stretford End, Kippax and other famous terrace names were demolished to make way for a safer, sanitised form of football spectating. Grown men cried crocodile tears while bulldozers moved in and took the roof off their beloved Northbank, Highbury. With the bulldozers came the merchandising and the fashioning of an army of erstwhile hooligans. Now they can sit with their designer shirts and branded pretzels, then cheer when prompted to by the electronic scoreboard, and the loudest sound in the stadiums is that of the cash register. And while the record company executive knows the clock can't be turned back, he isn't sure about the price of progress. But the man on the satellite TV tells him it's progress, so you'd better believe it . . .

Harry didn't move with the times. He didn't care about all-seater stadiums because he was punching people out from seats long before they'd knocked down the terraces. 'Listen mate, after we had lost 6–2 at home to Man U in the League Cup, I rabbit-punched this Manc bastard and sent him spiralling down the steps, then a few of us gave him a kicking. Shitbag shouldn't have been in the east stand.' Harry had a funny way of looking at people, but it wasn't my job to tell him. Nobody wanted to be seen looking at Harry's eyes. Harry hadn't seen them in the mirror himself for a long time. Quite what he did see when he looked was pure speculation. Harry's Saturday consisted of a line of charlie (cocaine to send him across the road to punch some hapless rival fan) then some after-match billie (speed) and loads of lager in the evening to keep him loud and on form. Whatever you do, don't make eye contact with Harry or else he will talk to you all night, I was told. Sound advice that I once (but only once) ignored at my peril. Harry was too crazy for me so I was always deep in conversation and just hoped that somebody else would be mug enough to get their earhole chewed off.

One night Harry had run through his usual repertoire of fights where we 'dun 'em, run 'em and stabbed 'em' with a guy who didn't know how to avoid conversation with Harry. Attempting to change the conversation, he then remarked that Harry's eyes looked as if they were bloodshot. (Wrong move, my old mate; bet you find another pub to drink in after the match next time!) 'What are you trying to say, eh? That I'm on drugs? Okay, so I like a puff and a bit of billie but I'm no junkie. You're taking the piss . . . go on, clear off before I stripe you,' and he said it two inches from the guy's face at full volume while everybody else looked at the floor. Harry wanted Arsenal to be known as 'the guvnors' with Harry chief guvnor, although the reality was that there were old faces who commanded far more respect than Harry. Guys who had used their reputation and muscle to move on from the world of football hooliganism into bodyguarding and security. 'Nobody messes in our manor nowadays,' was Harry's line. 'We run West Ham everywhere,' but Harry couldn't run for the bus 90 per cent of the time as he was too far gone. Harry also suffered from acute paranoia and imagined that people were after him. (He even heard I was after him once.) Harry should have gone out with the Bay City Rollers but there were people like him at every ground. Forty-somethings with fading tattoos, limited vocabulary and an overdeveloped sense of their place in the respect table of honour. The reality was that the guys who Harry thought he had run had sold him a line of charlie the previous evening.

Sitting in front of me in the east stand was a middle-aged man. Every Saturday he went through his ritual. Five minutes before half-time he indulged himself in his little ceremony as he nipped out for a drink, returning five minutes into the second half. Things were grim at Highbury in those days with a bad team. As summer drifted into autumn to the harsh chill of winter, only the diehards could muster any enthusiasm. The tunnel seemed to go on for ever with no light at the end of it. As the results got worse, so did the man's drinking. Five minutes got to ten, then fifteen either side of the break. Once he returned with ten minutes to go in the match, saw Arsenal concede another goal, then abruptly left. The last time I spoke to him he was drinking out of a hip flask early on in the game. He turned to me as Arsenal conceded an early goal, offering me a drink with the words: 'Watching Arsenal is enough to drive a man to drink.' One day he left the seat in front after ten minutes of the first half and never returned.

2

A GLORY DAY AT THE NATIONAL
STADIUM

'Listen, lads,' said Tony Madden. 'The pub will be open for breakfast at 8 a.m., so I will meet you at 7.30 a.m. outside King's Cross then we can walk up from there together and get in. He is only letting local faces in because he doesn't want to get a tug off the Old Bill.'

These were heady days for Arsenal fans as everybody sensed that a new era was about to come about. Sure, there had been false dawns before and, as for all football fans, hope springs eternal, but a new mood was amongst us and everybody loves to be there at the christening. This weekend we would be playing the mighty Liverpool at Wembley in the Littlewoods Cup final, a team synonymous with success and, for me, with the most disgusting fans in the country. Arsenal's new manager George Graham (nicknamed Gorgeous George because of his suave good looks and iron-willed discipline) had, in a short space of time, transformed Arsenal from an easy touch into a major force. This would be the first big test and we were taking the strain and big match nerves as only we could. Friday afternoons at work just before a big match were hell. I have never had one where the whole afternoon wasn't just a blur and work was pushed around my desk while the clock moved ever slower until 5 p.m. To make matters worse there was a whole Saturday to endure, as the match had been switched to a Sunday afternoon 4 p.m. kick-off, but at least you could spend the Saturday afternoon telephoning friends to confirm for the umpteenth time that you would indeed be at the rendezvous point, lager in hand.

This was our first big cup final since Brussels, so to a man all the old faces were at the 7.30 a.m. Sunday muster at King's Cross. Even a lukewarm Burger King with dank fries for breakfast tastes good when the excitement levels are this high. I had kissed my fiancée goodbye just over an hour previously and promised her that should Arsenal win I would propose. The standing joke amongst my friends was that Arsenal would never win the League Cup (renamed the Littlewoods after a benevolent sponsor) and I would never get married. The walk up the Caledonian Road past the mixture of drunks, pimps, prostitutes and down-and-outs who used to frequent the surrounding streets makes for an interesting introduction to any day, let alone a cup final day. All human life was there but unsure of which stage of its evolution it was in. The compulsory lurch from the drunk offering sherry was received by TC. As a group we have always looked upon moments like this as a lucky talisman, a sign of good luck, so if it doesn't happen immediately then we walk back around the block until it does happen.

'You lot are bloody loony,' my father used to say. 'There's something wrong with you. You can't go drinking this early in the morning.'

'Atmosphere, Dad.'

'Atmosphere rubbish, it's just an excuse to go drinking with your deadbeat friends.'

'I didn't realise you had such a high opinion of my friends, Dad.'

With this in mind, and much to my father's disgust, I had taken my younger brother along. So far his education in life had consisted of a few drunken sorties with the Essex oiks who inhabit the money market which he worked in. I promised to take him to meet some real drinkers. Up the hill from King's Cross we walked with only talk of football crossing our lips. It was like a school reunion with people coming out of the woodwork with tales of derring-do about how they had obtained tickets. Mick was there along with Tommy. Mick was a drinking legend who could fall asleep standing up and still not spill his pint. As I had brought my younger brother along I took great pleasure in telling the story about how Mick had taken his brother drinking one Christmas Eve and got him blind drunk. When his younger brother vomited the contents of the evening's drink on the pub floor, Mick had slapped him for wasting good drink. To Mick, meeting this early constituted a proper drink and all this handshaking and embracing outside the station was a waste of valuable drinking time. With kick-off still nine hours away, I imagined that the atmosphere at the pub would be subdued with bacon sandwiches and orange juice being drunk.

Round the back of the pub we crept, like agents from a John Le Carré novel doing a recce for a big Berlin spy exchange. A bang on the back door and in we crept through the kitchen, to be met by a wall of heat and red-and-white bedecked Arsenal fans. The disco was blaring, moisture from all the sweaty bodies was running down the walls and the DJ was leading the chorus of Arsenal, Arsenal, Arsenal. People were three deep at the bar and four barmaids were serving lager for all they were worth and listening to the corniest chat-up lines in London. It was only 7.45 a.m., but people had either been at it all night or were very early risers. It transpired that the pub had opened at 6.30 a.m. and some very serious drinkers had taken occupancy. Mick, who felt that his position as number one in the serious drinkers' league had been usurped, promptly sank his first lager in five seconds.

The pub was heaving, the atmosphere was electric and the collective belief was that Arsenal's invincibility would carry us to victory. The DJ put on the victory march and to a man everybody sung it. 'March on, March on, March on to Victory.'

I only knew the first line, as did most people, but we sang together. If it is possible to get intoxicated without drinking then this would have been the moment. I could have walked across hot coals, as could everybody else in that room. We knew that our emotions would go through the wringer in eight hours' time so now we would bask in the anticipation of our forthcoming glory. Too many of us had seen it all before, but somehow this seemed different. We had a player called Charlie Nicholas who was a big-game player, a player who could turn a match with one piece of skill, but more than that we actually had a manager who inspired confidence in us. It didn't matter that we had lost our previous two matches: the manager said he believed we had played well, so if he believed it so did we. Not only that, we were The Arsenal and our time had come. Liverpool had seen the glory, but thanks to their fans we would not be going into Europe should we win the match, as the Heysel stadium disaster had resulted in an indefinite ban on English clubs from European competition.

By 9.30 a.m., the whole pub was heaving, so people spilled out on to the streets. The landlord was appalled. 'Licensing laws, lads, this pub doesn't open until 12 o'clock.' It was useless trying to speak to people as the sun had come out and the drink had overcome any ability to reason, plus I could not see the police attempting to shut this pub without starting a mini riot and most of the police would probably be earmarked for duty at Wembley later in the day.

Back inside the music played on, led by the redoubtable DJ. Gary Glitter sang 'Come on, come on, do you wanna be in my gang?' OH YEAH, we shouted together. We were in the greatest, most formidable, gang in Europe. We drank to that. Loads more lovely lagers darlin'! Frank, whose sobriquet is Pisshead Frank, was well on form and needless to say living up to his name with the rest of us imitating him. Frank is an interesting character (as long as you're not picking up his bar tab) who manages to get drunk without ever seeming to buy a drink. Frank has modelled his life on two Hollywood blockbusters, *The Deer Hunter* and *One Flew Over The Cuckoo's Nest*. Consequently, on occasions like this he staggers around the pub like Jack

Nicholson as R.P. McMurphy, holding an imaginary bullet as Robert de Niro did, saying 'this is this'. Unfortunately he usually has a glass in his hand and as he slurs it sounds like 'this is piss'. I actually saw him get thrown out of a pub by a landlord once because he thought he was insulting his beer. At times like this I always dig out my silk scarf, *circa* 1971, as it brings me luck. It doesn't matter that this scarf has seen more Cup final defeats than victories; I, like nearly every football fan, have a superstitious ritual which is guaranteed to bring victory.

While the music played we sang and danced, for we knew that our time had come. Only a couple of weeks previously we had vanquished our greatest rivals and most hated enemy, Tottenham Hotspur, in one of the greatest semi-final comebacks in recent years. Three times we were behind but the unfailing spirit had manifested itself in a last-minute goal. After it was all over we had celebrated in their back yard.

Someone came up to me and said that I had taken a photograph of him and his mate at the 1979 FA Cup final. Sure enough I recognised his face. I had looked at his picture hundreds of times since and wondered if I would ever see him again. TC was doing his favourite trick and kissing all the girls as well as the men. Dave Wingate, who always acts serenely and keeps his thoughts and nerves in check, was up on the seats and dancing to Kool and the Gang's 'Celebrate'. People were walking holding their fists clenched and shouting 'Yeah,' just like they'd clinched a big-money deal. The communication between us was as profound as any between lovers. Actually, it's more so, because there is no need for reciprocation as we all love the same thing, but the thing we love is so big that we can all have some with no jealousy. This love of ours demands no requital or pledges of affection, yet we give our love unconditionally and pledge our allegiance for life. Kick-off was still five hours away, yet the proximity of the match had heightened our powers of consciousness so every sip of lager tasted like the nectar of the gods. Meanwhile the adrenalin flow enabled us to drink more than we would be able to under other less exciting circumstances.

At 12 o'clock the landlord opened the doors and everybody spilled out. With gaps appearing in the pub the frenetic atmosphere dissipated slightly, but the drinking rose, as did the music. Now the locals were coming out of their houses to applaud us. We obliged with a conga, the lager got spilt, and Mick scowled!

'Those scouse scumbags won't be having none of this. They're probably just starting their first pint,' said Steve Ashford, the thinking man's cynic and Arsenal through and through. I maintain that if someone cut off his head the word 'Arsenal' would run through him like Brighton Rock. I am sure that other football fans do celebrate like this, but to us, we were the only ones who did. The Liverpool fans, they had seen it all before, they had won everything. Coming to Wembley was blasé, old hat to them. Well, I have never lost the buzz that a walk up Olympic Way gives me; the first sight of the long road up to the stadium has never failed to make my knees go weak. When I lose the goosebumps on my neck when I glimpse the twin towers, first from the train, and then as I emerge from the underground walkway, then I will call it a day. Today, with two hours to go to kick-off and nine miles from Wembley, I already had the collywobbles inside. I wanted to see us win but more than anything I wanted to wish away the next five hours and wake up with Arsenal having won the cup. If I could avoid the gut wrenching, teeth grinding and feeling of sickness when we go a goal behind or (the unthinkable) lose, then I would. I would be going to the black hole of emotions and beyond, then look back and say it was the greatest day of my life, and I had paid good money for it. Just waiting for the postman to arrive with the ticket is hell incarnate.

I needed the loo. It is a fact of a football spectator's life that one often hears some of the strangest stories standing next to a complete stranger in front of a urinal. It is definitely a football fan's trait to talk to the person at the urinal next to you. Doing it in any other toilet in Britain would probably result in a punch in the teeth, but football fans talk to anybody who stands next to them. This guy was definitely the worse for wear, but I wondered how I looked. (It was like the scene in the film *Papillon* when the guy looks at Papillon and asks him how he looks. The guy is falling to pieces after two years in solitary but Papillon tells him: '. . . you look great.') Yeah, we both looked great.

'You know there's a slasher crew coming down to do our firm.'

'Who told you?' I asked.

'They done a little Chelsea firm at Euston last Saturday.'

'Really?'

'Yeah, they ambushed 'em in the road that runs between the station. Chelsea ran like dogs but they caught one and kicked him to the floor, then they chased the others for a few hundred yards. When they couldn't catch them they came back and gave him a real stanley job. Noughts and crosses all over his back. Said they were going to do a few Gooners at Wembley.'

I have heard horror stories like that on many occasions about Liverpool fans' use of their favourite slashing weapon – the Stanley knife. 'Hello, cockney, have you met my friend Stanley?' are the words no London fan wants to hear when he meets a group of scousers, yet despite this I informed my soothsayer urinal friend that there were too many of us for them to threaten us. His parting shot should have been haunting, but was forgettable: 'Sure, but don't let the bastards catch you alone.'

I left the toilet and started thinking about getting to the ground. Two double-decker buses had been arranged to take people to Wembley. I didn't fancy that and was seconded by my brother to go in a minibus with a group of friends, people one has never met before but drinking mates for the day and someone to reminisce with at future meetings. The journey to the ground would be interesting as a new law had been passed which forbade the drinking of alcohol on transport taking football fans to matches. A stupid catch-all law passed in haste by a politician who saw football as an easy way to posture and look tough, a cheap quick way to try to win votes, and as stupid laws go this one was ignored. I had a more pressing problem in the shape of an acute prolapsed disc and could not sit down for any length of time, so I lay on the floor of the minibus while everybody spilt their beer over me. I had a nice new leather jacket on which was suitably beer-stained by the time I got to Wembley, although at the time I didn't care about such trivialities. More pressing was the need to be able to drink while lying down.

As we approached Wembley the back doors of the minibus were opened and all and sundry were treated to a rendition of 'The Famous Arsenal', with one young guy hanging out the back like a circus monkey.

At a set of traffic lights a group of about 30 scousers stood malignantly. Perhaps it was the slasher gang. I had retold the story, probably embellishing it a bit with the retelling. 'Oi,' our circus monkey shouted. 'Are you the wankey Toxteth slasher gang? Or are you just the run-of-the-mill horrible thieving scouse bastards? Either way you're about to lose.' With that the van sped off, with our circus monkey gesticulating that he thought they were wankers. I had no doubt that this spirit of friendship and camaraderie was being repeated at all junctions leading to Wembley. Occasionally it would lead to fisticuffs, but with the police being out in force nobody wanted to get arrested before and miss the match.

'Is it always like this?' Simon asked me.

'No, this is as good as it gets. It's downhill all the way from here as expectation turns into reality,' I replied. He looked at me as younger people do when they are unsure of the relevance of the comment and think you are in the early throes of senile dementia.

I have never been to Wembley and not stopped to admire the 'The End is Nigh' brigade. They stand there imploring us to repent our sins before Lord Jesus because the Lord is coming. And if I had a pound for every time the reply was: 'Well, if he does come then we'll sign him up.' But not everybody is polite. Sometimes they get beer thrown on them, yet they stand there with their unshakeable belief that the end is nigh. Every time I go back to Wembley their faces look the same – tired, weary, caused by worrying too much about an event that may or may not happen. Even my father reckoned that the worst gutter drunk has more going for him than the sad-looking Wembley God Squad. Yet, in a way, I suppose they are right, because in a couple of hours' time, after 90 minutes of excruciating excitement, 50 per cent of the crowd will feel that the end has indeed come. It is another purely English tradition; I have never seen the God Squad at any European match.

The walk up Olympic Way was like a Herb Alpert record, with every step hitting an empty beer can and creating a sound which enhanced the songs we were singing.

So to the final hurdle, actually getting in the ground. Just before we got in we pulled a good scam right under the noses of the police. A few young guys were milling around the entrance with no tickets. Wembley is an old ground with expandable metal grills so these guys had an idea to use physical strength to expand the metal grills and squeeze through the gap. We created a diversion by doing our best barber shop singing, and while all eyes were upon us the group did it and all five of them sneaked in. Richard Attenborough in *The Great Escape* would have been proud of us. Good deed of the day over and so to our seats. My father was already in position.

Arsenal were away to Luton in the third round of the FA Cup. The temperature was just above freezing with snow lying everywhere and around 15 of us got in the Luton members' bar, thanks to a steward we knew, around 10.45 a.m. I had just finished a book on the Russian liberation of Berlin, so the part where they drank vodka while dancing to Tchaikovsky outside the Reichstag *touched a nerve. I figured that the Russians had been to Dante's inferno and back to take Berlin, and we would take our emotions close to the edge of hell before we saw Wembley's twin towers and met the God Squad, so we decided to toast the third round of the FA Cup every season with a vodka salute. Whilst our single-glass salute has become a regular fixture the Luton initiation ceremony got a bit carried away. By the time we left the bar to the cries of* prost *Luton Town FC's vodka stocks were seriously depleted. The government, in another knee-jerk reaction to a football-related violent incident, had recently made it an offence to enter a ground while drunk. I bet that our breath was flammable at 20 paces. As we got near the turnstiles we all pretended to be sober, but kept giggling like schoolboys. One officer asked TC if he'd been drinking. 'Just a couple, occifer,' and we all burst out laughing, but this officer spared us all with a stern lecture about what he could do if he wanted.*

'Been drinking, have you? Look at the state of you. I get you the best seats in the house and you turn up like Dean Martin. And if you start singing "Little Old Wine Drinker Me", I'll belt you.'

Not for my father the niceties of telling me I looked great.

'And, not just satisfied with getting yourself in a mess, you take young Simon out and get him plastered.'

No time for excuses or more parental lectures as the match was under way. Despite the fact that I had been at it for so long, I didn't feel too bad. To hell with how the rest of the breakfast club felt, my metabolism means that I sober up really quickly. The game was even and we all cheered madly, aided by the fact that the drink was acting as a massive upper. To our left where the Arsenal fans were ensconced was a cacophony of noise and colour.

However, an error in defence, a cross and the ball was in the back of the net. Not only that but the unimaginable had happened. One of the greatest truisms in modern English football was staring us right in the face. Ian Rush, a goalscoring legend for Liverpool, held this unique record. Every time he had scored for Liverpool they had never been on the losing side. This had been going on now for over 100 matches. I looked at my father and the same thought crossed our minds, and at the same time it would have been going through the mind of every Arsenal fan in that stadium. If people could receive messages by telepathy then 48,000 messages would have hit the wall at the same time: when Ian Rush scores Liverpool never lose! Brian Moore, the ITV commentator, was saying exactly that on the live TV transmission. This was it, the dream was dead. Now we had another 70 minutes of torture followed by weeks and months of torment while crowing scousers gave smug grins which said 'I told you so'. This is the moment when the drink becomes a massive downer, enough to make you think about joining Alcoholics Anonymous. During the French occupation of Vietnam the soldiers used to suffer from a spiritual disease called *la cafard*. Its symptoms of occasional fits of depression combined with an unconquerable fatigue would sum up how I would be for the next few weeks after we had lost.

However, the match didn't develop like that and Arsenal pushed and probed. Suddenly it was Arsenal who were calling the shots and finding the space. If our players didn't believe the match was already lost then why should I have negative thoughts? Then Davis, our slick midfield player, surged into space and put in a shot but it came off the post. I can't take this; why me? Why couldn't it have gone in? Deep breaths to weather the feeling of helplessness. The tide was flowing our way because of the force of our will. We were turning the match but we couldn't get the ball in the net. Come on You Reds. It isn't easy to sing when your stomach is churning up from the inside like a recalcitrant cement mixer, but you will your vocal chords to react to sing. Another run forward by our tireless right back,

Anderson, another shot off the post. I don't believe it, but before the guts can churn one more time the ball is in the net. Whoosh. Yes. Charlie Nicholas.

Charlie Charlie! Charlie Charlie!

The man next to me who hated jocks, wops and niggers two minutes ago, now loves the world; he even loves his wife. He loves me and he's dancing with me. It doesn't matter how often you think about how you are going to celebrate a goal – and all football fans think about this sublime moment – the actual moment lasts only a millisecond, but it's heaven. It is like the splitting of an atom. The actual splitting creates the power. Everything else is a corollary from the initial split. The hugging and the kissing is the release and reconciliation of the passion.

Half-time and the compulsory urine flowing out into the walkways all over your shoes. People urinate where they stand, or in sinks because they have been drinking since 7.00 a.m., while people have animated conversations and exchange banter (this is where the big knobs hang out). If you love Charlie Nicholas clap your hands, so 1,000 people start clapping together and some wee on themselves or the guy standing next to them because they are so keen to clap their hands, as they push and shove each other because the entrances and exits to the toilets are not big enough. This is our national stadium yet the drains can't cope with 50,000 people going to the toilet within a 15-minute period.

Having pee on your shoe is part and parcel of the day out. But nobody complains about getting peed on because moments like this are what dreams are made of. The money men and honoured guests don't see this because they are enclosed in their glass towers eating smoked salmon canapés with a Chablis 79. At 1–1 with the force of will on your side it doesn't matter. Nothing matters: the mortgage, the clapped-out car, the redundancy notice or the slasher gang waiting outside. Only football can replace reality and substitute it with something better which is often worse. For 48,000 Arsenal fans this wasn't the time to analyse. I was in these toilets in 1978 when we were getting murdered by Ipswich (although we were hanging on at 0–0) and nobody said a word to each other because the opposition had grasped the mettle. Today was different. There was laughter, backslapping and a shared knowledge that the drains were worse than last time we were here.

So the second half progressed; it's nip and tuck with us getting on top. Then George pulls his master plan. He starts to warm up Perry Groves. Now Perry is one of us because he charges around the pitch like a headless chicken giving his all, but he's fast, direct with it and he upsets defenders who hate lunatics running at them at speed. He plays the way we drink beer or we would play if we had been fortunate enough to be signed by The

21

Arsenal, so we love him. We love him so much we nicknamed him 'Son of Graham', and 'Tin Tin' because he looks like him. His popularity judged by the number of nicknames he has, as Oscar Wilde put it.

Perry comes on and immediately beats the full-back for speed down the line. Go Tin Tin! He's got his confidence so the next time he gets the ball he goes again, aiming at the line, and he goes past his man, will-o'-the-wisp. The cross is good and Charlie hits it, deflected. We all see the ball going in but it is like a slow-motion film. The goalie is straining to get the ball and it's moving so slowly. We're on our feet in the limbo between life and death. Just one more inch takes us to nirvana. The goalie's face changes from excruciating effort to the look of horror as he realises it has crossed the line. For one second 48,000 suffer the *petite mort* before the volcano erupts to signal the glory is ours as the ball eventually reaches the net. Celebrate isn't the correct word as the Arsenal fans around me erupt. Even my father leaps off his feet to join in. At that precise moment absolute disaster strikes as I get a shooting pain down my right leg and my back gives out. I stagger to the back of the seats and limp painfully down to the concrete concourse which runs under the stadium. I just need to lie down on my back for a few minutes and let the pain subside, but first I must find a concrete area which doesn't have puddles of wee on it. I don't mind a few beer stains on the old leather coat, but pee as well? Everyone will think I'm a Hells Angel.

Lying prostrate completely still in or around a football stadium is not an advisable activity as it tends to arouse the suspicions of the police. 'Okay, sonny, up you get or you'll get thrown out for drunk and disorderly.'

'Piss off, plod, my bloody back's in spasm.'

Expression changes from you're a nuisance to quick I've got a chance to do something useful. 'Don't move, son, I'll fetch the St John's Ambulance.'

Christ, I don't believe it. We all love the St John's Ambulance and they do a great job at all sporting venues, but they are all volunteers and there is nothing worse for someone who wants to be left alone than to be bothered by an unpaid volunteer. They usually have the zeal of a moonie and the hide of a rhinoceros, and my two friendly stretcher-bearers, one older and kindly looking with a younger helper, were no exception. Over they bounded with their fold-up stretcher and box of bandages. The glint in their eyes told me that I was about to endure the insufferable. After-match conversation with Harry looked fun by comparison.

'Okay, son, where's the pain?' one asks.

'I never knew I had so many dads.'

'Don't try to move, we'll have you in the ambulance and in hospital before the final whistle.'

'I don't want to go to hospital. I just want to be left alone for a couple of minutes.'

'Right then, let's have you up on your feet so we can see where the pain is.'

'Can't you just piss off and pretend you haven't seen me?'

And then the slightly older one of the two said the immortal words:

'Oh no, it's more than my job's worth, mate.'

They just couldn't understand why I started roaring with laughter, which sent sharp sciatic pain down my left side so the more I laughed the more my face screwed up with pain. The younger one quipped in: 'Well, we might not be able to produce miracle cures but we do produce lots of laughter.'

'Sod it. I'd rather have plod give me a hard time. Thanks, but no thanks guys.'

With that I stood up and limped back to my entrance and pretended to go back to my seat. The two of them gawped at me with a look which couldn't understand why I was refusing their offer of a lift to hospital. Obviously they had not had much to do that day. It's a pity the drain cleaners aren't so zealous, then there wouldn't be so much pee on the floor at the stadium.

A Manchester United fan got stabbed coming out of Seven Sisters station before they were due to play Spurs. He was rushed to hospital and was stitched up. He declared himself fit to watch football as he had a seat ticket so he discharged himself from the hospital. As he left the hospital and waited outside for a taxi he was speaking to the same two ambulancemen who had run him to the hospital, who got another call to return to the ground where another incident had taken place, so he jumped in the back and got a lift to the ground. When the ambulancemen got to the incident near the ground and opened the back doors the Manchester United fan got out. Standing there open-mouthed was the same police superintendent who had helped him into the ambulance not two hours previously. He thought he was seeing a ghost. The Manchester United fan was oblivious to the look on the policeman's face and was only interested in getting in to see the second half.

The rest of the match was a complete blur as I was in so much pain and I couldn't sit down at all, but the final whistle went and I cheered along with the rest. At moments like this I always feel a serene calm come over me as I have lived every kick and shot along with those players. My father was not impressed by my problem.

'Get yourself off home and lay off the booze.'

'I can't think of a better painkiller,' I said.

Off to a Tony Madden boozer just up the Caledonian Road where entry before the 7 p.m. legal opening is positively encouraged. No problem as long as pimps and drug pushers are your preferred company. 'Salt of the earth, mate. Someone's got to dispose of the black economy profits.'

So we reassembled in this pub and as each person entered we regaled each other with our own worst moment. When O'Leary nicked the ball off Rush's boot. The shot from Nichol that hit Steve Williams. Our clarity in remembering every last detail would fascinate any psychologist, especially as we had been suffering from *la cafard* from Ian Rush's goal until we equalised. And everybody who walked in said the same phrase.

'When Ian Rush scores Liverpool never lose!'

No matter how many times we said it we all burst out laughing. We even made it the password for everybody coming in the pub. When somebody pumped the juke-box, every song we sang had a line which somehow incorporated the magic phrase. We were happy, beyond reproach. Then around 7.30 p.m. a group of seven scousers walked in, but they didn't bother us, in fact their entry made for better pantomime. They took our banter in reasonably good humour, but they had no choice as we outnumbered them fifteen to one. However, one of them didn't and he perched himself by the juke-box and glared at every single one of us every time we dared to laugh. He had a tough-looking face, a type that looked tough because he had a few acne scars which made it seem as if it had seen its fair share of right handers. Unfortunately for him he was just drawing attention to himself and the more he glared the more we looked at him when we laughed. His eyes were pure hatred, and if looks could kill we'd have been stone dead.

'I'm gonna knock him out, just for fun, for a laugh, ha ha ha,' sang Mick to a record on the juke-box. 'No, let's really wind him up until he cracks,' I said, pulling Mick back. I walked over to the juke-box with everybody watching and put on some Tamla Motown. He stood there staring at me, proving how hard he was compared to us cockneys. I put my face right up to his until it was about two inches away, Harry style. 'When Rush scores Liverpool never lose,' then I walked away back to the bar.

Ian from Bristol was watching him closely. 'He was gonna go for you.'

'Well, he'd better have some more then,' I said. I shouted over to him. 'What happens when Ian Rush scores?' He ignored me but he wanted to kill me. No doubt if he could find a few more mates then he would. A couple of the other scousers challenged us to a game of pool for money and we obliged. When they potted the first ball the roar went up from everybody.

'Ian Rush has scored!' Then to a man every head turned towards the juke-box and roared at our friend. 'When Rushie scores Liverpool never lose, ha, ha, ha.' Nobody in our group of around 14 felt sorry for him because he was nasty. He wanted to do us all because we had won, yet all he was doing was making a rod for his own back. I said the famous phrase so many times that people thought I was a record stuck in the groove.

Tony Madden walked over to the juke-box as he had tired of a constant diet of Tamla. 'How's your sense of humour, bypass wack?' said Tony in a mock scouse accent. At last the silent nasty said something. 'Hang on,' said Tony, turning round to us, 'It talks as well as glares.' I thought that this was the moment when he'd overstep the mark and we'd give him a right kicking.

'You think you're clever, don't you?' he said to Tony. Tony paused for a second, put his hand on his head to imitate The Thinker, then held his head as if about to come out with some profound wisdom. 'Yup, I suppose we are,' he said in the mock accent.

'Well let me tell you this, cockney. You've had a good day out today.'

'Affirmative,' chipped in Tony before he could finish. The scouse continued with an edge developing in his voice.

'You've had a good day out today, but how many good days out have you had in Europe?'

'One, wack, but thanks to you lot we won't have too many more, will we, plank?' Within a second Tony had turned the scouse sneer into a gawp. Tony continued. 'You ain't clever enough or hard enough to perform the way you are so why don't you do us all a favour and go back to Liverpool before your bird sleeps with your brother.'

Our scouse friend realised that he was close to a beating so he left. His mates looked at us and shrugged their shoulders as if to say that his problem wasn't theirs. As he went out the door I opened it for him.

'See you, Rushie. See if you can score with King's Cross finest.'

'You're dead, shitbag,' he shouted back at me; then he was gone into the melting-pot of people that is King's Cross.

As I staggered the short distance back to the station it did cross my mind that our nasty friend might be lurking with the slasher gang, but my main aim after a good day and night was to put one foot in front of another. It doesn't matter how good the celebration was and how much fun you have, the hangover still feels as lousy the next day. When you finally arrive at work people expect you to be happy but you feel so bad that people can't understand why you aren't full of beans, as every form of laughter feels like a herd of buffalo stampeding inside your head. To make matters worse I fell asleep on the train and ended up in the sidings at the end of the line, getting woken up by a cleaner then paying a fortune to get a taxi home.

3

SUPER SCOOP

'Never let the truth get in the way of a good story.' Whether or not this is true of the press, this almost certainly applied to events in Stockholm in September 1989, and what a good story it was, especially for the undercover reporter working for *Today* newspaper. The events in Stockholm caused a reaction quite out of proportion to actual events. The Prime Minister of the day, Maggie Thatcher, even talked about banning the England football team from playing abroad!

Amongst all football fans, and especially Arsenal fans, there is a theory about the press which is probably completely prejudiced. They all indulge in too much pre-match hospitality then fail to appear for the second half of the matches, then write the match report using their cliché books and journalist notes from university. This would explain why they always seem to watch such a different game from the rest of us. It would also explain why Arsenal are boring and lucky while Manchester United are exciting, West Ham cultured and Wimbledon hard. The old story about the American pressman who stated that he only became a bastard when he sat in front of the typewriter rings true when you read some of the excesses perpetrated by the sports press over the years. All in the name of reporting a game of football.

For my own part I have allowed myself to take offence at some of the comments written about Arsenal. Seeing myself as a latter-day Captain Avenger I have even written to some sportswriters, threatening them with a smack in the mouth when I see them at the next match. Some of the sportswriters take me seriously enough to write back dissuading me from such a drastic course. All have replied in one shape or form. Jeff Powell, of *Daily Mail* fame, even researched one of my comments, got the wrong answer then wrote back gleefully saying I was wrong. Patrick Barclay, of *The Observer*, on receipt of one of my letters advised me to seek the solace of pretty girls. Part of my problem can be explained away by a secret wish to be a part of the sportswriting *cognoscenti*. It is the secret wish of every fan who watches a match, just as every sportswriter believes he is really the best manager the England football team never had.

Once, in my dim and distant youth, when Arsenal were enduring a particularly bad run of results and the press were really sticking the knife in, I made a hit list of journos that I wanted to sort out, then made an assault upon the press-box at Stamford Bridge, shouting out that so-and-so's mother was a whore. As the match was between Spurs and Chelsea my father, who was with me at the match, quite rightly commented, 'Well done, son. Not only will the press become more one-eyed about Arsenal, but can now comment rightfully that their fans have become deranged losers who didn't know which ground they were attending.'

I armed myself with some sound advice from my father: 'All you need to be a football journalist is the ability to start a sentence with "Notwithstanding", then be able to use the words inveigh, boring and predictable within the first three sentences. Your drinking habits will get you accepted and you can pick up the nuts and bolts as you go along.'

I used to read the reports from the tabloid journalists about the England fans which were at odds with the stories I heard as well as contradicting my own experiences. What all newspapers needed was an intelligent hooligan who was accepted by the main thugs, someone who knew a preposition from a malignant disposition and could bring the real stories to life. With Clive James not being affordable, I decided to put myself up for the job.

Prior to every England away game I would bombard tabloid and serious editors with a new angle as to why they should be employing me. I used to finish with 'of course I would want to be paid for this and I would expect you to cover my travelling plus out-of-pocket expenses, but my fees are very reasonable when you consider the enlightenment that your readers will achieve. A small price to pay, don't you think!' I even included my father's famous sentence in one letter. It began with 'Notwithstanding', but the rest of it was so unmemorable that it got even more 'thanks but no thanks' replies than I normally got.

Despite being armed with a conviction that I was the next sportswriting F. Scott Fitzgerald, I received more rejection notices than a tone deaf cabaret singer. However, the climax of the 1990 World Cup qualifying campaign was coming up and England only needed two points from two away games, Poland and Sweden, to be sure of qualifying. For some reason the game in Stockholm seemed to touch a raw nerve with everybody taking an interest in the England fans' ability to cause mayhem. At the time English clubs were on an indefinite ban from European competition. The Football

Association were lobbying hard for reinstatement as the crowd problems in England had decreased dramatically. (Crowd problems in Europe had risen at the same time.) Unfortunately, in power at the time was a government still using fan violence as a political football, and using every outbreak of violence as an excuse to show how macho they could be. It would also, after the deaths at Heysel, take a politician of immense courage to recommend the reinstatement of English clubs teams, lest their fans cause mayhem again and finish a politician's career. Why risk that when 'wait and see' wouldn't lose one vote and when the right moment did come they could use it as a vote-winner?

Whatever caused the interest in England fans travelling to Stockholm, I was suddenly topical and received two letters saying that employing me as a roving hoolie-watcher (war correspondent) was a good idea. The first was from *The Sunday Correspondent* and the second was absolute heaven from *Today* newspaper, offering to pay not only my expenses but also a minimum of £300 for articles published. *Today* was a new newspaper owned by the powerful Australian tycoon Rupert Murdoch, a man who had really shaken up the cosy world of newspapers.

The Saturday prior to my departure I went into The Swan public house at Chelsea and spoke to a few of the Chelsea lads who were intending to travel to Stockholm via the *Tor Britannia* ferry from Harwich to Gothenburg. They were happy to meet me in Stockholm and I came clean with them by telling them that I was going to write about my trip.

'About time the press told the truth,' someone remarked.

On Sunday, 3 September, I was on an SAS flight to Stockholm as a fully fledged member of the press corps (even if I called them 'core' in my ignorance, although the editor of *The Times* corrected me in very correct tones), working officially for *Today* newspaper as their undercover hooligan reporter. I had with me my trusty notepad and pencil plus a John Le Carré book because I felt like a real-life spy. More importantly I had an expense account and a hotel booked and paid for by *Today*. The expense account meant I was really at the races as a reporter. The England team party which included assorted pressmen were booked into the Royal Viking hotel (*Today* didn't book me in there, though, but a smaller hotel one mile from the city centre), but would not be arriving till the Monday, so I had 24 hours to get streetwise and spy out the main action areas. All the papers were making noises that there was going to be trouble so were getting ready to send out their heavyweight news teams on the day of the match. There had been the usual build-up plus the fact that Stockholm had a hooligan group called the 'Black Army' who had modelled themselves on the worst excesses of the England fans. Big game, huge expectations. No tickets for the England fans who are going to travel anyway, with the usual dumb press questions to the Stockholm police chief:

'How will you deal with these troublemakers?'

'We will treat them as gentlemen and visitors, then expect them to behave in a civilised manner.'

'What about the clash between our thugs and your Black Army hooligans?'

'I see no real problems as the England fans will be made very welcome when they arrive.'

That answer really cocked up the journalist who asked it as well as causing consternation within the Tory 'hang 'em, flog 'em and take away their passport' brigade who were calling for all ports and airports to be sealed off to stop the hooligan scum trying to buy a ticket for a game of football.

Stockholm is a beautiful city and I cannot imagine a better place to spend a few days with my wife. To have come here with her and an expense account would have been heaven. As it was, in my first 12 hours, I seemed to be the only England fan in town and although I went for a boat trip and had a nice lunch I couldn't find any fans, let alone a story, despite cruising nearly every bar in the city centre. Add this to the fact that I was expected to file copy (telephone in with a story) every six hours, and I found my first few hours as a journalist extremely boring. I started wishing time away, then I had my first stroke of luck. Wandering into a bar I came across a group of three English guys, one of whom was coloured, accompanied by a stunning looking woman. The loudest one among them called out to me.

'Here for the match?'

'You bet I am,' I replied.

'Come and join us. We've got another of your lot here,' he said, pointing to the third guy in the group. I walked over and he stood up, offering his hand.

'My name's John, this my pal Andy,' he said, pointing to the coloured guy, 'and this is my wife Susanne.' The other guy was a squaddie from Germany, originally from Birmingham, called Phil who had arrived earlier and was after a match ticket, but his priority was, like all squaddies, to sample the local brew first then continue sampling it. John then spent the whole afternoon regaling us with stories about his life in Stockholm and general brinkmanship.

John Leach was a wide boy, wider than the river Thames; a north London chancer who could make you laugh, but you wouldn't want to lend him money. He had money which he may have made legally or not and wasn't afraid to spend it. The Costa del Sol in Spain is full of people like him. He wasn't what I would call good-looking, but he had a confidence that certain men have around women which makes them attractive. His wife was absolutely stunning, with blonde hair, clear blue eyes and a smile that could have graced the front of Vogue *magazine, she was that elegant. John had come here for a holiday, or to escape the taxman, had met Susanne, then stayed on at her parents'. John was one of those people who told you he knew the people whose pictures were in the glossy Sunday newspaper magazine supplements. When he went out for a drink it was with these faces. Back in England he knocked about with some of the Spurs players, especially Pat Van Den Hauwe, whom he considered a mate. John might well have been a bullshitting name-dropper, but the fact that his wife would turn heads at a Hollywood film première gave him credibility with me.*

John's wife was also an invaluable source of information. Where the ground was, where the red-light district was (absolutely crucial for any journalist looking for football fans) and where the rough areas of the city were, plus information about the Black Army and crime levels. Susanne also told me about the special football match bus trips. Ticket touting was illegal in Sweden with big fines for offenders. However, to get around the law travel agents were offering a bus trip around the city with free entry into the Rasunda Stadium to see the big match on Wednesday, Sweden v England. At last, I smelt a story. The name Colin Ward would be hot on the wires tonight.

I travelled up to the ground via the red-light district which was empty. 'The Swedes tired of all that sex bit years ago,' Susanne had informed me. At the ground I went in the main entrance and showed my press ID card to the girl on the desk. It read BBC Frank Partridge, Radio News and Current Affairs, Sports Correspondent, and it had the address of the BBC on it along with Frank's office, home and car-phone numbers. I had met Frank a couple of days earlier and arranged to meet him on Tuesday dinner-time in the Royal Viking Bar, and he had given me his card. I had contacted Frank and he had wanted to talk to me to get some information, as he felt that there was a story developing around Stockholm and he would be out there to cover it for BBC *Newsbeat*, a midday current affairs programme. As Frank wasn't here in Stockholm yet I decided to use his card to gain entrance to wherever.

The receptionist looked at me. 'Who do you want to see?'

I didn't have a clue. 'Who is here?' I asked.

'Mr Lennart Johansson.'

'Lennart Johansson?' I looked puzzled.

Mr Lennart Johansson, the Swedish FA President, Chairman of UEFA and Vice-President of FIFA, the world football governing body.

'Yes, he'll do.'

This was comical. Here I was being shown into the office of one of the most senior men in football, impersonating a BBC journalist without a clue what I was doing there. However, my stupidity and ability to smile got me out of a corner because he was desperate to explain how the English press were getting all worked up about nothing and they were not expecting any trouble. He was such a big friendly man that I felt sure he would send me on my way with an Abba greatest hits collection or a Volvo dinky car, but he didn't. He took me out into the stands and showed me where the England fans were going to be put and how they had kept some space over to put any extra ticketless fans (you understand that that is our little secret) and to the right where the Swedish fans (plus Black Army) would be standing. Pride of place in his tour was the heated seats which warmed people's bums on cold nights. My comment of 'Doesn't do much for the piles' went right over his head. I couldn't imagine Graham Kelly, Secretary of the FA, offering a stupid-looking journalist a tour of Wembley, although this might be on once they get the drains fixed.

Mr Happy Swede was very confident that there would be no trouble, but I got the feeling that this man would look on the bright side of almost anything. 'We are very confident that there will be no problems.' I asked him about the bus trips. 'Of course, as a journalist I would like to buy one of these for one of my friends who is coming over here from Germany.'

'Well, Mr Partridge, you must understand that the reselling of tickets is against the law in Sweden so the England fans will not be able to purchase them outside the ground, but they can go and purchase one from a travel agency. I will give you the address for your friend, but you must understand that the tickets are about five times face value.'

'No, whatever, he's got plenty, that would be brilliant. Thanks very much Mr Johansson.'

So I left (or Frank did) with the recommendation from one of the most powerful figures in football of where to buy a ticket which circumvented the strict Swedish ticket-touting laws. The irony was not lost on me.

At the ticket agency I paid my 300 kroner (£30) and obtained my bus ticket. You will be given your match ticket at the end of the tour, the pretty Swedish agent informed me. 'Which end is the ticket for?' I asked. 'Just so I will know where to meet my friend after the match.'

The young lady showed me a ticket and it confirmed my suspicions. Any England fans buying these tickets would be smack bang in the middle of the Black Army faction. A recipe for absolute mayhem. It was early Monday evening and I had a red-hot story. I sprinted from the taxi back at my hotel, almost forgetting to pay the fare. I wrote the story then telephoned the copy desk, asking to speak to the sub-editor, Jeff Sweet. In all newspapers it is the sub-editors (subs) who really make the paper work. They hassle the journalists, rewrite the stories and generally kick ass to make it happen. Journalism, especially tabloid journalism, is now. News becomes old news very quickly and these guys live close to the edge as they make hundreds of decisions a day as to what is news and what isn't.

'What's happening, Colin, any fighting or riots?' he asked disdainfully.

'Listen, Jeff, I have got the story of the trip so far. The Swedes are selling tickets to England fans for the Swedish end which is circumventing the strict fan segregation policy. That means that any fan buying these tickets will be right in their end, right amongst their Black Army who have pledged to give the English hooligans a lesson.'

I said this without drawing breath and expected a shout of 'hold the front page' to go up. Instead I could feel his indifference coming at me down the line.

'Listen, that sounds like a job for our news boys. You liaise with our man when he turns up. You stick to drinking with the hoolies and getting some real stories. Stuff like that is out of your league,' then he transferred me to the copy-taker.

Later that evening I was in a bar and a guy fell off his bar stool and through the window. The police turned up and asked the England fans to pay for the window. When they refused the police arrested them until they paid for the damage, then released them. When I telephoned this in his reply was: 'Fucking marvellous, mate, you're earning now. Now this we can use.' Welcome to the real world of tabloid journalism, Colin.

I popped in this bar which Susanne had recommended called the Café Opera and I flashed my Frank card at the barman, who informed me matter-of-factly that the friendless army of English hooligans was on its way. All the bars would be employing doormen for the duration. Sitting at the bar was a Scottish expatriate called Jerry who'd been unemployed in England but was making it here and more. The fact was that this man was the most one-eyed bigot whom I couldn't have had more than ten minutes' conversation with, and who hated Maggie Thatcher so much that I actually found myself defending her, despite the fact that I had no time for her at all. Notwithstanding his bigotry, he summed up the whole Stockholm trip in one wry comment: 'In a city where beer is five pounds a pint and 90 per cent of the people speak better English than the England fans, then the impending arrival of England's lager culture is not seen as a major event.'

'Well, it's big news in England,' I said.

'Well, it would be in a country where the two most powerful people are women and the third most powerful is an Australian man with a tit fetish.'

'That's who I am working for – the tit man.'

'That's how bad it's got. He now employs second-rate journalists,' he said without a trace of humour in his voice.

I have come to realise that all jocks have to obtain a degree in pessimism before they are allowed to get a job abroad. I bet the ugly bastard had a tasty Swedish bird and yet he was still sitting in the Café Opera bar hoping to meet an Englishman to take the rise out of. I returned to my hotel, fast becoming disillusioned with this journalism lark and convinced that all English hooligans could smell me coming at 100 yards and immediately moved on to deprive me of my genuine 'English fans run amok' story. Ironically, all the lads who had travelled out earlier were in a bar only 50 yards from my hotel but I consistently missed them as I walked past.

I telephoned in with a small report then went for another drink with John. When I arrived back at the bar the squaddie was a faceless drunken mess and in grave danger of becoming a public nuisance. The vocabulary had degenerated to 'fuck' every other word and his sorry life history of 'fuckin' punch-ups' was unfolding. The trip to Gibraltar where he had fought the matelots (sailors) in every pub along the main drag was one of the funnier ones. More fights in one evening than Frank Bruno and he'd won every one! Not only that, but he was calling John's wife 'luv' or 'darlin' and was informing the coloured friend of John that 'you ain't a bad bloke for a darkie'. John was getting the hump. I was all for buying him more drink but John was appalled at the thought.

'When, as a reporter, your day is as mind-numbingly boring as mine has been then you'd look at that squaddie as extremely newsworthy,' I said to John. John roared with laughter and decided I was unprincipled enough to be okay. He explained to me that Andy was Des Walker's cousin (due to play for England against Sweden on the Wednesday) and he wanted to go down to the team hotel to have a drink with Des. I was welcome to come along as long as I didn't bring drunky. I left drunky to his devices and departed with John, Susanne and Andy.

At the Royal Viking hotel, with the arrival of the England team, they had put someone on the door to stop England fans pestering the players. That is one of the sadder aspects of modern football. Players are shut off from all fan contact and now live in a sealed world surrounded by agents and press and other assorted hangers-on. The doorman was given short shrift by John and his wife, so in we all went.

As we got in the lift and the doors were about to shut a large gentleman made a dash to get in. As he got in a realisation dawned upon his face that perhaps he shouldn't have rushed to get in. The portly gentleman who entered the lift was none other than Graham Kelly, the Secretary of the FA, a man who has been described by various people as having a charisma bypass.

John smiled at him as he didn't know him from Adam. 'Hello.' (It reminded me of the funny sketch performed by Peter Cook and Dudley Moore on *Derek & Clive*: Hello. You provocative bastard, how dare you say hello to me.) This innocuous friendly greeting almost sent Graham into tears as he thought we were all the dreaded football fans the FA love to hate. Graham turned away and John looked at me with an expression of disbelief as to why this guy should ignore him. 'Got any spare tickets, Graham?' I asked out of mischief. He ignored me so I prodded him in the back. 'Oi, fat boy, I'm talking to you. Don't turn your back on me.'

Graham turned around and looked flustered. I thought he was going to cry. 'There are no tickets. The match has been sold out for weeks so you shouldn't have wasted your time coming.' He said it in a monotone voice like he was making a speech. I could almost imagine him rehearsing it in front of his mirror for moments such as this, plus judging by the way he was standing he seemed to have messed his pants by being in the same lift as us. This is probably the closest he has got to real excitement in his life!

Faced with such indifference I reverted to fan speak which left Graham no wiser as he had decided long ago that travelling England fans were all bad. The sooner we stopped travelling then the more time he could have enjoying his gin and tonic with the rest of the FA International Committee. 'The story that this match is sold out is crap . . .'

Why is it when you get a chance to put across a coherent point you always end up using words which reinforce their view of you as a stereotyped thicko, so adding justification to official stupidity. I only wish I could insult eloquently when petty officialdom makes my blood boil. Before I could say another word the lift stopped on the first floor and the doors opened. Graham got out as quickly as he could. John, seeing that the guy was a buffoon, sensed that he just wanted to get out of the lift, so he made a comment for the hell of it. 'Did you get a good hiding for laughing when you were a kid?' and as he left the lift on the first floor: 'I thought you was staying on the second floor.' As the doors shut I saw Kelly breathe a huge sigh of relief.

On Tuesday morning I was up with the lark and down at the railway station checking every train that was due in. I telephoned in and heard that there had been trouble and a reported death of an England fan upon a ferry which had been forced to turn back due to rioting. The rumour mill was in full swing and I wandered around the station nodding to and exchanging pleasantries with other England fans who were in the station. Everybody including a contingent of riot police was waiting for the next train due in from Copenhagen which would have a number of England fans on board. Just before the train pulled in I went over and had a chat with the Stockholm chief of police who was here to supervise the orderly arrival of England fans. As the England fans shuffled up the concourse they were met by a line of Swedish riot police along with girls handing out accommodation addresses. Fans looked lost but I couldn't spot any of the Chelsea fans I had agreed to meet. I asked some Leeds fans if they had been on the ferry and if there were any Chelsea fans on the train from Copenhagen. They shook their heads then shuffled off. I was wearing a brown leather jacket and had short neat hair, rather like a policeman would wear it. I settled down to await the next train and my pals from Chelsea. I pulled out my little red notebook and started to write notes for the story I needed to file. Unbeknown to me a couple of the Leeds fans had been watching me, and seeing me ask loads of questions, speak to the Swedish policeman, then pull out a little notebook was all the proof they needed that I was in fact an undercover police officer. In retrospect it seems hilarious – me an undercover policeman – but the level of paranoia in everybody in that city and especially amongst the England fans was running that high. Trains came and went over the next few hours and still my Chelsea colleagues never materialised. I realised that they were not going to turn up when the riot police started leaving.

Little did anybody in Stockholm know that the incident on the ferry had caused all the press back in England to go on a hooligan red alert. It was like someone had pressed the nuclear hoolie button. All that day the news editors were running around their newspapers like lunatics during the full moon barking orders. The constant requests for politicians' quotes about the forthcoming violence were creating a form of paranoic hysteria. I likened it to the panic which came over America when H.G. Wells' *War of The Worlds* came out and people ran for the hills from an imaginary alien invasion.

I walked towards the door of the Royal Viking and found my way blocked by a burly doorman. I flashed my card and walked past him to the desk where I asked the receptionist to telephone Frank Partridge. 'Who shall I say is calling?' she asked.

'Frank Colin Ward. Tell him I'm at the bar and ordering drinks on his room number.' I walked to the bar and ordered a drink.

'Shall I charge this, sir?'

'Yes, please. Frank Partridge. Room 157,' and duly signed my chit Frank Wank.

'Thank you, sir.'

In Sweden lager is sold in different strengths: 1, 2 or 3, with number 1, the strongest, being the most expensive, so I stuck with it.

A lot of the press were in the bar plus two ex-footballers: Ray Clemence, the goalkeeper who had played for England over 50 times, and Trevor Brooking, the ex-West Ham player who had played nearly 70 times for England. Both were here to work for TV and were surrounded by a number of pressmen. One of my press heroes was with them, Mike Langley, of *The Sunday People,* and such is the way when you finally get to meet one of your heroes – the actual moment is rather disappointing. Here was a man who had actually inspired me to want to be a sportswriter. A scoop with attitude who always got the right punchline. A man who could sit hunched over his manual typewriter making the keys sing. Yet standing in front of me was an old, tired-looking man with droopy eyelids. At least he was drinking Scotch, but only sipping it, and he was holding the glass with his pinkie finger pointing upwards, like a San Francisco poof. And to top it all he had a sort of handbag slung over his shoulder.

I was looking over at Mike who was in the group surrounding Ray Clemence. Ray, like all footballers, was used to people staring at him (Ooh look, there's Ray Clemence), obviously noticed, said something, and a couple of the press within the group turned around and looked at me. They probably thought I was a groupie so I went and sat down and watched the press from a comfortable leather armchair a little distance away. These were the guys who had given successive England managers a hard time, yet I wondered what sort of people they were.

As I looked around I suddenly realised I was sitting in the middle of the most exclusive club in the world. The English sporting press was a club which conferred massive benefits. These guys travelled the world watching England play football, staying at the best hotels with an expense account. There was *bonhomie*, laughter and camaraderie amongst the different groups who had settled down around the bar, especially amongst the senior group around the two ex-England internationals. I couldn't hear what they were talking about, yet I assumed they were talking about football. Imagine being paid to talk about football. Any football fan would give his right arm to do that, especially as he does it every night for nothing. Sure, they were slightly arrogant, but that came with the territory. Football is an obsession, sometimes even a diversion from life, but it is safe to say that in England what these men wrote had more cause and effect than any other form of writing. This knowledge made these guys cocky.

It was summed up for me when David Rocastle, the Arsenal footballer, cut through the bar area. One of the press called out to him by his Arsenal nickname which only those who knew him used: 'Er, Rocky, can I have a word later?'

'Yeah, later,' replied Rocky, as if to say much later, like next year later.

The pressman muttered something then I heard him say, 'he's only young, he'll learn the ropes.' Like Rocky was a dog who had to learn how to behave in their company; but Rocky was like a lot of young blacks who have come on the scene: they are proud players because they've had to fight to get where they are. (When Rocky didn't make the final squad for the World Cup finals, the sports boys made up a story that he had stormed out of the hotel after a row with Bobby Robson.) Sadly, Rocky never did learn the ropes as his career went into decline when he reached his mid-20s.

Then Bobby Robson walked into the bar area closely followed by John Barnes, a footballer whose skills could only be described using adjectives such as silky and refined. Immediately, journalists were up and talking to Bobby, asking him this and that about certain players. Who is injured, what formation did he expect? This was a big game and Bobby looked under pressure, yet he talked to them with his trademark smile and made his facial expressions when he didn't want to say too much. Bobby was big on facial expressions, but it's not until you study him close-up that you realise how much Bobby used to say with his face. Bobby was a proud man who hated failure. He was once sacked at Fulham by the Chairman, Ernie Clay, who later committed suicide after his business ran into problems. In an interview when Bobby was asked about this he made a comment which, although containing no malice about the dead man, spoke volumes about Bobby Robson's force of character and the sort of attitudes his teams would take on to the pitch tomorrow evening. 'The man sacked me . . . said I couldn't take the pressure, yet we all saw what happened when he was under pressure.' Bobby was getting irritated by the constant banality of the questions so someone tried to collar John Barnes as he walked back through, but he rode the comment like he rode a good tackle and he glided away. And the look a couple of the scribes gave him was almost sexual because John looks good even when everybody else looks bad. Yet as he walked out I heard one say 'he's a waster. He'll find a hole to hide in tomorrow when the going gets really tough.' As I looked around at the faces around the bar it dawned upon me that I had gatecrashed a bigger event than I had imagined.

Bobby excused himself, but politely said he would be back later. And as soon as he had gone the comments around the seats where I was sitting started.

'The man's on the edge.'

'He doesn't know his own mind.'

'He'll pick the wrong side tomorrow.'

I wonder how many of these people could live with the sort of pressure they were putting Bobby under, yet he still spoke civilly to people who he knew would rubbish him as soon as his back was turned. Looking at the way they mocked Bobby behind his back, I doubted many of them could.

I looked at their faces: there was no expression, just comments. But the guys at the bar were just looking serious, and even if they were making comments I was out of earshot. You see, they had progressed right up the pecking order to be the confidants of the two ex-England internationals, Ray and Trevor. I looked at the way they spoke and looked at the two players and I saw something different. Whilst the sportswriters may never have played or reached the supreme level of athleticism these two had, their ability to verbalise their grace and power gave them credence in the athletic world. For all my anger at the hypocrisy surrounding me I was jealous over the fact that I wanted to be where they were, because I felt sure that I could write about football. Yet what had I drawn? Phil, the drunken Brummie squaddie who fights his way around Gibraltar.

David Lacey of *The Guardian* came into the bar. As an avid *Guardian* reader I had been waiting for him as this man was a prince among paupers, the only writer who gets Robson and Rachmaninov in the same sentence. Sure, he had made some unkind comments about Arsenal, but so had everybody in this room.

David didn't look like a sportswriter. He looked like a primary school headmaster; he even had on one of those tweed jackets that they are so fond of. When David told me that he had never played football at any level, although he had refereed a few matches, it got me wondering about how he could talk about formations and tactical mistakes made by England managers. David also informed me that the same was probably true of most sportswriters present. David could see that his revelation that this whole hotel was made up of writers who had progressed from reporting about Friday night fights outside the local Indian restaurant to stating that England's midfield movement was prosaic by comparison to Johnny Foreigner had opened up a can of worms in my psyche.

Lacey heard the questioning tone of incredulity turning to anger and could see the way the conversation was going so dashed off after catching the eye of Bob Harris of *Today*, which had two journalists covering this match. Rob Shepherd was the other, here to cover the quotes. Rob came over to the bar and I thought it would be a good opportunity to introduce myself.

'Hi, Rob, I'm Colin Ward. I'm working for *Today* and I'm here to cover the fans' behaviour.'

'Wonderful,' he said. 'I'm sure it's going to be an exciting couple of days for you,' in a tone which said 'I don't care because I'm browned off about something'. I think it was basically because he was here as second fiddle to Bob Harris, a strange-looking man with big glasses and a garish dress sense which involved mixing brightly coloured shirts and ties. Nevertheless, Bob was the man who would be writing the match report, even if Rob felt he was better suited to the job.

I heard someone behind me. 'Excuse me, can I buy you a drink?' Standing in front of me was a diminutive character with glasses and, still angry from the brush-off I had been given by Rob Shepherd, I snapped at this guy who was trying to be friendly. 'No, piss off, I don't talk to the press. Plus I am waiting for someone.'

'Actually, I am not here with anyone and this is my first trip. My name's Pete Davies and I am writing a book about the World Cup.'

'Oh, sorry, mate. I thought you were a newshound who thought I was a hooligan and was taking the mickey.'

We got chatting and Pete's politics were very similar to mine. He told me that he was using his advance to take a risk and travel everywhere with the England team to write a book about the 1990 World Cup. 'I like to take risks. I am known as a bit of a risk-taker,' he said.

'Well, drinking with me is a risk, that's for sure. You stick with me and we'll stitch up the expense account of the BBC tonight.'

He looked impressed and when I told him what I had to do he seemed even more impressed, but he was just there taking it all in, listening and probing to give himself a writer's edge. Meeting pipsqueek Pete with the wire-framed specs, then seeing what he later wrote has taught me never to judge a writer by the way he looks. Pete didn't know what he was going to write but after the first three hours spent in the company of Fleet Street's finest he had already upset the apple-cart by asking a couple of probing questions which were frowned upon.

Frank Partridge came into the bar area. 'Want a drink, lads?'

'Yes, two more beers. Don't worry, I've started you a tab,' I said.

Frank looked puzzled, as did the barman when he signed Frank P on room 157. 'Cheers, wank,' I said, which made Frank look more puzzled. Frank was a typical BBC man right down to his paisley cotton socks so he didn't have time to waste making small-talk. It was straight down to business.

'What have you got, Colin?'

'The story of Stockholm so far.'

'Which is?' asked Frank.

'No chance, mate, I don't give away anything and neither would you. If

Today don't take me seriously by tomorrow then I'll sell you the only story that has broken so far.'

I looked around the bar and swept my arm across a broad sweep. 'This and the newshounds like yourself is the real story.'

Frank gave me his quizzical BBC look which said more than words ever could: 'Look, I'm the journalist here. I've done my indentures and stood out in the pissing rain and freezing cold interviewing absolute pillocks and you, a belligerent hooligan, tell me where the real story is,' but Frank was professional enough to know that I was news and he had seen enough of me in the bar to know that I was good for a story or two.

'Fair enough, I'll meet you for breakfast tomorrow. I bet you already know a good bar where we can have a beer.'

I was standing on the main drag which sweeps along past the parliament building and up through to the station. I saw five young England fans walk up past a row of neat clothes shops. The door was opened by one of them and they dashed in and grabbed a box of clothes inside. It was full of Burberry hats and they grabbed one for each of them and ran off up the road laughing, dropping the box which spilled the rest on to the pavement. I met them later, much later in the trip, and they were always good for a soundbite for any journalist. I watched them and I wondered at times who was chasing whom. I nicknamed the biggest one amongst them 'rent a quote'. They came from Carlisle and called themselves the Border City Crew. I could never take them seriously, especially as they spent the whole time walking around with these silly Burberry check hats on. It reminded me of the school coach trips to the coast I used to go on when everyone used to nick a silly 'Kiss me Quick' hat. How governments could worry about the arrival of this lot beggared belief, but the collective resources of every English national newspaper as well as a few foreign ones (which could have fed Africa's starving for some considerable time) were about to be spent writing about people such as those five whose acne was the most terrifying thing they had going for them. Frank met them early in his trip, resplendent in their hats. They complained to Frank that they were being picked upon by the authorities. Frank ran that verbatim in his first report as well as other rubbish they fed him, including their gang name. When I saw Frank later I informed him that he had been suckered. Frank, who was dumbstruck but took it well, stuck a lot closer to me after that.

Just before we left for our beer Pete Davies saw Bobby Robson come back into the bar. 'I just need a quick word with him,' said Pete and walked over. Bobby, in the meantime, had been collared by James Lawton of *The Sunday*

41

Express, a large man who could only be described as a bit of a 'Two Dinners'. Pete stood there waiting but was just in earshot of the conversation, like he was earwigging what they were saying. I was standing back a little further, not taking much notice. Bobby looked over at me and made eye contact. Perhaps something about my scruffy leather coat or general appearance unnerved Bobby, or he just felt claustrophobic with everybody milling around trying to get a piece of him, but he exploded and started shouting at Pete Davies. 'Do you mind? I'm trying to have a private conversation here. How dare you stand there listening to what I'm saying?'

Everyone turned around and looked at me, Frank and Pete, although most eyes were on me as I was the interloper. 'Time to leave, Frank.' Frank and I left with Pete scampering behind. There was something not quite right about Pete Davies and my suspicions were proved right later in the evening after I left early following a spat with some sportswriters.

I was looking forward to my beer in the Café Opera and picking the brains of an experienced journalist like Frank Partridge. He spoke with a BBC accent, but didn't have the BBC superior air about him and came across to me as a thinking man's journalist. Once inside the Café Opera Frank bought some beers but before we could settle down I spotted a group of sportswriters eating their meal. I walked over to where the eight-strong group were seated around a circular table. It included Harry Harris, *Daily Mirror*, plus writers from other papers including *The Time*s as well as Colin Gibson from *The Telegraph*.

I meant to make a joke with them as I felt sure they would have a sense of humour. After all, these were the guys who had spent the best part of their journalistic life making fun of successive England managers and got paid to do it. 'Excuse me,' I said in my best mock Swedish accent which in all probability sounds like all my other impersonations, a drunk Pakistani. 'I am looking for the famous English football hooligans who cause violence. Could you tell me where to find them?'

The completely humourless, threatening reply which came back shocked me.

'Clear off or we'll throw you through that window. Is that enough for you?' It was said with genuine malice. In the centre of the table was a plate of chips. I leant over to the centre of the table and picked up a handful of chips. 'Have some of these, sludge guts,' I said, then threw them violently at the person who had made the comment. They bounced off his face and napkin, landing in the lap of some of the other diners.

'Do you want to get up and throw me out?' I asked politely in my voice which had reverted to best London. Our brave friend stayed put. One of the other sportswriters interjected. 'We are having a meal here, so it was a little impolite to interrupt, wasn't it?' Assaulted by deadly logic I left them, after one final offer for one of our heroes to try and throw me out, shaking my head with disgust.

Breakfast with Frank was an illuminating affair. 'Why did you leave so suddenly last night?' Frank asked.

'I went over to make a joke at the sportswriters' table and by the time I had got up to the bar I couldn't find you and Pete.' Frank explained that they had found a seat in a bar downstairs and thought I was behind them. (Davies later told me that Frank had seen my words with the sportswriters and had immediately slipped away because he didn't want to be seen around me.) Frank told me a story he had heard over breakfast from the sportswriters whom I had a minor spat with.

'We were sitting in this lovely café restaurant when this group of National Front supporters came over and started threatening us. We had to help the management throw them out.' I am sure there was more about their heroic deeds but Frank only heard that much. I may look rough and ready with my leather coat and blondish red hair, but I have never been mistaken for a group, and as the doorman was not letting in any England fans, then it had to be me. It makes you wonder about their mentality and their whole *modus operandi* when you hear things like that.

'Do you know what that Pete Davies said to me after you left the restaurant?' Frank asked.

'No.'

'He told me that you were going to stitch up my expense account. Bit naughty, that.' I laughed. 'Listen, Frank, I only said that to test him out, but I'll put Davies down on the hit list and sort him out when I see him.'

Frank continued. 'The funny thing is that bastard stitched up my expense account. I ended up carrying him back to the hotel.'

Whilst this was probably true, Frank was so busy being a BBC man that he didn't have time to be himself, to let go and get pissed. Frank was in love with his job, so much so that journalism was his mistress. Later in the evening when Frank had consumed a few brandies, he confided in me that his marriage was in danger of going down the tubes because of the way he worked. Looking at Frank over breakfast, speed-reading all the newspapers coming over the faxes, I could see why. The man was strung out in the same way that the fans arriving at the station from an all-night bender in Copenhagen were strung out. But the hoolies were making it happen because they were enjoying it; Frank was doing it because something was driving him forward, and as the trip unfolded I would begin to see what was driving the likes of Frank.

Frank warned me to be very careful what I said to people as I wasn't in an honourable business. 'Careless talk costs lives. The fact of the matter is, Colin, that your mob (hooligans) have much greater ties of honour than us lot (journalists).' Whilst I didn't agree that hooligans were my mob, I understood his sentiments.

Frank Partridge broke my ticket-touting story on BBC radio *Newsbeat* although for some reason he left out the part about how he had obtained the story. Within a few hours the Travel Agents were raided and all the bus tours were cancelled with the tickets being confiscated under Swedish law.

My first and only report came out on Wednesday morning (although they did use quotes from me) on the inside back page of *Today* newspaper, under the name Mike Roberts, as I didn't want my real name being used as I was really into this John Le Carré thing. Under the main heading

AS ENGLAND FOLLOWERS TOE THE LINE IN SWEDEN
Police army subdue fans

the article appeared as follows.

Mike Roberts is one of 150 England fans in Stockholm – a city living on its nerves awaiting the main tidal wave of support today. This is his report:

The desperation of the long distance England fan was aptly illustrated by the few arrivals at Stockholm Central station from Copenhagen at 7 a.m. yesterday – a scruffy bunch in their late teens and early 20s.

None of them looked tough enough to warrant the huge security operation ordered by the Swedish chief of police, who is using his transport police as a paramilitary force with riot equipment. The fans, many of them with shaved heads and pigtails, shuffled aimlessly through the station looking tired and gaunt, a world apart from the smartly dressed Swedes hurrying to work. The riot police – expecting a cross between Genghis Khan and Adolf Hitler – seemed surprised at their meekness.

This ramshackle lot looked at the floor and waited for the riot police to return to their vans having heard that all England fans will be sent straight home.

Fears allayed, they are happy just to have gained entry into Sweden. Friends meet them and exchange information. 'Is anybody in town yet?' someone asks. 'No, there are only 60 of us.'

'Any trouble from the Black Army (the street gang who follow AIK Stockholm)?' No, apparently all has been quiet.

Normally, the local boys would have been out in force by now and there would have been plenty of action. In Stockholm, however, little has happened apart from five arrests late on Monday, with everyone released yesterday after paying for a broken plate-glass window.

Talk turns to the match and lack of tickets. Those unable to afford £30 on the black market for a terrace ticket – let alone the £90 demanded for a seat – are hoping the police do the usual thing and let them in. 'If we are mob-handed they will just have to let us in,' was one opinion, while someone else felt that a couple of hundred might try to kick the gates down.

The last scenario sounds improbable because the overall mood is muted. The death on the ferry and the friendly Swedish attitude has had a calming effect – for the moment. But a big rush in new arrivals is expected today and then, anything could happen.

Hemingway? No. Proud? You bet I was proud, so I went looking for a well-known journalist who had been the recipient of one of my 'smack in the teeth letters' after he had dared to suggest Arsenal copy Spurs if they want to play good football. The letter was tongue-in-cheek and he had replied in kind. He was a superb writer and I had been dying to meet him so now that I was a proper journalist I could question him on level terms. However, he was otherwise engaged on extra-marital activities so I considered it unprofessional to interrupt. This actually elevated him in my estimation because he was bald, even if the other sports boys heaped scorn on him as he sat in the Royal Viking lobby with a gorgeous blonde woman. Frank told me that he pulled on every trip. He had been voted the journalists' number one puller!

On the Tuesday morning there was a training session at the Rasunda stadium. Above the ground's main stand there was a restaurant. The press sat in the restaurant and watched the players go through their paces, and from this session they deduced that Robson was planning to play Waddle and Barnes to nullify the threat of the Swedish full-backs. Bobby Robson wanted to stop the fast Swedish forwards making direct runs at the English back four. After the training session some of the press, who fancied they knew about tactics, said things like 'Eckstrom and Magnusson's pace will slaughter Butcher' and 'Our midfield will get murdered', but never to Bobby Robson who was always deep in thought or conversation with his assistant, Don Howe. Don and Bobby were football thinkers, always analysing when together, so the press psychobabble would have been mocked by these intellectual football giants.

Later in the day I met four blokes from Luton. Two of them were absolute screams: Diddy, aptly named because of his lack of height, and Ray, who was only just slightly taller. I accompanied them to the Under-21 match which was being played in Upsala, a town remarkable for the fact that it didn't have a single bar in it, or if it did I couldn't find one, and that's a first. However, while the England fans spent the sunny afternoon swigging from warm lager cans we descended upon the town's plushest hotel. Inside we came upon the Swedish Under-21 team who looked so young and fragile that even Diddy looked big compared to them. The Swedish Under-21 manager was quite happy to talk football to us and as there were a couple of livewire Black Country humour merchants who followed Steve Bull (the Wolves striker who was playing for the Under-21 team) everywhere and gave us constant renditions of 'Woolly Bully, Woolly Bully', it developed into an interesting pre-match beano. The Swedish Under-21 team looked terrified of us (unlike the rest of Stockholm, who looked mildly bemused by us) and seemed quite glad when their coach turned up.

Inside the ground there were a couple of policemen but access around the ground was unrestricted with only a steel tube around waist height as a barrier. As I was walking down the players' tunnel I bumped into Bobby Robson who looked a bit worried to see the same brown leather coat there. Diddy and Ray went and sat in the press-box. The press were horrified. 'This is for the press only.' 'No worries,' replied Diddy, 'Ray here is going to report on the fight I'm about to start.' He then jumped up and down and shouted 'Help, we're being attacked' and ran out of the press-box on to the pitch where the two teams were coming out. Diddy then proceeded to trot out to the centre of the pitch and help collect the players' track suits. When he trotted back he went and sat down in the dug-out next to a perplexed Bobby Robson and Don Howe. After about 20 seconds a smiling Swedish policeman showed him the way into the seats behind. And that's how it was: relaxed and fun.

The Swedish crowd of mums, dads and children enjoyed the match and England got run ragged by a Swedish team with pace and movement who ended 1–0 winners. The Wolves boys sang Woolly Bully while Bully played a stinker, but everyone went home happy, and the press reported that Nazi salutes were made by the England fans. I saw some wallies and thickies, I heard some Woolly (Bully), I even saw some sillies, but not a Nazi, and I was being paid to find them. Rob Shepherd did the match report for *Today* as Bob Harris was above following the Under-21 team to a provincial ground. Rob's report was about the performance of Paul Ince who was due to sign for Manchester United. The actual match was deemed to be worth one line, such is the attention span of the tabloids.

At half-time I bumped into Bobby Robson again who hurried away, then at full-time I went over to shake his hand and have a word. The poor man looked more frightened than cry-baby Kelly in the lift the previous evening.

I think he thought I was a crazed stalker. Later that evening I popped into the Royal Viking to leave a message for Frank saying where I was, and just as I came out of a side door Bobby Robson was getting out of a taxi. He turned round to see me grinning 'Hello, Bobby, are you following me?'

Bobby shouted 'Hello, son,' and ran past me like I was an escaped zoo lion. His facial expression of shock horror told the whole story.

Three doors down from the Royal Viking was a little bar. They had put a large Swede on the door as a bouncer, but his method was to be so polite when you entered that the thought of upsetting him was tantamount to treason. He was as big as Dolph Lundgren, yet as you walked in he offered to hang your coat up as it was against house rules to wear your coat in the bar. The England fans had been drinking in there since Sunday and it was a nice friendly atmosphere. Two factors changed all that. First I walked in and the whole bar started staring at me. Perhaps Bobby Robson had put out a contract on me. Then, the real reason unfolded when a guy decided to sit down next to me. I wish he hadn't because he had a nylon England shirt on and he had been wearing it for over two days. His odour was so overpowering that you had to breathe the smell in up your nose a second time because your sense of smell couldn't believe that anything could be that bad the first time. Also, the lights were on but nobody was home. After informing me that Dolph had a glass jaw – he knew because he had done a bit of sparring ('Yeah, mate, I can see that from the state of your chops') – he then proceeded to tell me how Hull had run West Ham. Judging from the amount of half-wits who tell the 'we dun West Ham' stories in foreign bars, it would seem as if half of the East End travels abroad with a black eye. When West Ham came into the bar later the 'we dun you' stories abruptly ceased.

'Everyone in here reckons you're an undercover policeman,' he said to me.

The words of John McEnroe sprang to mind: 'You cannot be serious!' I can't remember what I actually said, but try as I did to convince him I wasn't a 'copper', he wouldn't have it. 'No, one of the Leeds lads said he saw you writing some stuff in a little book after you were asking some questions.'

That was all the proof everybody needed. Despite the logic that an undercover policeman wouldn't really write up his notes in a public place, which was staring him in the face, he wasn't having any of it.

The debate about my status as undercover police was raging when Frank walked in. I even showed 'Stinker' some of the notes I had written, to which he replied, 'That doesn't prove anything.' He got up to go to report back to his mates and Frank thought he was a bit obnoxious.

'After two days in that shirt I think he's about as obnoxious as he can get,' I said.

'You've got problems,' Frank said. 'You're not one of us and you're not even one of them.' Frank looked smug, but as he unwound a little he let his guard drop and started talking about the journalists' pecking order which everybody had to conform to. At the top were the heavyweights led by Hugh McIlvanney. At the bottom were the tabloid newcomers like Rob Shepherd who had to know when to ask a question. Journalists had to play a sort of Eton fagging game to get accepted in the pecking order, so when a new boy got in they had to play the game the correct way or get ticked off. Outside the pecking order and absolutely contemptuous of all of them was Brian Glanville of *The Sunday Times*. A man who considered himself an intellectual giant (he spoke fluent Italian) amongst pygmies. When Frank told me about the bald journalist who'd been nicknamed 'shagger' (of course he loved his kids, but he had natural urges when watching pure athleticism) and the journalist who liked to get tied up and whipped, I listened intently. When I enquired as to the names Frank went berserk in a BBC accent. He was worried that his talking to me could upset the whole equilibrium so I politely stopped asking.

As the evening wore on Frank, who was drinking brandy again, looked tired. Frank's mistress, the BBC, was a demanding lover. Unlike most lovers who are happy to go to sleep after receiving their quota of love, a good story from Frank created the need for Frank to do it again. Added to this was the pressure that if he didn't perform there were at least 20 others who would give up their cosy semi to be here. I looked closely at Frank. Did I really want his lifestyle? The news boys from *The Sun*, *The Guardian*, *The Daily Mail*, *The Star* and *The Mirror* entering the bar *en masse* was the second act that caused friction. These guys were on the hard edge of journalism: they called themselves 'The Rotters' and the crumpled suits stated that they had come direct from the previous story.

They had notebooks and started asking questions. Andy Russel from *The Daily Star* asked me a couple. 'Go and file some copy,' I said for a laugh. He pounced on me. 'You know a lot, who are you working for?'

I replied, 'Nobody, I just know my journo words.' He confided that they were getting nothing and they were all desperate. The heat was really on all of them to deliver the story which was definitely going to happen at the match. 'It's gonna be big', they all said, but nobody thought for one moment what they would do if it wasn't. I remember reading about the US colonel in Vietnam who, on the arrival of a full helicopter of journalists, insisted on cranking his men up to get them a story, adding: 'Don't worry, guys, I'll get you a few dead bodies for your story!'

Andy Russel was asked by 'Stinker' how he justified what he did. A reasonable contribution although it could have been his shirt talking. His reply shut Stinker up and put him up in my estimation. He said that if nobody read what they wrote then they would all be redundant, but until that happens he needed to work to live. I could live with that, after all I was here selling my soul to Aussie Bob for a few pieces of silver. It was only a few years ago that I had worn a badge stating that I wouldn't buy his papers. Andy spoke to Frank and me. 'At least we are above board. *Today* have sent an undercover fella out who is travelling with the real hooligans. And all of us are dying to know who he is.'

Separate groups within the bar were getting angry about the stupid questions they were being asked. Eventually all the news boys left together. Dolph the doorman told me that he wouldn't allow any more reporters in his bar as it caused friction with these lovely fans who had been so well behaved. I took some of the reporters' names because I could see this developing into the only real story of the trip. News reporters attacked in city centre bar. As they went outside I followed to speak to George Jackson of the *Daily Mirror*, a silver-haired man who, it has been reported, so enraged John McEnroe that his entry into the press conference would send John apoplectic. Before I could speak to George I was accosted by three Portsmouth fans and another West Bromwich guy who didn't like undercover policemen.

'You're undercover Old Bill.'

'No, I'm not.'

'Yes, you are, and I'm going to have you.'

'Really?' I asked mockingly.

'Yeah, me and you round the back. Come on.'

'Well firstly there is no back, secondly I don't want to fight you because I'm not a policeman, but thirdly, if I am and you do me you're gonna get nicked because I have a journalist as a witness.'

My logic temporarily stopped his alcohol-fazed brain from working.

'Well if you're not Old Bill then name me some names who you are here with.'

'I had arranged to meet some Chelsea lads but they were on the acid ferry that got turned back.'

'Bloody convenient for you, wasn't it?' said my West Brom mate.

I wasn't impressing them and the other two Portsmouth lads were shaping up to give me a wallop, as was the other obnoxious brummie who was mouthing at me, asking me where I was staying and saying 'search him for a radio'. He went to touch me.

'Keep your hands off, ugly,' I said as I pushed him back, then I just walked away saying that I was going to get my mates. I had five paces on them and thought that if they tried to follow me then I would break into a run. They had drunk too much to chase me and I fancied my chances over 50 yards against Linford Christie if I was being chased for a beating.

When *The Daily Mirror* printed George Jackson's riot report it had a quote from Chelsea fan, Colin Ward.

The day of the game and the car drop-off area in front of the Royal Viking became a focal point for the England fans who massed outside, drinking and singing. The news boys waited like vultures inside the hotel and the police stood perplexed. Occasionally, someone would do something stupid and would get admonished by a Swedish policeman. Every so often I would pop in the side entrance of the hotel. I introduced myself to the *Today* news man but got a frostier reception than I had the previous day off Rob Shepherd. I observed the pecking order which existed. The sports boys were number one and so looked down their noses at the news boys. The news boys really worked their butts off. For them they had to deliver the story. The pressure was on. The pressure on the sports boys would come immediately after the match when they had to deliver a succinct report under the tightest deadline imaginable. Everyone seemed to be looking at me. I was getting paranoid.

Frank Partridge filed a report for the midday edition of *Newsbeat*. Based upon what he had seen going on around the city he filed an honest report in which he felt that this trip was the start of a new era of supporter behaviour and it would be the bridgehead which enabled English clubs to gain entry back into Europe. Frank had hit the nail right on the head, yet in six hours' time would be seen as the biggest iconoclast since Winston Churchill was reviled for saying the Germans were a threat to world peace in the 1930s.

I saw Pete Davies who was scurrying around the hotel. 'I can't stop as I am going to play football for the English press against the Swedish press. Then it's back here straight to the game and fly home,' Pete said to me breathlessly. Pete was in it now and it was sucking him in to the full. Now he would get a chance to play in the same team as Ray Clemence and Trevor Brooking. He could live out his boyish fantasies along with the other sports boys who were fit enough actually to play the game. And while Pete ran to live his dream, some of the other sports boys drank while they ridiculed Bobby Robson and waited for the Swedes to destroy the 'leaden-footed English defence'.

The news boys all hunted together and late in the afternoon they disappeared to the ground where they anticipated the news would happen. Around 5 p.m. the England fans outside the Royal Viking stirred, and, as one, around 150 of the chanting fans marched across the road and up some steps towards the underground train station. Along the road a couple of boys ran into a shop on a shoplifting grab raid and in the rush to get out without paying the glass door got shattered. The sound of the glass smashing set off a small chain reaction. A bus full of terrified Swedes had a window smashed then a bottle got thrown at a police car and the animal broke into a run after some imaginary Black Army. They were whooping and shouting and as they got to the bottom where the subway was the riot police descended on them and held them all. They were taken into preventative detention. I walked back up the road with Diddy and Ray, but we saw no other news boys. I maintain that this was the riot of Stockholm. The innocent residents of one Stockholm street had been subjected to one frightening minute. It was unnecessary, it was embarrassing but that was it. More to the point, no news boys saw it except myself.

We stood in the centre lane of the dual carriageway and watched the England team get on the bus. The England players looked unsure of what they were supposed to do, almost as if they had been instructed not to acknowledge us. John Barnes gave us the thumbs-up, delivered with a precise rhythm. Then the press boys came out to jeers, catcalls and the wankers sign from Diddy and Ray. As the England team coach pulled out I walked up to the front and banged upon the window where Bobby Robson was sitting. His facial expression of 'Oh no, not the brown leather coat again' sent Diddy and Ray into fits of laughter.

On the train from the city centre out to the Rasunda stadium the Swedish fans drank beer and chanted 'We will kill the English' and 'We shag women and we drink beer', while the English fans behaved and sang 'Ingerland' and the riot police looked on.

At the ground the news boys were scampering around like plains buffalo, stampeding up and down the road in a pack, every shout starting another stampede to find the story. No England fans had tickets and none were trying to get them. It was felt the Swedes would let us in. I saw Owen Bowcott of *The Guardian*. His eyes were rolling, his mind was chasing the story. He was speaking at a speed which indicated to me that he was high on adrenalin. Had he interviewed a fan speaking like that he probably would have suspected they were on amphetamines.

'Have any of you lot got tickets?' I asked.

'None of us are going into the ground as our copy deadline expires halfway through the match. We have all got to file some early stories. Did you see the riot in the town earlier?'

'What riot?' I asked. But Owen didn't answer because he didn't hear it.

None of the news boys heard that because they had all seen and heard about the riot in the town earlier and that's what they were going to be reporting in a short while.

'The riot where Bobby Robson shot at that nutter with the brown leather coat with the magnum 45,' shouted Diddy.

'We heard it was wild, shops were looted and police cars were turned over. People are in hospital,' said Owen, walking away up the road at speed with some other news boys. The awfulness of the situation began to dawn on me. The news boys had decided *en masse* to report what they had heard about the riot in the town earlier and that's the petrol they would be putting on the fire back in London in less than an hour. Putting out the fire with gasoline.

I spotted some skinheads milling around just by this grassy bank. 'Stick around here; something's gonna happen,' I said to Diddy and Ray. About two minutes later six enormous skinheads came walking up to the group of England fans, about 25 strong, including us, standing on the grassy bank.

'You pig fuckers,' shouted this enormous skinhead in a Swedish accent.

'Jesus, they ain't Abba come to sing "Dancing Queen",' said Diddy.

We all stood there looking at each other, thinking, 'Shit, he's a big bastard.' And we all pretended he wasn't talking to us. Then another one lurched forward and hit an England fan who went backwards and ran. With that Ray ran down the bank and chinned the huge gorilla. Diddy jumped on his back and got flipped over into a group of shrubs. Ray was hitting this huge skinhead who couldn't believe he was being attacked by this little Englishman. Diddy was crawling out of the shrubbery saying 'Help me, ginger', but I was laughing so much I could hardly stand. Then everybody came to life and the England fans attacked and four of them ran, leaving two to take a beating. Diddy jumped out of the shrubs and was replaced by the gorilla who was trying to get up while Diddy, Ray and a host of others kicked themselves while they tried to kick him. Within 60 seconds it was over. The police came and arrested the two skinheads. The news boys came sprinting through the subway, their view blocked by the bodies in between. Unless you were there you couldn't imagine it. Frantic faces, running for all they were worth, faces red, panic etched in every straining muscle, holding the front of their coats with one hand so their notebooks didn't fall out. When they got to the bottom of the bank the England fans were laughing.

'What happened?' they asked frantically. They were almost pleading for a story. The looks and shakes of the heads they got back said that if you need to ask then you wouldn't know even if we were to tell you. Owen Bowcott actually said 'please help me' when asking me to tell him what I had seen.

I shook my head along with the rest. This was the only major fight of Stockholm. For 30 to 60 seconds it was comical, like a Charlie Chaplin movie, but nobody told the news boys that.

While the England fans walked to the stadium the news boys scribbled frantically, asking questions of fans who had come from behind them but were happy to give a quote about a non-existent fight they had been in to get their names in the paper.

'Listen to me,' shouted the Swedish police chief on a loudhailer. 'We are going to let you in to watch the match, so please don't push. There is plenty of room for all of you. Anybody who has purchased tickets for the other end can use them to gain entrance to this end. Do not try to get in the other end as you will be sent back around here.'

So I waited outside until the last of the England fans had got in and all that was left was the news boys, who were standing outside comparing notes and swapping stories that they were going to file. A Swede came up to me and offered me the best seat overlooking the England fans so I went in while the news boys filed their early stories. Whatever happened in Stockholm was caused by the need for the news boys to file their stories by 7 p.m. While the match went on the petrol got poured on – by the tanker load. By the time the match ended mass hysteria had gripped everybody. The wires were alive with riot stories. Nobody filed a story which matched that of Frank Partridge's earlier in the day.

During the game some of the boys smoked dope, some took speed, but they all cheered the England players while the Swedes made monkey noises when England's black players got the ball. A fight broke out amongst the Swedes at the opposite end where England fans would have been had the black market source not been eliminated by Frank's report. At the end it was 0–0 and Terry Butcher had played a blinder, his head split open, covered in blood, like he'd been caught in a real riot.

'He was one of us, a fan, prepared to spill his blood for his country. We were proud. We had come, we had seen and we had conquered. We felt so good walking out of that ground with the whole Swedish army escorting us back to central station. It feels good when it's like this. I'm so proud to be English,' said Ray, but it could have been any one of a thousand.

Bobby Robson spoke proudly of his team epitomised by his captain, Terry Butcher. Actually, we'd survived by the skin of our teeth and a miracle save from the England goalkeeper, Peter Shilton. Bobby spoke of the trench spirit and of guts. Bobby could have been one of us, and we loved him too. (The next day some of the press mocked Bobby Robson over his use of military metaphors to describe a football match.) While the fans basked in the glow, the news boys filed their copy. As the wires brought in the reports from Stockholm the sub-editors shouted out more instructions to their news boys who delivered the stories on cue. Meanwhile the England fans walked back to the station surrounded by half the Swedish army and 1,000 belligerent Swedes looked for aggro.

Back at the station I was approached and accused of being Old Bill for the umpteenth time. Ray gave the guy short shrift. When I told Ray that I was going back into the city centre to look for a story, Ray offered our friendly big-mouth a chance to come along. Our friend refused, saying that there might be real trouble out there. Looking out from the safety of the station area into the dark empty streets, which looked menacing under the yellow glare of the sodium light, it looked stupid to go back into the city centre, but I was determined to get a story

So we went back into the centre and could find no smashed windows aside from the one I had seen broken earlier. The streets were empty and echoed to the occasional shout as people kicked tin cans or shouted. Bars were shut with police vans driving around. I was the only journalist out on the street looking for a story. The rest were safely cocooned at the Royal Viking, writing what their subs back in England told them to.

Back at the station it was bedlam as news crews with light wanted interviews with hooligans, and not just English news teams: there were Germans, Norwegians, and Americans along with other nationalities. The boys in preventative detention had just come back from a big sports hall where they had watched the game on giant screens drinking free beer while they cheered England on. They were put on trains to go back to the ferry. All I could see were callow pasty English youths, who were proud of their country, who had attended a game of football which had ended 0–0. England needed one more point to qualify for the World Cup finals in Italy so there was a certain feeling of anti-climax among the fans. Certainly nobody was worked up enough to riot as most were exhausted.

I went back to my hotel with Diddy, Ray and two other lads and telephoned in to be met by an incredulous Jeff Sweet on the line.

'Where the hell have you been? This is the biggest night of violence ever and you have been missing for eight hours.'

'That's the story, Jeff. There is no violence. It's quieter than a Sally Army booze-up.'

'Don't give me that shit, the wires here are on fire with violence. There's a bloody riot going on, shops are being looted. People are getting murdered out there and you're sitting in your fuckin' hotel room. Get your arse out there and get the story we're paying you for.'

'Jeff, I am telling you that that is the story. Damn you, the press is the story. They've inverted on their own bullshit. It's a house fire. It's spontaneous combustion with every story fuelling the fire even more.'

I was really angry. I had been where it mattered when it mattered. I had even risked physical damage to go back into the city centre to see how much damage had been done, yet here was some idiot 800 miles away telling me what was happening.

'Bollocks,' Jeff shouted.

With that I put the telephone down and went down to the bar where the lads were sitting. 'Five beers, strength 1, put them on my room tab,' I said. 'Who's paying for these?' asked Ray. 'Rupert bloody Murdoch,' I said, and I lifted the glass and gulped it back as did the others. The first was for my resignation as a journalist, the second was for Bobby Robson, the third for Terry Butcher, the fourth for England. We stopped counting at four and Rupert paid for them all. Everybody liked Rupert.

The next morning I went back into the Royal Viking which resembled the morning after an all-night card and lager session. Sitting in the lobby were the news boys who had been up all night filing stories about the riot. They looked terrible, strung out with creased clothes and sweaty shirts that clung to them.

'Shit, the wires are down to London, I can't file that story about the double-decker bus getting turned over.'

'How many are in hospital?'

'Fifty, I've heard.'

'Four stabbed. Hundreds arrested.'

The *Today* newshound told me that he was too busy to talk to me. The sports boys went into breakfast looking at these bleary-eyed scribblers, high on caffeine, nicotine and adrenalin, with incredulity. They had done their jobs the previous evening in 40 frantic minutes immediately after the match. I looked at the news boys, awestruck, yet finally saw what was driving them on: fear. Fear of failure, fear of not delivering the goods, not producing for the mad sub. The fear was in their faces, just as it had been in the faces of those Swedes sitting in that bus, but the bus never got turned over, the truth got turned over. I didn't have the fear or dishonesty to lie on tap in me so ultimately I discovered that my dream was dying in front of my eyes.

England fans who'd slept overnight turned up at the station that morning to have a microphone thrust in their faces.

'What do you think of the riot?'

'What riot?'

And the camera crew would run off to find someone else who did know about the riot. When they couldn't find a rioter they filed stories anyway about the terrible carnage and destruction that had been meted out by the disgusting English hooligans. I saw Frank, who looked tired. 'Off home to see the wife?' I asked.

Frank looked at me, dressed in his best travelling cottons which were creased through too much air travel. 'I know I said I was going home, but I've been asked to go to Barcelona to cover the World Athletics championships.' A chance to chase another story had put the light back in Frank's eye. A glint was also in the eye of Bobby Robson who saw the brown leather coat for the last time with a satisfied facial expression.

The aftermath of this reporting was almost catastrophic for football. Politicians reacted as only they could, threatening to ban football itself. Maggie Thatcher declared war on the hooligan scum as only Maggie could. No inquiry was held into the mass hysteria of Stockholm. When the truth was finally exposed many months later, it rated as a small news item, as the truth was seen as an expendable commodity where football fans were concerned. Nobody defended the travelling England fans. Nobody dared because the media onslaught against them would have finished their career. Graham Kelly and the FA said nothing, which spoke volumes for the FA. TC, who lives in Victoria, met all the Today *people at a pub party a few weeks later. They were talking about this nutty ginger-haired reporter who went missing when the going got tough. TC laughed.*

By the time my wife met me at the airport, all the journalists who had participated in the story of Stockholm had moved on and filed more stories than I would ever do in a lifetime. In war truth is the first casualty. I had come to Stockholm as a war correspondent and learnt this lesson the hard way. On the flight back I read *Flying Visits* by Clive James and dreamt of the stories I would never write.

4

THE DOLLAR BOYS

Bobby Robson
England Football Manager
The Football Association
16 Lancaster Gate
London

Dear Mr Robson

You probably remember me from your trip to Stockholm and I would like to take this opportunity of apologising for any distress or alarm my appearance in the brown leather coat might have caused. I am unable to go to Poland because my wife is expecting our first child but the lads will be there and I fully expect us to get the point we need to qualify.

The reason I am writing is over the unjustified vilification you are receiving from some sections of the press, and not just from the tabloid nasties. I shout as loud as the next man and don't always agree with your team selection, but when you start getting called 'Plonker' and the abuse takes on a personal level then it's time to retaliate. I remember reading about when you chinned Mick Lambert at Ipswich. Why not do the same again and chin the journalists who call you names because the players have a poor game? Better still, why not offer them outside for a lesson or throw them out of your press conferences? It's no good them saying that they are only acting under orders; that defence was ruled null and void at Nuremberg.

A few of the chaps are going to have a word in Poland. These chaps are not renowned for their ability to reason or listen to excuses, and have been known to use the odd expletive deleted, as they said in Watergate.

Minimum, your protagonists are going to get the 'Full Monty' verbals.
Yours sincerely

Colin A. Ward

Bobby Robson replied to this letter with the usual 'Thank you for writing', but from the rest of his letter it did seem as if there were other fans apart from me who felt that Bobby Robson was getting an unnecessarily hard time. Okay, so Bobby did use ten words where one would do and a paragraph when a sentence would suffice, but this man was one of us, in so much as he loved his country.

Clemmo was a Leatherhead legend. Clemmo could drink for England and frequently did. He was the only man ever to drink the top shelf in The Railway – you know, one measure of each of those funny coloured bottles of liqueur that every landlord brings back from obscure bars in Portugal, Spain and France and puts up for show in his pub. Twenty-three measures, and the retelling of the story never fails to make me sick. Clemmo had a face similar to Robert Mitchum with a long body and arms which gave him a trademark right hook uppercut that used to come at opponents from the floor. He was still sinking them and throwing them at 50 years old, but better drinking company I've yet to find. Clemmo used to pepper his conversation with the conjunction 'but', especially when he was angry. 'Everyone's entitled to an opinion but that's out of order.' It was the introduction of the 'but' which made one know there was going to be a rider. Two 'buts' starting consecutive sentences prefaced a right hander. Clemmo decided that Poland was the trip for him. I had informed him that it was one of the cheapest countries in Europe. When I informed him that I had met a guy in Berlin who told me that Warsaw had an incredible underground scene of music and drugs, he stopped me.
'Everyone's entitled to do what they want but drugs are wrong.'
'Okay, Clemmo.'
Clemmo was tour leader for a gruesome foursome which included his son, Harold and Jerry. They were on the seven-day tour organised by the Polish national tourist agency. Warsaw for a couple of days then down to Katowice for the game. Katowice, in Silesia, is the equivalent of Middlesbrough on a bad day: tough and dirty with a thick black layer of soot on everything because of the poor quality coal that they burn.
Jerry and Harry were local men who thought that Leatherhead was the centre of the universe. Quite why they went to Poland is beyond me. It's guys like these two who built Benidorm and Lloret de Mar with their all-

day English breakfasts. 'What's wrong with being patriotic?' they used to say to me when I rubbished the Queen and the politics of England in the pub. Absolutely nothing, it is an honourable trait, but reading *The Sun* does not prepare guys like Jerry and Harold for the deprivation that was Poland at the time. I told them my best Polish jokes to prepare them for the culture shock: 'What have USA and Poland got in common? You can't spend zlotys in either country. What's 500 yards long and eats cabbage? A Polish meat queue. What do you call a pretty girl in Poland? A tourist.' They didn't get my jokes in The Railway but they soon did in Warsaw. More to the point, they were also going to sort out the lousy unpatriotic sportswriters for Bobby and England after we had qualified for the Italia 90 World Cup.

There were 50 people on their tour and Clemmo summed them up. 'Good English boys. They love their beer and football and like a good time. Okay, there were a few arseholes sitting at the back giving it all that Nazi stuff, but that's their problem.' Clemmo had been to the European Championships in 1988 and had seen a side to the Germans that he didn't read about in *The Sun*. 'What a great people, tremendous sense of humour. Great drinkers, and so hospitable.' So people being Nazis was an insult to the Germanic people.

'Hello and welcome to Poland,' said the tour guide who looked like George of *George and Mildred* fame and had a permanent smile the whole trip, especially when he got some of the lads to change dollars for his zlotys. (Everyone had bought dollars at the airport because someone had told them that they were of immense value.) When someone pointed out his striking resemblance the name 'George' was on him. His impersonation of the sitcom star even extended to George wearing crimplene trousers and a bri-nylon shirt.

George thought Warsaw the finest city on earth and tried to tell the lads about its culture before the Russians came. Nobody took any interest and everybody was astounded to see long queues of cars near every petrol station. George explained that cars were abandoned near a petrol station when they ran out of fuel because nobody was sure when the next petrol would arrive.

When the lads got to the hotel they tried to head out to find a local bar. All they found was empty shops and queues for everything. When Jerry and Harold stopped outside one empty shop with a Polish flag in the window two women started queuing behind them. After 20 minutes they found a taxi, but no sooner had they got in it than the driver explained that he needed to get some benzene. He drove them to a run-down council estate, every bit as grim as those in south London that they knew. They were ready to run as they expected to be attacked by a mob after their money at any moment. Next thing the driver appeared with another guy with Russian army jerrycans. It transpired that the residential flats had petrol stored in them. Those flats must have been an absolute death-trap.

On the way back the taxi with the lads in got stopped for speeding by a policeman. After the driver got out and paid a spot fine/bribe, the driver explained that the policeman had stopped the taxi because it contained England fans who must have had money.

After two days in Poland the lads were ready to go down to Kraków to see the England Under-21 match. When they got on the coach George had other ideas: 'Today we are going on a cultural visit to see some Polish history which will finish at one of our famous monasteries.'

'He's not for real,' said someone.

'Piss off, we want to go to the Under-21 game. We're football fans, not bleedin' culture vultures.'

The coach was stopped and Clemmo explained: 'I understand that you are keen to show us your country, and we are really honoured, but the boys are getting a little restless and want to go to the England Under-21 game.'

'Our driver has a tachograph on and cannot drive all the way to the game, plus he must buy some fuel, for which he needs hard currency.'

'How much?' asked Clemmo.

'Two hundred dollars,' said George.

'Listen, lads,' shouted Clemmo, 'It's four dollars per man and Smiler here (pointing to the driver) takes us to the Under-21 game, or it's a trip to the monastery. What's it to be?'

Two hundred dollars was collected faster than you could chant 'We love you Georgie, we do, Oh Georgie we love you,' which went up as the bus pulled away. And the comments of 'Christ, they look scruffy,' and 'Look at the state of their cars' could be heard all the way to Kraków. At the game the man on the turnstiles started charging one price as the first went in then started putting the price up as he went along. The ones at the back paid twice as much as the first, but it still only worked out around 20 pence when the black market exchange was calculated. The ground had huge floodlight pylons which had no bulbs in. One of the lads cracked a funny which nobody else understood, based upon Winston Churchill's comment after the war. 'The bulbs are going out all over Poland.'

Every England trip has a resident goon on his first trip and Poland was no exception. You can spot them a mile off on England trips. They walk around the airport departure lounge with a beer in their hand, even at 7.30 in the morning (which is flat, because they haven't bought it for drinking but for show) and a permanent painted-on smile. They want to be liked by everybody, yet ultimately try the patience of a saint. This guy came from Nottingham and became known as Norm. At the airport he kept staring at everybody. With his short, tidy hair, Jerry said he looked like a policeman. It was a mistake because Norm latched on to Clemmo and their group. All he did was get on everybody's nerves with his constant drone of conversation and desire to do stupid things which nearly caused a riot. 'We're having a bloody scream. Fuck off, Polak. Look at all these dollars, loads of money,' he shouted at a group of miners in Kraków, then started waving a wad of money at them. The boys thought it could get no worse, but no sooner had they only just survived that when he trashed his hotel room, throwing a chair out of the front window five floors up which just missed a woman passer-by. He just about had time to walk into the lobby of the hotel when the police stormed in and nicked him, dragging him away.

'Thank God for that. Peace at last,' said Jerry.

George explained later that evening.

'Norman . . .'

'Call him Norm the Storm, George,' said Clemmo, interrupting.

'Norman Storm (everyone fell around laughing) is being held for attempted murder.' Clemmo, along with nearly everyone else, erupted into laughter, but some of the other northern lads thought that everyone should chip in to bail him out.

'Spend money on that time-waster, you're having a laugh,' said Jerry.

Norm did finally get released and came into a packed breakfast room, and promptly started throwing bread rolls. Clemmo stood up and pointed the finger at him.

'Now you listen here, you twerp. Everybody here is just about fed up with your behaviour. You nearly got us all killed in Kraków and you nearly killed some innocent woman when you threw that chair through the window. Everybody is sick of you and if you put one more foot out of line then I will personally smack you in the teeth. Do you understand, Norm?'

'Yes, Clemmo.'

'Right, we can substitute that speech for grace.'

All the England fans and other people in the room started cheering and clapping Clemmo, led by the ubiquitous George, who was wearing his best purple bri-nylon that day.

At the end of the trip Norm was seen sitting on the stairs close to tears. 'Why doesn't anybody like me?' he asked, but nobody bothered to tell him.

Other fans were staying in the Grand Hotel and Clemmo was invited up to the room of a group who had come over from Kent. As he entered the room the bed had a pile of money which nearly went up to the ceiling. This group had changed all their money up into zlotys on the black market then found out they were absolutely worthless. They were playing three-card brag and drinking blue label Smirnoff vodka. The opening bet was one million zlotys blind. The next guy went open with ten dollars which went into a separate pot. One million zlotys was worth ten dollars in this card game. 'See us lot,' one of the card-players said to Clemmo. 'We're all millionaires.' When the chambermaid came in to clean the room the lads had a bet. They put five dollars, a bar of soap, a Mars bar and 5,000 zlotys on the bed. They all bet which order she would take them in. After she was invited to choose she took the dollars, soap, Mars bar, and went to leave without the zlotys. For entertainment value she was given the zlotys as a tip.

The Grand Hotel in Warsaw looked like any one of a number of buildings that one sees in the Eastern bloc. The architecture was great but the Russian occupation since 1945 had made everything seem joyless and bland. Winter was settling upon Warsaw which made it seem even more drab, and everywhere they looked they saw unsmiling faces, endless queues and nowhere to get a drink. 'No bloody wonder they love their football out here, it's all they've got.' However, on the third floor of the Grand was a complete floor of prostitutes and that is something none of the lads had seen before.

The first night in Warsaw Clemmo went out for a drink with the boys to find a local bar. There were bars but none had any drink in them. They found a night-club full of sad young Poles shooting needles up their arm. 'Christ almighty, what have we come to?' said Clemmo upon returning to the hotel, so they stayed in the hotel after that.

Traf was from Manchester and everyone liked Traf as much as they disliked Norm. Traf was always on the move, twitching, unable to sit still. One night they were sitting in the bar when he came bursting in. 'Lads, come on,' he said excitedly. 'There's a big group of Polaks out there giving it the big one, chanting Poland and goading us.' Harold went out and had a look. There was a subway and Harold didn't like the look of it. 'It's an ambush,' said Jerry, but Traf rounded up a couple of the lads to go and sort out these Polaks. Traf limped back into the hotel about 20 minutes later holding his back in agony. 'Poxy ambush. The bastards lured us down into the subway then bricked us. I got hit in the back.' Traf sat there moaning all night. Everyone agreed that Warsaw wasn't so bad after all.

The second night three lads walked in: Andy, Billy and Nick. They hailed from Bedfordshire, were loud, funny and brash and called themselves the dollar boys. Clemmo immediately struck up a conversation with them. They were contract plasterers whose job it was to replaster the British Embassy as every so often the walls were stripped out to search for bugging devices.

They spent all their time travelling around the world replastering all the embassies. The dollar boys thought that being in Poland at the same time as the England match was bliss. As the evening wore on the dollar boys told some interesting stories.

'Do you know that we are not allowed to tell you how much plaster we use to redo the walls at the Embassy?' said one.

'Yeah, the Commies might be able to undermine the defence of the British Isles.'

These boys had travelled around the world replastering British embassies and had to sign the Official Secrets Act which limited what they could talk about. When they did talk about life on the front line of international spying then everybody listened. 'Spies don't look like spies, they look like school swots. Most of the real spies are electronics bods. They tell us that spying is about listening to radio messages and nothing like James Bond, but occasionally we see spooks.'

'Spooks?' someone asked.

'Yeah, real stern-faced bastards,' said Andy. 'We saw two yesterday when you lot turned up. So Billy here is having a bit of fun and asks them if they were in town to brief the Polaks on our finest hoolies. About two hours later we get asked to go and visit the head honcho's office. He reminds us that we have signed the Official Secrets Act and all that garbage.'

Andy piped up: 'Real serious he was an' all. I reckon that they were over here because of you lot and what happened in Sweden.'

'Just think, James Bond tangling with us lot.'

'Don't worry, Traf'll get him a hiding.'

'Yeah, and at midnight, if James sticks with us, he gets to meet the dollar girls!'

That's what they called the girls on the third floor because that's all they accepted, but Billy, keen for everybody to know his proudest moment, took the lads upstairs for a tour. 'See her,' he said, pointing to this tall blonde woman. 'I had her for zlotys.' In a country where zlotys were worthless it was his proudest boast, and no other England fan, not even the millionaires, got to make that boast during the trip, try as they might.

A group of Palace fans moved into a hotel in Dusseldorf. Also in the hotel were a group of Millwall fans. For three days they lived in each other's pockets, drinking and laughing the night away. On the day the Millwall fans moved out of the hotel one of the Palace fans got the room keys of the Millwall fans and went around and shit in their beds. What did you do that for, he was asked? 'So the krauts would remember all Millwall fans as a bunch of shits!'

Clemmo, Jerry and the others came back to the hotel the day before the game and were grabbed by this animated character called Alf who supported Queens Park Rangers. Alf lived in a twilight zone where people were judged by their class: supreme, top, first, etc. Whilst it was thought that supreme was best, Traf entered the breakfast room one morning to be informed he was exquisite class. Alf was a sometime man – sometime back in 1982 he did a day's labouring. 'Shit, that was hard work, no wonder the spades don't do it.' Now he did deals in drugs or 'whatever them yuppies want. Real yuppies from the monied upper classes, not the new money, they're a nightmare. They want a line, they bell me on me mobile and I deliver, cocaine, billie, or E. No heroin [people who buy that are too freaky] or dope [the spades class that as their domain and get angry if you take their income].' Alf was making a fair living in the west London yuppinomic zone. 'ET' Alf was constantly trying to telephone home to keep in touch with his man, who was keeping business going while he was in the 'Polish enterprise zone', as he put it. No morning was complete without Alf chiding George over the state of the telephone systems. 'Don't worry, George, I'll do a deal to get a dozen of BT's finest to travel with us next time.' Alf could seemingly be miles away, then just as you were about to walk away he would repeat the last line of the conversation. Alf thought little of the NF thickos. 'Low wattage,' he used to say.

'What do you mean?'

'Bit dim, ain't they. Shout "muck up hoddie" and they'll come running like a sheepdog.' Then he would shout 'Muck up hoddie' in a mock high-pitched voice and go off laughing.

'Quick, come upstairs with me and see what I've got. And bring a camera. You are never going to believe it, it's blinding,' shouted Alf. So up they went and into his room where there were two blokes flat out on the bed, completely out for the count. He flung open the wardrobe. 'What about that, then?' he said proudly. Hanging up were two immaculate Polish army uniforms complete with caps. 'Deserters, they're bleedin' deserters and I've got their uniforms. I'm gonna sell them for about £250 quid each back in London. Those bloomin' yuppies are gonna wear them to their fancy dress parties. I can see them now, marching around the room boasting where they come from, especially as I'm gonna tell 'em that we mugged them. They get off on all that violence kick.'

'What about them two?' asked Clemmo, pointing to the two young Poles lying on the bed. 'I got them pissed on cheap vodka and my duty-free. I'll let them sleep it off. They think I'm gonna smuggle 'em back into England, but by the morning we'll be gone to Kraków and they'll be on the way to the salt mines.' Alf was so infectious with this scam that everybody laughed.

Lying on the bed were two crew-cutted Polish conscripts who didn't look like they would ever wake up. Alf had swapped their Polish army uniforms for two pairs of Adidas track suit bottoms ('nicked 'em down Oxford Street, well cheap, eh?') and two T-shirts. One of then had 'Prisoner Cell Block H' written on the front. 'Mark my words, that shirt will go down a storm in Warsaw High Street.' On their feet were their army boots. 'Funny thing is that they wouldn't give up their boots for anything. Look at the state of them. Adidas track suit bottoms and Army boots. It won't catch on.'

Everything Alf said was funny and after more of Alf's duty-free everyone retired to bed.

The next morning the two Polish army guys were gone, along with everything that Alf possessed, although they did leave him the Prisoner Cell Block H T-shirt. In the breakfast room Alf was not fazed. 'The funny thing is that they didn't go through the door because it was still locked from the inside, and we were four floors up. They must have been members of the Polish State Circus to get down from that height with all my gear.' By the time breakfast was over Alf had a new scam organised for Shepherd's Bush market; he was going to take back large denomination zloty notes and frame them, then sell them to trendy yuppies for a large profit.

Later, before the match, Clemmo bumped into Alf who'd scrounged some gear up off the other lads which made everybody laugh. Anybody else would have been gutted to have all their gear nicked but not Alf. He was laughing about it: 'No, fair play to 'em, I'd have done the same thing myself. Real top-class performers. Perhaps I should have smuggled 'em back to Blighty!' Then Alf was gone, looking for another money-making scheme. As Alf reasoned, the only purpose to come to somewhere like Poland, in conjunction with watching England, was to see how people survived under such harrowing circumstances, then take their best scams and adapt them for Shepherd's Bush, 'the centre of yuppiedom', as Alf put it.

George organised a coach trip down to Auschwitz. Everybody who went in as a human being would come out a different person, despite the different ways they dealt with the incomprehensible fact of four million dead. Most of the fans were shocked into silence. Jerry summed it all up: 'I've stood at the top of Wembley Way waiting for mates for 30 minutes and people have streamed past me like a constant sea. When I have met them there are still people coming out of the stadium behind us, but that's only 100,000.' A couple of wags sent a postcard to Colin Moynihan, the Sports Minister, from Auschwitz, which made everybody laugh. On the way to Auschwitz the morons at the back of the coach sang 'Zyclon B, Zyclon B, Zyclon B's the gas for me' (to the tune of Stars and Stripes), and shouted how they were

gonna spray NF on the gas-chamber walls. Whatever class they were it was
low and low wattage was close to no wattage.

On the day of the game the police put men on the door of the hotel to stop
the England fans getting out. Not that there was anywhere to drink so they
stayed in their hotel. By now boredom had set in so the lads started to play
jacks, which basically is a mad drinking-game where the loser gets to drink
horrible concoctions of alcohol. Jerry, being a local man, got stitched up big
time and ultimately ended up missing the match, fast asleep on the hotel
floor. Clemmo went to leave the hotel to go to the game wearing his best
blue anorak, which was a prize he had won in The Railway. It was a
corporate gift from the brewers Fosters and had a huge F logo on it. Clemmo
had consumed a fair amount of drink and was stopped at the door of the
coach by a Polish army three-striper who spoke good English.

'You have been drinking. You shouldn't go to the game.' He then
remarked that he liked his jacket.

'Well you can piss off you, stupid Polak, cos you ain't having it. It ain't
for sale.'

With that, the rifles were up and Clemmo was in the back of the van to
be joined by his son who had left the hotel with a bottle of orange juice
containing vodka. Within minutes they were joined by around 12 others. As
they drove them away the three-striper spoke to Clemmo: 'I like your
jacket. I am sure that if you were to swap your jacket for one of our finest
army coats then you would be sober enough to go to the match.'

'Clear off,' said Clemmo. 'I'm English, and we don't succumb to
blackmail.'

So they took them all to the nearest police station where they all were
subjected to the old-style breathalyser. Chalk line across the floor. Walk
eight feet with their finger on the end of the nose. When every England fan
passed the officer was dumbstruck. Just as it looked like they were going to
be released to see the second half, a couple of the lads started chanting Lech
Walesa's name, which caused anger amongst the army, so they were driven
to a larger police station where they went through the ritual again. In the
meantime Clemmo's original drunkenness charge was being changed to loss
of his wife as his joint passport, which had his wife's picture on it, was
causing the Polish police all sorts of problems. When a senior officer driver
appeared he ordered all the England fans to be released, but three-striper
wasn't very forgiving: all the England fans supported a revolutionary, he
had no Fosters coat and he was no closer to finding the mystery of
Clemmo's missing wife, so he drove them to just outside the stadium so
they could hear the cheers of the match, as a form of punishment.

And while Clemmo defended the honour of England by refusing to give the army man his Fosters coat or reveal his wife's whereabouts in Poland, the England team defended their goal while the Poles threw everything at them. Only a point was needed, but England would have to earn it and the Poles would have to take away England's place in Italy by winning the match. The irony of all this was that Clemmo would have given the Pole the jacket if he had been in the bar with Clemmo before the match and Clemmo had liked him. (I've never known Clemmo to dislike any foreigner once he met them and started drinking with them. Frogs became great French people and Yanks became superb Americans.)

Back at the stadium the Poles threw the kitchen sink at England. Peter Shilton, the England goalkeeper, made two breathtaking saves to keep England on level terms.

When the match ended Clemmo, his son and the rest of the drunks were thrown out of the van and headed back to the hotel. 'They don't tell you about that in the tourist brochures,' said Clemmo's son. Only one thing for it – have another drink, especially when Alf bounced into the bar with a cut above his eye where he had been hit by a flying stone, and declared: 'First-class rearguard action. Ironic, that. We're going to Italy now following a retreat the Eyeties would have been proud of.' Nobody knew whether he was talking about the England performance or his retreat after the game from the ugly Polish fans. More guys returned to the bar saying they'd been attacked by a huge mob of stone-throwing Poles.

'Did you run?'

'Too bloody right we did.' They all ran. Ran for their bloody lives. They ran to cheer England on another day, in another godforsaken hell-hole where the local lunatics try and decapitate you on the day of the match with a half-brick.

That's not how the tabloids saw it, as it was only England fans who caused trouble at games like this. The police told the press that they had arrested England fans who were absolutely stoned, far too drunk to see the match, but nobody in the press bothered to check it out. When, during the press conference, a bloodied and beaten England fan had entered the room causing uproar, the man from the FA had stormed out, swearing about stupid fans, not bothering to ask if he could help him or anything humane like that. Get that Good Samaritan out of the press conference; my job depends on you lot calling them moronic Nazis.

Night comes early to Silesia in October with all the pollution in the air. Not that any of the lads noticed, as the hotel bar had plenty of drink, even if it was East German Seck – sparkling white wine which was a little too sweet, but better than the best French champagne at times like this. At last a reason to celebrate: Italia 90 beckoned next summer. Clemmo surveyed the top shelf but it was empty so he stuck to genuine Polish vodka from the freezer with the corn stem and husk left in it, while Alf regaled everyone with yuppie women I have slept with, and Traf twitched his way through every victory toast. Jerry moaned that he could have spent his money by going to the Costa Brava for a real holiday, but the truth of the matter is that all of the lads would look back on this trip with a great deal of affection, even if they wished they had done the three-day trip.

The lads on the five-day tour were on a shuttle between Warsaw, Kraków and Katowice. Whilst the England team were flown out immediately after the game, there were still some press left in the Holiday Inn the morning after the game. It transpired that some of the press were staying on overnight, as one of the lads came back into the hotel stating that he had seen one with a bleach blonde prostitute down the road. While the lads had celebrated and felt pleased, the sports press seemed to feel cheated that England had qualified.

In the morning there was a tense atmosphere, as hungover England fans and the press mix as well as petrol and water. The England football team, having fought for their lives in a very hostile environment against fast, incisive Polish players, had to endure the abuse of the press who called them horrible names – Donkeys, Slow-witted – and concluded that it was a waste of time England turning up in Italy. The England fans who had endured the insufferable, who were too young to be there when the Poles knocked them out prior to the 1974 World Cup, had spent the previous evening celebrating with Polish vodka that tasted like paint stripper and pretty girls who definitely weren't tourists. What motivated the sports boys to rubbish England, its best footballers admired by all the Polish people the England fans spoke to? There was also a little resentment that they had seen the rough end of the stick from hostile Polish fans yet would probably be painted as the aggressor once again.

Jerry had a stinking hangover, but more to the point he had come a long way to a country that was more boring than a wet January afternoon in Eastbourne and had missed the only possible reason for coming somewhere such as this: the game itself. He spotted some press sitting haughtily at a table and walked over to give Rob Shepherd of *Today* a piece of his mind. Rob made an unwise move and ignored Jerry. Jerry was a local man who loved football – you'd have to, to play in some of the leagues Jerry once played in. Jerry would have given his right arm to have played football for his country, as would any of the fans who followed England. For most fans, meeting and talking to their heroes gives them some form of pub kudos. If Jerry could write he would write about the magnificence of England, how they stoically repulsed the mass waves of Polish fervour and unflinchingly threw their bodies in the way of desperate Polish long-range shooting, a desperation forced upon the Poles by the inbred spirit and *esprit de corps* of England, our England. The initial Polish cavalry charge reduced to despair by 11 heroes.

Jerry once played against a pub team in south London where the entertainments manager was Charlie Kray, so he knew about people coming at him in a threatening manner, but ignoring people was not big on Jerry's list. So Jerry did the most un-English thing one could ever do – he spat green brought-up phlegm over the side of Rob Shepherd's face then walked away in disgust. Harold said later that Rob pulled out a hankie to wipe his face and turned to the other sportswriters and said: 'See, this is what we have to put up with in places like Poland when they put us with them.'

'Whatever you put up with from us, it's nothing compared to what Bobby Robson puts up with from you lot,' said Harold sneeringly. Rob wasn't on his own, yet nobody got up to help Rob who just sat there with it running down the side of his face.

At the side of the breakfast room were a number of small flower vases. This being Poland there were no flowers in them. As Jerry returned from the toilet the lads were launching the vases at the press, like a fusillade of Katyusha rockets. After the last vase had smashed, when the press stopped cowering, the boys left laughing. Bobby Robson was back in England but, had he been here, I am sure he would have managed a wry smile under his ambassadorial nice-guy exterior.

Clemmo and the other three caught the train back. They travelled first class for 70 pence and were met in Warsaw by a pensive-looking George who was worried that some of the lads had not returned. Every time someone else came back, George's smile got wider. These were all his boys and he was proud of them.

As the lads went to board their bus to go back to the airport to return home, George stood in the lobby, adorned in his best bri-nylon. He declared England to be 'the greatest country on earth with English football fans VC class (Alf's coaching after he had come back from the match with a slight cut), as nobody else comes to Poland for a week's holiday'. George loved Poland and fervently hoped that by the time we came next time his wonderful country would be in better shape. (Clemmo declared on the plane home that he would never willingly go to such a deprived place again as long as he lived.) George wanted to spend all his life working as a courier for English football fans, while the man from the FA was quoted as saying to the press after the match that English football fans shouldn't have come. They weren't welcome.

Like all England fans I believed that England could go all the way in Italy. Only four years previously, Argentina via Maradona had cheated us out of the World Cup with his 'fist of God' goal then gone on to win it. I met Hugh McIlvanney, chief football writer of *The Observer*, at an awards ceremony in London before Italia 90. This man had really passed his cynicism degree with flying colours (guess what, he was Scottish) and he berated me for believing that England could go all the way in Italia 90. He mocked England, who had only won the World Cup in '66 because they had played all their matches at Wembley, the Hungarians had butchered Pele off the park and a friendly referee sent off the Argentinian Rattin in the quarter-finals. (Of course he mentioned the Russian linesman. I have never yet met a jock who doesn't mention him.)

So I shut him and the rest of the press boys present up by telling him a story about the real world football fans operate in. In my best east London accent I told him about the Toxteth slasher gang and how the slashed Chelsea fan was still going because he loved the game. 'Tell me you love the game as much as he does,' but he couldn't because he lived and operated in a world which had no comprehension of how it really is for many fans. The other writers present were shocked by my vitriol and looked at the floor, as if I was Harry.

England went to Italy with the sports boys mocking their chances. The fans who went had belief in their chances. The aftermath of Stockholm meant that England had been given Sardinia for their group matches. An island was meant to help security matters. There was also, according to the press, the grudge hooligan match between England fans and the Dutch.

Maggie Thatcher was the most responsive Prime Minister in history. An event always had to have a reaction, so after the Stockholm riot she had threatened to ban England from Italia 90. (No need to look at the facts dispassionately then have a reasoned response: these are football fans so give them both barrels then ask them if they are dead.) The only person who took this seriously, apart from Dennis Thatcher, was the malignant midget she had appointed as Sports Minister, Colin Moynihan. This was the man who got so worked up when the England hockey team won the gold medal in the previous Olympics that he ran on the pitch to celebrate. Nothing wrong with that. Perhaps he understood the passion of football fans. Not a bit of it. Football fan in Italy equals thug, so he promptly told the Italians that our fans were animals, which gave the worst elements of the Italian riot police *carte blanche* to beat the brains (or lack of them – but when has it been a crime to be thick?) out of any England fans they saw fit.

Not only that, a new ruse was invented: arrest people and ship them home summarily without charge or reason. When an airliner was chartered to ship home troublemakers and exactly the same number of fans were arrested as there were seats on the aeroplane, even the most vigorous cynics raised an eyebrow. The Foreign Office can turn a blind eye to human rights abuses when it suits our trade requirements, so it won't matter if they turn a blind eye to a few football fans being mistreated. Unfortunately, one of the guys arrested was a guy who was on holiday in Rimini with his wife and family. When he popped out of his hotel to get some cigarettes he was rounded up along with other England fans after an incident in a bar. His only crime was to answer the question 'are you English?' with a yes. The next morning he was back in England after being arrested and deported along with 350 others, which just happened to be the exact number of seats on the aeroplane.

While Colin Moynihan was saying that the England fans were getting what they deserved, the local Sards were taking them into their houses and stopping the riot police dishing out unfair beatings. Keith Chitty took his wife to Rimini for a World Cup holiday but came back after seven days. 'Listen, ginger, it's like nothing I've ever experienced before. That midget Moynihan has whipped the Italian police up into such a state of paranoia and hysteria that it's no fun. Being English is worrying. I know we've been in some hairy situations before but it's really frightening out there. Be careful if you go!'

On the field, despite being written off at every turn by the sports boys, the English got to the semi-final and got so close. On the night of the semi-final against Germany the whole country came to a standstill. In the final gut-wrenching moment England had lost. The fans cried, as did Paul Gascoigne (Gazza) who came back a hero. Now there's a guy who really is one of us. He even has a mate with a stupid nickname: Jimmy Five Bellies. In the focus on the football it was suddenly realised that the fans had behaved. Bobby Robson retired as England manager to go to PSV in Holland with the best wishes of the nation. His facial expressions told us that he was sad because the story could have ended oh so differently.

After the World Cup the unnecessary heavy-handedness and stupid establishment behaviour was cited as being justified because there was no trouble. The faces were the same, but all of a sudden the perception changed. The Trafs, Alfs and Clemmos who had gone to Poland were there along with even more low-wattage types, but the news boys could not distort the truth as the hooligan story had long since become tired and hackneyed. The boobs were still on page three but the front page titillation using the hoolies was old now.

Maggie Thatcher invited the England football team to 10 Downing Street because football was now good. Maggie, like all politicians, was quick to bask in someone else's reflected glory. With the whole country shutting down the night England played the semi-final, football was seen as something that could raise her popularity. The decision to reinstate English clubs to European competition was now becoming less of a political hot potato, so suddenly, with the blue-rinse pass-the-buck brigade discovering the existence of football, English clubs got their long-awaited return to European club competition. For real football fans this was a moment that many had been dreaming of for four years.

5

ALL-SEATER

Football had meandered along for over 100 years. The shape of the stadiums had not changed despite there being huge changes in society. Up until 1989, the only new stadium built in 100 years had been Wembley in 1923. Football seemed to have a limitless capacity for self-destruction with an infinite ability to survive and soldier on much as before, but when Maggie Thatcher came to power that changed. She felt the need for a knee-jerk reaction after every football-related incident. A reported punch-up on the Saturday would result in a law being passed in Parliament the following week regardless of whether the press were overloading on hooligan hype. Always a one-word answer. Any new law which would curb football hooliganism was taken on board with a zeal bordering on fanaticism.

The greatest threat to the future of the game was not provided by the hooligans but by the government decision to make it compulsory for all football fans to have ID cards to be able to enter a football stadium. Despite the fact that every football hooligan carried an ID card in the form of a passport when they travelled abroad, which didn't stop one foreign drink or punch-up, it was deemed that ID cards would have to come in. As usual the logistical and financial side was never looked into by Maggie, who shouted ID then left her lackeys to translate it into action. As Thatcher herself had stated (in one sentence), the money could come out of transfer fees. She cited the transfer of Gary Lineker to Everton for £900,000 as proof enough of football being cash rich, not realising that the money Leicester received for Gary Lineker was used to keep the club going for another season.

Football started to worry because the very essence of its existence, the spontaneity of the game, the essence of people suddenly deciding that they wanted to attend a match, the *raison d'être* of the game, was being threatened. Football started to work together against a common enemy for the first time in its history. Suddenly football started to lobby as a group and perhaps this was the point when football realised it really could become an effective marketing force. Maggie was getting warnings from her ministers and MPs that mixing politics and football was not a good idea but she needed a face-saving get-out. It came in the shape of Hillsborough, a tragedy which created the nightmare scenario of people being asphyxiated in a public place. I remember being at Highbury that day and the whole stadium going quiet when the terrible truth started filtering through.

It was so appalling that Lord Justice Taylor was appointed by the government to report on the reasons for it. In Parliament, the knee-jerk reaction was to ban the football terrace. Lord Justice Taylor's report on the tragedy painted a gloomy picture of the terraces, yet the terrace wasn't dangerous in isolation. However, a compromise was needed by the government. It seemed to go like this: if football accepted the full recommendations of the report without argument – which included accepting money to outlaw the terraces – then Maggie would drop her ID scheme and retreat honourably. Football would now be marching to a different tune.

It was only five weeks after Hillsborough. Arsenal travelled to Liverpool to play the final match of the season and had to win by two clear goals. Everybody said they couldn't do it. Before the match the Arsenal fans applauded the Liverpool fans who reciprocated because they were sure to win, so plaudits from cockneys were accepted. Liverpool in their own back yard were invincible, but truth was stranger than fiction and Arsenal won the match and the championship with the most incredible last-minute goal the world had ever seen. Liverpool fans cried, yet they were great sports because they had suffered the unimaginable, so we felt sorry for them. Never again could the spectre of violence rear its head around football. Lawrence and Steve had been to the match and felt euphoric that they had witnessed the match inside that stadium. For the rest of us the match was played out live on Friday evening TV. They walked into a chip shop about half a mile from the ground and ordered some food. A young lad, about ten years old, was standing in the shop. As soon as he heard the cockney accents he darted out of the shop. Within seconds a Liverpool fan was standing in the doorway. 'We've got you now, you cockney bastards.' Outside he heard the young kid shouting: 'Quick, they're in here.'

This couldn't be happening. Only two hours earlier, before the match, the Liverpool and Arsenal fans had been united in their grief. Lawrence, who had opened his fish and chips, pushed them into the scouser's face and Steve kicked him straight in the balls. Down he went, covered in fish and chips. Out the door went Steve and Lawrence with ten scousers coming after them. The little kid was shouting, 'Get the cockneys, do them.'

Down the road they ran and started getting away as the scousers had had to run some way to get to the fish and chip shop and were short on puff. Lawrence later told me that while he was running he was pissed off that he'd wasted good food on such a lowlife. As they sprinted down the road they approached a pub just as a guy was coming out with his girlfriend. One of the pursuing scousers shouted 'Stop them, they're cockneys!' With that the guy who had just come out of the pub pushed his girlfriend aside and tried to trip up the two fleeing Arsenal fans. They escaped, but Lawrence said he has never forgotten the look on that arsehole's face or the shouted comment of the girl: 'I hope they catch you and kill you.'

Many words and much wasted rhetoric had preceded Lord Justice Taylor's report, but this time the writing was on the wall and was acted upon. The report was written by a man who wrote like a better-educated football fan (one of us). He talked about the degradation of the human spirit that the cramped terraces produced, of poor toilet facilities, the stench of urine and stewed onions. Not that terraces had to be like this; it was just the way they had been allowed to develop. Most football fans accepted this as a way of life, just as most British people accept the fact that pubs shut at 11 p.m. Suddenly people who administered and ran football had to think about spending the money which had slipped through their hands (into someone's back pocket) since the end of the Second World War on improving facilities. Money would be provided by diverting some of the tax money which the government had been taking from the pools levy into building seated areas where terraces existed. (Successive governments had also removed millions from football, thank you very much.) The all-seater stadiums went up. This would improve spectator behaviour. What it couldn't do was remove the dark side that is inherent in everybody and manifests itself in a number of football fans.

In tandem with this the police also got their wish for more resources to fight the war against hooliganism. Despite the fact that incidents at football matches had been declining, the police had perfected their marketing skills when it came to getting more resources. With new technology making it easier to identify people who caused trouble the police marketed their needs cleverly. The politician in the police needed a success story, so why not introduce an undercover intelligence unit to produce results? When the unit was set up incidents at football matches were already decreasing in a country where violent crime was rising so fast that old people were afraid to venture outside their houses. When Midget Moynihan and the other MPs were cheering the eventual end to hooliganism thanks to our ever-vigilant undercover police operation, a statistic was unveiled by the press. During the previous year 6,147 football fans were arrested against 17,000 racing fans, of which 600 were arrested at Royal Ascot! However, once the establishment juggernaut is let loose in the UK it gains a momentum of its own which cannot be diverted by a simple matter called the truth.

'I was in Vinos the other Friday straight from work, drinking the best shampoo as it had been an absolutely blinding week. I had earnt a bundle. I had gambled on the Deutchmark falling against the yen and it had fallen faster than shares on Black Monday. I was drinking with that Stefan from Spurs when my mobile rang. It was that nutter Mo from West Ham. "We're having an off with Millwall tomorrow morning at 8.00 a.m. at London Bridge. When we play you in a few weeks then perhaps we can organise something along these lines." I thought it was someone having a wind-up, but it was kosher. The geezer's off his trolley.'

Mark, a face at Chelsea who worked on the money market, asked around and evidently the worst elements among the real nutters have taken to telephoning each other. West Ham started this fashion off when some of their faces started moving into the rave security scene and used their mobiles to organise it.

The police undercover units were a great success. After a number of dramatic show trials the ringleaders of these disgusting fan gangs were jailed. Unfortunately, many of the policemen were later found to be telling lies so the fans were released after their sentences were quoshed. However, the illusion had been created of a sport involved in a war. There was a war on and, as I found out in Stockholm, acceptance of casualties, among them the truth, was necessary to win this war. The young police who had written the bad scripts, which passed the initial screen test in court only to fail when scrutinised, were taken off the undercover football case and put back on to the street. Some, no doubt, went back to Stoke Newington where the local blacks were screaming that the police were planting drugs upon them or indiscriminately beating them up. The police did have some good ideas. One of them, getting themselves known to the main faces of all the different firms and letting the main faces know that they knew what they were up to, was very successful. The police units who were charged with spotting the hooligans began to know more about the hooligans themselves than they did about their own wives. They even got to know each other on first-name terms.

Some of the undercovers began to enjoy the lifestyle the hard-core firms had. The camaraderie, banter and verbal shenanigans along with the violence, which the undercovers said they never indulged in (although one or two of the lads on one trip said they did when it was found out at a subsequent show trial that one of the nutters was actually undercover 'Old Bill'), made undercover a good number. As most of the hooligans didn't care who they drank with and weren't exactly candidates for *Mastermind* they were never in any really serious danger, so undercover was a good assignment. The hooligans were playing a game which politics demanded the police play as well. With their resources, of course, they could play it better, especially with the security services giving them tactical support. That's all it was to the hooligans: a game. The really nasty types weren't football hooligans; they were violent people who had managed to criminalise a whole section of football spectators. The focus given to them was totally disproportionate to their influence to cause trouble, yet the laws passed were given the English treatment: 'We must oppress every football fan in case the nutters do anything.' The people who saw it as the great threat to society failed to realise that it had all happened before with mods and rockers, skinheads and the like. Would the drug culture or whatever else replaced it be easier to control?

Henry was off down to Spurs to see his beloved Chelsea and was looking forward to having a nice day out. He'd come from a party where he smoked some of the best Thai grass he'd had for a long time. The hard core of the main firm was breaking up. Jock was inside on a coke-dealing charge and Ralph and a few of the lads were more interested in the fruit machine scam than fighting for Chelsea. Just before he left he dropped a small piece of black into the top of his jean jacket. At the entrance to the Chelsea end there were numerous coppers searching all the fans for weapons. The young policeman felt the small lump in the top pocket and pulled it out.

'What's this then?' asked the policeman, knowing full well what it was.

'Lebanese black,' replied Henry.

'What's it doing in your pocket?'

'For God's sake, you're searching me for weapons, not dope. Dope is hope. If we all smoke this at every match then you lot don't have to be here.' The policeman was not impressed by Henry's logic and warned him that he was confiscating the dope.

'You have it on me, mate, smoke it later, chill out.'

The policeman was humourless and flipped when he found a packet of papers.

'You were planning to smoke this inside the ground.'

'Well, I wasn't planning to eat it, was I?'

Henry was most aggrieved when the policeman arrested him and stuck him in a van. Back at the station the desk sergeant was not impressed with the over-zealous PC.

'There are real criminals out there,' said the sergeant, shaking his head.

'Yeah, and I just wanted a quiet afternoon chilling out,' said Henry.

The sergeant, despite being discontented with the PC, was not impressed with Henry. 'If you screwed your loaf a bit more and didn't forget you were in London not Amsterdam then we'd all have had a better afternoon.'

Possession of enough black to smoke two spliffs was not considered a serious enough offence to hold Henry and he returned in two weeks to receive a caution. The officer who administered the caution apologised for wasting everybody's time.

Supporting the team through thick and thin would try the patience of any saint. Now fans would be asked for more money to finance the construction of the all-seater stadium. None more so than the hard-pressed Chelsea fan. Supporting Chelsea over the last 20 years has been a real love affair of the heart, as every one of them has never known from one season to the next whether or not they would still have a ground to support the team in. Back in the late '70s and early '80s the biggest threat to football's existence was not the hooligans (despite what the press said) but the greedy property speculators who moved into football clubs under the guise of benevolent saviours. 'I love football, always have, so the chance to acquire this club with its wonderful history (read £20 million freehold value) was a chance in a million.' Chelsea survived by the skin of their teeth thanks to a tenacious man called Ken Bates who bought Chelsea (and £5 million of debt) for £1.00 and the collapse of the property market which sent the property holding company who owned Chelsea into liquidation. Other clubs like Brighton and Fulham were not so fortunate.

Crystal Palace were bought by Ray Bloye in the late '70s. Ray was never one to miss an opportunity. My father had caught him stealing meat on Smithfield market many years previously when he was a boy. 'Once a crook, always a crook,' my father used to say. Ray went on to make a lot of money in the meat industry, but the meat industry is a very insular world so my father and Ray crossed paths a few times. My father predicted that Palace would be finished with Bloye in charge. When Bloye took charge of Palace they owned huge tracts of freehold land behind their goal and had a bedrock of firm support from a large catchment area. When Terry Venables was the manager they were predicted to be the team of the '80s and were promoted to Division One with a 50,000 crowd fervently cheering them on. Bloye went in there and used all his own companies to run everything that moved at the Palace. When Bloye left the best players had been sold for millions, the freehold land had been sold to J. Sainsbury for over £1 million (a supermarket was erected where a football stand should have existed) and the club was £2 million in debt.

During this period my father was involved in a spat with Ray over some freehold properties which an elderly butcher owned but had got himself into problems with. I answered the telephone one evening and informed my father it was Ray Bloye. My father took the phone. In between swearwords about his behaviour towards this unfortunate butcher he delivered a tirade about Bloye's activities at the Palace: 'Bloye, you're a petty thief who used to nick chickens off other butchers' barrows on Smithfield. You were a two bob thief then and you still are. You just can't stop yourself. I predict that when you are finished at Palace they won't be able to afford their own shirts. Now piss off my telephone.'

'You hear more bullshit per hour from the Chelsea boys than any other group of fans I have ever met.' That comment was made by a West Ham fan who hated laughing more than Graham Kelly, if that was possible. Whilst this isn't strictly true, I knew what he meant. Some of the stories I have heard in pubs *are* true. Des White was a pretty boy, not as pretty as Ricky Wallace who only pulled the right side of the fence, but pretty enough to pull both ways. It didn't matter to the lads at Chelsea that he was this way inclined because sexual preference wasn't a criterion for coexistence. He had stood his ground at Manchester when so-called hard cases had shit their pants running from the red army and he always stood his round. When he talked about pulling he never mentioned which gender he was pulling. It was unnecessary to mention this as everybody who was anybody knew. If you didn't know you were a nobody so you wouldn't have questioned him about it. Always good for a story, some apocryphal, some true. He frequented a world of clubs where some of the highest decision-makers in the land (senior civil servants) hung out, in the literal sense of the word. When he told this story in the pub everybody listened.

'I was with someone the other night and they told me that we were being targeted by the big firm.' When he was asked what he meant he explained that the collapse of the Eastern bloc meant that there was probably going to be a lot of MI5 and MI6 out of a job, so they were setting up telephone taps and targeting football hooligans to produce information dossiers to justify their existence to Ministers who were setting budgets. He even quoted the relevant legislation: '"any offence involving conduct by a large number of persons in pursuit of a common purpose". If that ain't us lot looking for an off with West Ham then I'm Tutankhamun.' Some of the information is being drip-fed to the police to lobby for favours. The undercover police operation is seen as security services' operational sphere.

Des said they'd try an experiment. Chelsea were due to play away in the north-west so Des telephoned around ten or twelve of the lads who were in on it. They picked a train leaving King's Cross and told certain people that different firms would join the train at different places going north, to outwit the police so they could cause mayhem before the police got their act together. When the train in question arrived at the destination three Chelsea fans got off, to be met by 100 northern police and six London special spotter police. Henry, who was on the train, burst out laughing.

'Expecting trouble, boys?'

'Not from you lot,' snapped back an angry London policeman.

'Well, you must have been expecting something, there's enough of you,' said Henry, laughing, as the three of them walked out of the station.

Everyone was a lot more careful about what they said on the telephone after that.

I remember an animated conversation once between my father and his friend Vic Warden on the way to Chelsea one day. My father was arguing that the money from the huge 40,000 crowds in the '50s and '60s had been siphoned off by unscrupulous directors who ran football for their own ends. His logic was that the wage costs were extremely limited and none of the income had been used for capital expenditure on stadium renewal, so it had to have gone somewhere. I was just a small lad and coming out of that match I chased after George Eastham for his autograph. George was the man who had won a historic court case which enabled players to be transferred from one club to another. Before that case players had been treated like slaves, unable to move from clubs, trapped like a Charles Dickens novel in the Victorian football workhouse. Some say his action was the start of the slippery slope to rampant commercialism, but it was the realisation that the amateur negotiation of TV rights was losing a fortune and that individual team fan loyalties were an untapped commodity which really changed the game. The three disasters of Heysel, Bradford and Hillsborough were the final actions which shocked everybody into the frantic change which gripped the game. Terrible disasters had happened before and sparked nothing more than promises to make things better. The hooligan era had precipitated more government legislation than the terrible loss of life at the two previous football stadium disasters at Bolton and Glasgow Rangers. Whereas before the people who ran football would talk of bolting seats on to the terraces, the talk was now of whole new stands and new grounds on greenfield sites.

Trevor Phillips was a brilliant marketing man from Unilever. He was also a tough negotiator. He realised the power of football and how the creation of competition between TV companies could negotiate extra money, so when the Football League appointed him as Marketing Director he knew what he had to do. His realisation that football fans were an untapped commercial commodity was nothing revolutionary, but he and other marketing men were replacing the ex-professional footballers in marketing departments everywhere within the game. Once the people in power realised that all-seater meant loads more income which the fans would gladly pay, then the floodgates were really opened. Grim commercialism replaced the effervescent benign smiles.

Silver, of West Ham ICF fame, was doing an interview for The Face *magazine. 'Nah, the violence has passed, it's long since gone. You know when you go to your cousin's wedding and the guy turns up dressed in the Teddy Boy stuff with the velvet collar drape and sideburns, everyone looks at each other because they know they used to do it but grew up. All the main boys have moved away into the rave culture. There were 5,000 of them boys dancing in a field a few weeks ago, Chelsea, West Ham, Spurs, even some fridges from Millwall.'*

The Arsenal shareholders' AGM used to be a sedate affair with between 15 and 40 people attending, depending on the team's fortunes. My father used to go along to the club on a Monday afternoon and end up having a Scotch session with Dennis Hill-Wood. My father reckoned the great man could put a bottle back and still imitate an Alex James body swerve. (Alex James was the 1930s Scottish equivalent of George Best.) He used to pick up an invite to be a guest in the directors' box from the director Rev. N.F. Bone for a match later in the season. As the club shareholding got more widespread, the AGM was switched to a London hotel. A couple of years before my father's death a 'new money' man called David Dein bought his way into The Arsenal. Dein had made his money in commodity trading. Plenty of people like Dein were coming into the game. Some say they blew the cobwebs away, others say they hijacked the beautiful game. For me the jury's still out. The fans were too busy cheering their team on or queuing up for tickets to notice.

Peter Hill-Wood became Chairman of Arsenal Football Club on the death of his father. On the day in question I was haranguing him about the new shirts which Arsenal were wearing. 'Only two seasons ago we were wearing shirts that made us look like Wimbledon ball boys, now we have got shirts that make it look like we have been run down by tractors. When will it end?'

81

'It's a bloody disgrace,' shouted out one old boy who looked as if he was old enough to have seen Alex James play. Peter Hill-Wood looked flustered, so I sensed the moment was right to go for the throat. I asked him who made the decisions about the shirts? Whether it was Arsenal or their sponsors JVC? He looked at his Managing Director, Ken Friar, who said something and shook his head.

'It was a commercial decision,' replied Peter.

'How much are Arsenal being paid to look stupid?'

He looked at Ken and the same mumbled conversation.

'A substantial amount of money,' he replied.

By now I could hardly keep the anger out of my voice. '100K, 200K, 300K. Are Arsenal selling their soul for 40 pieces of silver? Can I have the assurance from the club that Arsenal will remember their traditions when they next negotiate the new shirt contract?'

'Hear hear,' shouted the crowd and started applauding.

Peter Hill-Wood gave that assurance in just the same way as the United States Government signed a treaty with the Sioux Indians ceding them the Black Hills of Dakota in perpetuity, then took them back five years later when gold was discovered in those hills.

The next time I attended an AGM the venue had been changed to the new Arsenal Clock End complex. Peter Hill-Wood was flanked by the 'new money' man, David Dein, and was dismissive of my questions about the new shirt contract. In a surreal, almost stage-managed atmosphere, the answers flowed off the tongue in a way of which a slick, seasoned American politician would have been proud.

'It's the world we live in. They're in the fashion industry now; it's a commercial decision,' said a smiling Hill-Wood. 'People love to wear these shirts. We might even have an Arsenal shareholders' tie done. As long as you don't object to the design changing every year,' said Peter Hill-Wood. As he made the final comment he gave a smug look towards me. The assembled throng cheered and the Arsenal Marketing Manager gave me an all-knowing smile. He later told me that he knew where I was coming from but my insistence that Arsenal stuck to tradition had to be reconciled with progress. All over the country fans were being told that tradition would be upheld . . . as long as it didn't interfere with the profit margin!

As the all-seater stadiums went up, so too did the ubiquitous luxury box. Now the clubs were attracting corporate money. People were prepared to pay huge sums to be wined and dined before the match, then watch the game in consummate luxury behind a glass screen. Some clubs even threw in the chance to be seen fawning around a star player. Watching these middle-aged businessmen with their shirt buttons close to popping out around their grotesque extended bellies talk animatedly to a young uninterested footballer is one of the more perverse aspects of corporate hospitality.

'Great day out. Avocado prawn cocktail for starters then the full monty. Two bottles of the finest to wash it all down and all paid for by that creep who sells us vegetables. Met the players after the match. Gosh, they're ever so small when you see them close up.'

'What was the game like?'

'Dunno, I was too busy looking at the waitress's tits and getting smashed.'

With this money flowing into the clubs the real fans should have got better facilities, but all they got were more requests to pay extra for less with bond schemes and higher prices for merchandise produced by exploited children for pennies in the Far East. So the peasants revolted, having had enough of being spoken to like morons, so they started publishing their own magazines. They called them fanzines. In them they mocked the clubs who wanted their money but not their input. So the clubs started banning them from selling these magazines inside their grounds, then copied the best ideas into their own programmes. While the 'new money' corporate clients got woozy on *vin de table,* the fans peddled their vision outside while the rain trickled down their necks.

Around about this time I saw a debate on TV about the new way forward for football. Garth Crooks, a black footballer and Chairman of the Professional Footballers' Association, was on there as the footballers' voice. No football fans had been invited on to the show. The debate was chaired by Terry Wogan, who asked the question: 'Where is the intelligent voice of the football fan?' 'Tell him, Garth. Tell him,' I shouted at the screen. 'Tell him about the hundreds of new fanzines that are being published. About the way the fans are requesting representation at board level. Tell him about Rogan Taylor, the Liverpool fan, who has started a football supporters association. Tell him about Craig Brewin who was really slating Maggie Thatcher and other politicians such as the sycophantic Sports Minister of the day, Colin Moynihan.' So what did Garth say? 'Yes, Terry, it is a shame that no real spokesperson has emerged who can speak for the football fans. It would be nice if football fans could speak eloquently for their hopes and dreams.' Terry Wogan's insular BBC ignorance was acceptable as he only saw his matches from behind the glass screen based upon his researchers' information. Garth's reply showed how far across the River Jordan the fan had to row before he could reach the other side. (Garth later became a BBC journalist who specialised in turning out smarmy, ingratiating interviews with players and managers.)

It was a big day at Spurs, the local derby against Arsenal. Tickets were hard to come by: the match had been sold out for weeks. The beer lounge for the executive boxes was packed as the wining and dining club consumed to excess until they were called for their pre-match meal. Jeans were banned so de rigueur dress was badly fitting suits, the jackets having spent too long hanging in the rear seat hook of the Sierra, and the seat of the pants much too long on the upholstery round the M25. While during the match the suits chewed on their canapés, the lads in the newly installed seats spat their venom and hatred at their opposite numbers, ripping out seats at the end of the match to throw across the lines of police and stewards. After the match two players who had participated in the game came into the bar area to see their friends. They walked in wearing designer suits, their eyes straight ahead as if all those people just didn't exist, not stopping to make eye contact with any one of those admiring glances.

For too long football had been run like a gentlemen's club. Deals on TV rights had been a cosy agreement. The television companies ran a cosy cartel which football didn't have the nous or inclination to break. Why bring more money in? It will only alert the tax man who might start to look at our gate-receipt fiddling. God forbid that we actually have to declare the full amount we take on the gate. Club chairmen understood cash money. The old-style chairmen understood cash money. One of them was Louis Edwards, the butcher Chairman of Manchester United who, rumour had it, used his cash money scooped off from his meat empire to pay cash to the parents of the best boys to ensure they went to Manchester United. Busby babes every one of them, their graceful innocence paid for in hard cynical handshakes and money exchanges in darkened rooms.

When football had previously tried to break the TV companies' cartel it was half-hearted, but the entry of Murdoch and his satellite TV changed the picture for ever. Huge amounts of money were needed to finance the building of these new stadiums, then pay for the players who were going to grace this brave new world. With the plans came the new money men with their marketing-speak executives. In staccato bursts they would enthuse about response levels, percentage returns and sales data. When fans complained that they were being asked to buy more and more and that their loyalty was being taxed to the hilt, the responses from the new executives were reasoned and factual, designed to deflect criticism into other areas. Managers were sacked on the back of poor results which reduced revenue, while the chairmen and marketing men stayed put. Their job was to implement new strategies to take in more money from fans who had now become customers.

The simple game of Finney, Mathews and even Eastham, the game which had been threatened by a few thousand pimply youths running across the terraces and on to the pitch to punch each other only ten years previously, was now being run by money men. Men so ruthless that they would see whole communities laid waste because the numbers on the balance sheet didn't add up. Men who would purchase the GNP of Africa while women and children starved to death. Which one had the greater code of honour? At least the pimply youths grew old with a love of the game and moved into a new era. Would the money men protect and nurture our beautiful game? The fans asked via their own fanzines because the clubs wouldn't tell them anything. Nobody answered because the money men were too busy negotiating with the biggest predator of them all. Rupert needed a strategy to anchor his satellite TV and football fitted that bill. Rupert, via his Sky network, offered huge sums to get exclusive rights to the English First Division. Rupert Murdoch, a man who ate up newspapers and TV stations faster than the Brazilians can burn the tropical rain forest. A man who saw football as part of his global corporate strategy. Football, the only true world game. A simple game of two halves, untouched for over a century, finally breaking into the greatest consumer market of them all – the USA.

'These constant shirt changes are a rip-off for young kids,' stated an irate fan. The marketing man had the smart answer ready. 'Did you know that over 75 per cent of sales come from 40 chest size upwards, which would signify that most of our sales are from adults?' The family enclosure at Chelsea told the whole story. Fathers and sons sitting together, both wearing their latest replica shirts. The father, shirt stretched over his beer belly, sleeves rolled up to reveal fading Chelsea lion tattoos (none of these dads would be a complete man without his Chelsea lion tattoo), singing 'the referee's a wanker' in unison with his son. Fathers and sons swearing in harmony and abusing the opposing star striker. A scene being repeated in family enclosures all over the country. One last shout of 'You're shit' before a trip to the club shop to buy more merchandise. The marketing men looked upon these foul-mouthed morons in marketing terms: WOYBIES = Well Off Younger Beer Bellies.

All-seater stadiums will stop the trouble. They will civilise the football fan. Just after Wembley was made all-seater, Chelsea played Middlesbrough in the Zenith Data Challenge Cup final, a worthless competition designed to extract more revenue from fans. Wembley is the marketing man's ultimate wet dream, as most football fans love to have a day out there. The marketing men have called it the venue of legends, yet when they bolted the seats on to the concrete terraces behind the goals they didn't leave enough room for anybody above 5ft 10in to get their legs behind the seats. Chelsea fans were unimpressed by this fact as they stood on the seats behind the goals while the rougher element waged running battles with their like-minded Middlesbrough counterparts in the tunnel under the stadium. Any unlucky loser in this pitched battle saw his blood flow away in the river of piss.

Chelsea away at Leeds. Yorkies (Yorkshire football fans) hate cockneys and especially Chelsea. What does a Chelsea fan call a Yorkie with the latest fashion? A Yorkie supporting Chelsea, cos you definitely don't see any native Yorkies like that. So spoke Soccer Steve on the train going to the midweek match at Leeds. Chelsea won 2–1 and the cockneys were cock-a-hoop. On the double-decker bus from the ground back to the station the bus was ambushed by a huge mob of Leeds fans throwing bricks and bottles, smashing all the windows. The windows that weren't broken from the outside were broken from the inside as the Chelsea fans smashed up the inside of the bus to throw debris back. Some of the fans ran off the bus with lumps of metal to chase away Leeds fans. 'A smashing time was had by all.'

After a few minutes of mayhem the police turned up and this 'two dinners' Yorkie senior police officer came up the stairs of the bus. Looking none too pleased he surveyed the destruction then shouted out his deliberation: 'Listen you lot. Sit down in your seats and shut up. Or else we will stop this bus and throw you off to the mercy of those angry Leeds fans and we will drive away and leave you.' This silenced the bus so the fat Yorkie copper continued, feeling very smug: 'And if that happens you lot will definitely be second best.' His smug, all-knowing smile was wiped off his face in a flash as Soccer Steve shouted from the front of the bus: 'Maybe so, Yorkie, but we'll be the best second best you'll ever see in your life.' The bus whooped and cheered as the Yorkie copper retreated, conceding that he would always be second best in exchanges like that.

Back at the station a small group of them chased around 15 Leeds fans who ran around the corner. As they'd had such a giggle on the bus everyone got on the train. As the train pulled out they saw a huge mob of Leeds fans waiting just up the road from where they were going to chase the Leeds fans. Everyone looked at each other with the realisation that they wouldn't have even been a good second best, just a badly beaten second.

Soccer Steve was so named because all he ever talked about was football. Everyone knew him as Soccer. He wasn't bad looking, but thought he was God's gift. His favourite saying was that ugly people were destined to support northern teams; real gargoyles had to support north-east teams. After a game at Oldham he pulled a barmaid in a pub. He reckoned she was dying to kiss a real smooth cockney so he waited till she came around to collect some glasses then gave her a real tongue-down-the-throat kiss. The landlord wasn't impressed. 'Okay, wise guy, now you've finished swapping spit with my barmaid you can get out.' Soccer loved to go north to watch football. 'The phrases they use in everyday speech are an edumecation,' was the way he put it. Soccer was involved in a bad car smash, losing all his front teeth. When I went to see him in Roehampton hospital I walked past his bed, not recognising him. One of his Chelsea mates had scrawled on his bed notes: UGLY AS THE REST OF US NOW, which even the nurses found funny.

When he got out he went away with Chelsea to see a midweek League Cup match at Bradford, still with severe bruising and facial marks. The match was rubbish, the ground was terrible and it was drizzling. Soccer was standing at the back of the terrace along with a couple of mates. At the back was a metal grilled exit gate which enabled people from the outside to see in. Standing outside in the dimly lit road were a couple of young Bradford lads, around 15 years old.

'Come on out and fight, you cockney wankers.'

'What you gonna do, bash us with your UB40s? Go back to your slums.'

The conversation went on like this until Soccer pulled out a 20 pence piece. He threw it at them. It hit the metal on the exit gate and made a pinging sound. 'Go and treat yourself to a Mars bar,' said Soccer.

One of the lads picked up the 20 pence and threw it back, retorting: 'No, you need it more. Put it towards some new teeth. Ugly bastards like you will frighten our dogs.' Soccer was lost for words, while the rest of the guys in his group fell about laughing. All the way back on the train the Chelsea lads taunted Soccer with the ditty: 'You're so ugly it's unbelievable.'

The full-time whistle went at Highbury. Spurs had won the first leg of the semi-final 1–0. Hatred filled the air. A Spurs fan taunted the Arsenal fans around him. The first blow made him laugh, the second made him draw a sharp intake of breath. While the police looked towards the terraces the Arsenal fans in the seats took it in turns to kick this rag doll along the corridor.

Henry struggled with the basics of the English language. He once informed a group of Cardiff fans that Chelsea fans were 'stuttle', which is why the Old Bill can't suss them out. The Cardiff fans looked perplexed and left not knowing that Henry meant subtle. Henry knew this guy who used to drink in the Swan before matches. 'He was a missionary in Africa.' I used to think it funny that a guy who had obviously done some good had found it necessary to go to football with the worst element of the Chelsea gangs. When I finally saw the guy I realised what Henry had meant to say. 'Henry, the guy was a mercenary, not a missionary.' Henry looked at me as if I was thick. 'Same thing, innit?'

Somewhere along the way the First Division became the Premier League with all the other divisions moving up one to become one higher than that which they once were. New fancy name to describe what was basically the same meant increased prices and the chance for the marketing men to sell the concept to a corporate sponsor for an ever-increasing sum. Now it was even acceptable to sell the name of the Premiership to a beer company. The same stuff that only a few years previously would have caused questions to be asked in Parliament. The same beer that used to turn the pimply youths into raving nutcases and lay waste to channel ferries and mainland Europe. The evil which had been banned from being drunk at almost every compass point in and around football grounds. It was money that was now talking, so those points could conveniently be ignored.

Ken Bates, the Chelsea Chairman, advertised in *The Financial Times* for a millionaire benefactor to help make Chelsea a great club again. His advert was answered by an ex-Shed boy who had made good to the tune of £150 million, Matthew Harding. But for the grace of God and a lot of hard work, Matthew might be sitting in the family enclosure with the other bellies. Now he could delegate his marketing men to exploit the love of all things replica Chelsea and an exposed tattoo. Elsewhere the story was the same. The seats were installed, crowds decreased in size but the revenue increased. Millionaire fans emerged from everywhere. Alan Sugar, the Amstrad owner, suddenly realised he was a Spurs fan along with other millionaires from every walk of life, such as David Sullivan, the man who liked boobs more than Rupert Murdoch. David owned a huge house in Chigwell, Essex, and everybody knew that the Essex man was West Ham, Arsenal, Spurs or even Leyton Orient, yet his love of football was reflected by his purchase of a club over 100 miles away: Birmingham City. Being associated with football was always good publicity. Now it was becoming a necessary corporate acquisition for self-made publicity seekers.

Arsenal fans saw their beloved Northbank torn down and were then told that they would be able to watch from the new structure if they purchased a bond which gave no rights except the chance to get in. When fans started asking about the new structure they were met with woolly answers. When Arsenal unveiled their model of the proposed new stand the fans argued that it wasn't large enough. Arsenal laughed until the Arsenal fans turned up at a planning committee hearing with their own architect who said it would be possible to build a bigger Northbank. The lads who cried when the Northbank came down now started to question the diet of garbage they had been fed. Islington council sent Arsenal away and back to the drawing-board. West Ham fans didn't like being told that they would need a bond to be able to get into their ground which they had been attending for years.

They objected, using all of the tactics they had learned as hooligans, and forced West Ham to look at a different way to raise the money other than milking the loyalty of the fans. Guys whose sole contribution to the football debate had thus far been 'You're Gonna Get Your Fuckin' Heads Kicked In' started to speak lucidly and coherently about the destruction of their beautiful game. Not that the money men took it all on the chin. One of the Arsenal fanzine editors overstepped the mark in his criticism of David Dein, Arsenal Vice-Chairman, and found himself the recipient of a libel writ which forced him to settle out of court and left him substantially out of pocket.

Meanwhile the police, who had told us for years that alcohol was the main reason for crowd trouble, saw a fall in arrest rates inside grounds despite the pubs opening all day Saturday, then all day Sunday. With their main reason for crowd trouble now sponsoring the game the police had to offer a new rhetoric to justify their stance on police numbers: we must keep our guard up because if we drop it then the hooligans will return and destroy the game. Incidents happened which gave the empty police discourse some credence, but only just. Millwall built a new ground just down the road from the dreaded Cold Blow Lane. Their new squeaky clean image with crèches and junior and family enclosures was too much for the die-hards who rioted when they failed to win an important play-off match. The shock of it had to be blamed on something when the truth of the matter was that these guys just reverted to type when they saw their dream of winning promotion to the glitzy world of the Premier League slip away. So the far-right conspiracy theory came up again. Extremists had planned it. The riot started on a pre-planned signal. I wonder if the extremists' planning would have been highlighted had Millwall won 2–0. Plus, conspiracy to cause civil disorder is still on the statute book from the last century so why didn't the police act before the match? While fans laughed at the conspiracy theory the news boys missed the real story once again.

Politicians banned drink inside the grounds, they banned drink on buses going to football. Running on the pitch became an offence. Standing up in an all-seated area was banned. It almost became an offence to attend a football match. With the authorities clamping down on anything that resembled passion inside the stadium, it became forgotten that football had always been played in an atmosphere closer to a bearpit than a ballet, where fans let off steam by abusing and insulting the opposing star player. The ushering in of the new era meant that bigotry and racial chanting became an offence. Never mind the fact that Arsenal players used to be spat at by north-east fans when they played there back in the 1930s because they were perceived as rich southern bastards. Although it was nothing new, as bald, black, yellow, Scottish and ginger players would testify. Bigotry and insults were now deemed worthy of a fine up to £1,000 and a ban from all football grounds.

A comedy film came out called *Ghostbusters*. T-shirts were printed showing the principal actors under the caption 'Our Mission: To Rid The World Of Ghosts'. A Chelsea fan took up the theme a few weeks before they were due to play Spurs, changing the theme to 'Yidbusters': 'Our Mission: To Rid The World Of Yids'. There were no racial overtones; it was mockingly aimed at their hooligan firm who called themselves The Yids. Nevertheless, the police arrested some young hapless Chelsea fan who tried to explain to the judge that he was wearing it for a laugh and he didn't know what Yid meant. The act which he had been charged under was brought in after the 1930s' riots surrounding the fascist Oswald Mosley, whose blackshirts were agitating Jews. The hapless Chelsea fan was fined £200.

Arsenal fans coined the nickname The Yids for the Spurs fans. The Spurs lads took the name and turned it on themselves as a sort of parody, calling themselves Yiddos. When Spurs signed Ronnie Rosenthal, a Jewish winger who ran around like a headless chicken and missed open goals when it was easier to score, the Yiddos took this Yid to heart, so the chant of 'Yiddo' meant he was one of them. When, during an Arsenal v Spurs match, Ronnie came off the bench, the Arsenal fans started baiting him by calling him 'Yiddo' whilst the Spurs fans chanted the same to signify their support. Technically, everybody was breaking the law!

Paul Ince, a black footballer with a well-balanced attitude problem (chips on both shoulders) left Manchester United to sign for Inter Milan. He moved from the cosseted world of the English Premiership, where fans were banned by law from calling him 'Sambo' or chanting monkey noises at him, to the frenzied atmosphere of Italy where the chant of 'Nigger' meant the fans respected his ability (bad players don't get insulted, they get laughed at). At the Milan derby, where no prisoners are taken, Ince was shocked to see a black blow-up rubber doll being hung from the upper balcony by the Milan Ultras, a firm who were as vicious and nasty as anything Millwall had come up with. Ince threatened to come back to England, saying that he hadn't come to Italy to be called 'Nigger'. The Italians didn't pass any laws to outlaw racial chanting, so Ince just had to put up with it.

Eric Cantona was sent off at Crystal Palace after kicking his man-marker off the ball. As he was leaving the pitch a Palace fan gave him a piece of his mind for the cowardly attack on a Palace player which had caused the sending off. Eric then attacked the fan, giving him the infamous kung fu kick which was shown all around the world. Eric, initially jailed by an unforgiving magistrate, was let off with some community service. Just over a year later Eric was allowed to come back and by playing good football ingratiated himself as a hero with the sports media, who voted him their player of the year. Meanwhile, around the same time the poor Palace fan was banned from the ground and ended up in jail after he tried to imitate Eric and attacked the prosecuting counsel when he was found guilty of using abusive remarks to Eric. The fact that 10,000 other Palace fans were guilty of the same offence cut no ice. Someone had to be seen to be receiving a sentence to show that football would not tolerate loutish behaviour. The poor Palace fan, Matthew Simmons, stayed banned from football grounds and never received the chance to rehabilitate himself.

A few months after the kung fu attack Palace played Manchester United in an FA Cup semi-final. During a pre-match drink at a Birmingham pub, a coachload of Palace fans were attacked by some Manchester United fans and a Palace fan was stabbed, then died as he fell under the wheels of a coach. His unlawful killing happened after some remarks about the Cantona incident got out of hand.

Banning drink inside the grounds didn't matter to the real nutters. They didn't care because whatever substances they were on they took them long before they went into the seats. But football profit margins needed those corporate customers to be able to drink, so skilful lobbying got the ban relaxed in the executive boxes. They still couldn't drink during the game, but they had to break from consumption at some point, even if the football was incidental to the event of attending a trendy football jolly inside the executive box. Eventually the fans were allowed to drink again at football but not while they sat in their seats watching the match. Now, after a small break, they could once again drink warm lager from plastic cups. Areas which once buzzed with the noise of singing and chanting became morgues with plastic seats inhabited by people eating bland food inside plastic wrappers, leaving at half-time to drink from plastic cups paid for with plastic money on the telephone. Arsenal built the new Northbank stand complete with refreshment areas and museum. Fans who initially tried to sing were thrown out by stewards. The silence was so alarming that Arsenal installed a singing area where fans who wanted to sing wouldn't disturb the peace of those induced by the marketing men to continue consuming. The writing was on the wall when, during the building of the stand, Arsenal painted a mural showing fans watching the match. With the politically correct lobby taking over football someone noticed that no black faces were on the mural, making it unrepresentative of Arsenal's support. No black Arsenal fans complained because they knew what role they were playing in Arsenal's support, but the black faces were painted in anyway!

In 1989 Arsenal passed a great milestone. For the first time they sat down 1,000 people for pre-match meals. This, combined with the rest of their marketing ethos, enabled Arsenal to achieve their goal of getting their income apart from gate money above 50 per cent of receipts. Their eventual aim of 75 per cent other income against 25 per cent gate money from the paying fan was in their sights. The other big English club involved in maximising their earning potential was Manchester United. In a year when Manchester United announced £21 million in profits, the marketing push saw their shirts change four times in one season. With fans hooked on the drug of becoming customers it was a great way to make money. Club-call lines were installed. Fans could now pay a ridiculous amount every minute to listen to a diet of nondescript drivel about their team. Of course it was profitable and of course the fans kept ringing in ever-increasing numbers. Other clubs took notes while in the boardroom across the country the latest copy of *Marketing* magazine became more necessary than a decent centre-forward. Glasgow Rangers, whose fans enrol their children for season tickets while they are still foetuses, started selling their own brand of beer. Meanwhile the man from satellite TV wanted to change the kick-off times almost as much as the marketing men wanted to change the shirts.

Manchester United were knocked out of the European Cup by Galatasary of Turkey. The holy grail which Sir Matt Busby dedicated his life to winning was to elude Manchester for yet another season. The football aspect of getting knocked out of the premier European cup competition was eclipsed by the tabloid headline the next day. 'This Defeat Will Cost £6 Million' boomed out of all the papers. It summed up the way football was second to the business of earning money.

Before the days of football violence, Elephant boys (south of the river) used to cross the Thames to battle with the East Enders. Millwall was south London, West Ham was east. Allegiance to their teams and areas exacerbated this century-old rivalry which seats could never take away. These boys loved to battle and seats wouldn't stop them doing what they did best. Just turning up on their manor was taking a liberty. Smashing up a rival boozer was really taking one. These boys meant it and up to the introduction of all-seater stadiums the death count stood at one-all. One Millwall fan dead on the underground with a West Ham boy stabbed to death at Charing Cross. While the rest of football spent till they dropped in their club shops and lived for the moment when the teams ran on to the pitch to the sound of their adopted anthem, these malevolents lived for the day they could ambush their counterparts and demolish the plate-glass window of a pub full of drinkers. Their numbers were dwindling but total elimination seemed as far away as it ever was.

Sitting in a plush Paris restaurant, at a business lunch, opposite a senior company director, it soon became obvious to me that this man was an Elephant boy. As the Sancerre flowed, his clipped marketing tones gave way to a guttural Bermondsey brogue. By the second bottle he was regaling his audience with tales of Millwall and his days on the halfway line (a forbidding terrace that ran the length of Millwall's pitch and was inhabited by the roughest kind that south London threw up). Nowadays he was one of the marketing men whose deal-making had helped get the money to rebuild the stadiums, like Millwall's redevelopment at Senegal Fields, yet deep down he hankered for the days when players and fans alike would fear to venture down to Cold Blow Lane. His favourite football story told animatedly at business lunches all over the world spoke volumes.

'Our favourite trick was just before kick-off. We would get an angelic little boy with blond hair and blue eyes and get him to poke his little arms through the fence with an autograph book. If any other boys tried to copy then their dads would pull them back because their dads were in on it. Then we'd point out the opposing team's best player and get him to call him over. As he stood signing the book a group of the lads, including blondie's dad, would shower the player with spit, right in his face. I never saw one that didn't jump back absolutely shocked, faces whiter than the Cliffs at Dover, especially when they used to look up to see the little boy laughing. I've seen visiting star players play absolute stinkers because of the Millwall welcome.'

When he finished the story he sort of sighed, as if he was sad that nobody would ever have to experience that once again. He looked at me and saw my look of shock. At that point he turned up the corners of his mouth and gave a little growl, like a lion who had just killed a gazelle, then he ordered another bottle of expensive wine.

Only a few days earlier I had read about Alan Sugar, Spurs and Amstrad Chairman, in Terry Venables's autobiography. The part where he walked around the boardroom repeatedly using the f-word made me think that perhaps English football's catalyst of change had been initiated by executive Harry types with an MBA (Master of Business Administration).

For many fans the road journey via the M1 meant spaghetti junction. Near this famous landmark which many fans have got lost in (rumour has it that a fan has been trapped in the road system since the 1970s, still wearing flares and listening to Abba records) is a famous red brick building. Its trademark red brick personified the old game which was built around the ethos of industrial muck and sweat. Seeing this building, with its smashed windows, the big words Fort Dunlop on the front facing the motorway, symbolised football's trip through time: still standing on firm foundations with a great tradition to keep it going. But with the change in football Fort Dunlop suddenly changed to TS English Partnership. It signified the end of football's attachment to the industrialised age. Now Fort Dunlop had entered the marketing age the age-old burden of tradition no longer needed to be hung around football's neck.

Now the travelling fans would have to look somewhere else for an omen or superstitious talisman that signified something from the past remained. But nothing could be found because the people who were driving the game forward could not see beyond the next trashy merchandising offering, so the money men felt at ease as they sold the heart and soul of football. At some clubs the fans clamoured to buy even more, so the money men thought hard to invent more than heart and soul. Whilst clubs inherited money beyond their wildest dreams it seemed worthless, as TV made everybody a fan and an expert. But an expert of what? Fantasy football, Sunday, Monday, Italian, Champions League. All of it sponsored by a willing corporate giant. Fans queuing up for tickets, only to be told they couldn't have their favourite seats because their seats were being occupied by advertising hoardings.

People who didn't know a half-back from a cut-back suddenly took up newspaper football, transferring players with imaginary money. Couch potatoes who, in the dim and distant past, wouldn't go within ten miles of a football stadium lest they smelt their own fear became experts, because the man on satellite TV had placed cameras in every crevice and threw money at the game so they could interview the players before the sweat had dried on their brows.

The players knew what TV meant. More money, not just a little more, but so much dosh they could snort and puff alongside film stars and afford to stand their corner. In four years the wage bill for the Premier League doubled to £96 million. Foreign agents practically lived in English hotels while they offered their star players to Premiership clubs. The English Premier League, in the land of bad food, poor weather, hooliganism and frantic physical football, suddenly became the happening scene, the place which every footballer had always dreamed of playing in, especially those deemed surplus to requirements in Italian football.

The great god that was TV money became so powerful that everything was geared to suit the TV schedule. Football matches kicked off at a time designated by TV to maximise ratings. European matches were spread over the week. Tuesday UEFA Cup, Wednesday European Cup and Thursday

European Cup Winners' Cup. Kick-off times were changed on the whim of the TV controller, while football tugged its forelock with one hand while stuffing the readies in the pocket with the other hand. Still the customers came, dressed to thrill in their shiny new uniforms, proudly wearing corporate sponsors' names on their shirts. The police got in on the act by refusing to allow any drawn FA Cup match to go ahead without at least ten days' notice. The whole mysticism of the FA Cup had been built around the drama being carried over from the Saturday to the following Tuesday or Wednesday. Now the magic had gone from the football cup competition watched by a world audience; its heart had been ripped out. The all-powerful marketing men within the major clubs didn't mind because more notice meant more time to fill the executive restaurant or sell ground perimeter advertising space.

6

HOTEL IRA

When the England lads first went to Copenhagen, the friendly Danes gave them as much 8.5 per cent Elephant lager as they could drink after they finished a tour of the Carlsberg brewery. Needless to say a lot of the lads were seen to be drunk. Whether or not the officials who organised a friendly international between Germany and England on the anniversary of Adolf Hitler's birthday had been at the same party is not known. Whatever, it was not considered a wise move as extremism in Germany had been growing for years, so the eventual cancellation of the match had to be forced upon the German authorities after anti-fascist groups threatened to disrupt the match. The German politicians did not want to risk the political fall-out, while the English FA didn't understand what all the fuss was about.

Dublin away is always a big day out for those England fans who are politically motivated. The National Front, Combat 18 and other silly fascist planks like to show the cowardly IRA how hard they are. For those who are not into politics it's still a big day out. At times it does seem as if everybody is doing a Nazi salute, but what else is everybody supposed to do with their arms when they are being demonstrative with the national anthem? Ask any England rugby fan what a day out in Dublin is like or just go there and do business with the Irish. Keith wanted to see England play in Dublin, so that combined with a cheap flight deal from Air Fungus meant that he was off and running for the European Championship qualifier. Flight out in the morning then an afternoon at Lansdowne Road, then home on the early evening flight with plenty of Guinness in between. Okay, so there was a chance that there could be a smack in the teeth, but the Irish only punch you for the crack.

Keith knew it would be a good day when the lads he met on the plane accompanied him to a city centre bar and the barman refused to serve one of the lads with a Guinness shandy. 'No way, lads, that's the destruction of our national institution,' said the barman sternly. The laughter could be heard all along O'Connell Street.

The Ireland v England football match had always attracted extremists from both sides of the political fence and today would be no exception. The previous time these countries were supposed to meet was in a friendly before the European Championships, but the Irish FA had decided to cancel the match due to fears about violence. (When the Republic played in Northern Ireland a few years later and had to get a draw to qualify for the USA finals, Republic supporters were advised not to travel because of fears for their lives.) Today the IRA had organised a march and stood around with collection boxes to raise funds for Sinn Fein. Keith was oblivious to the shenanigans of the idiots who represented both sides and had a great dinner-time which extended up until they left to attend the match; 'the most hospitable people on earth,' was his description.

One Irish guy summed it all up when Keith said he couldn't understand what all the crap outside was all about. 'While the whole world actively mixes sport and politics better than hops and water, you Brits bury your heads in the sand like ostriches, pretending that it will go away if you keep your upper lip stiff enough.'

'It's a pity you Brits can't get your knobs as stiff as your upper lip,' shouted an Irishman. 'Trust me, the Dublin girls know we can,' replied Keith.

The Tricolour and Union Jack-bedecked fans left the bar together, a mixed crowd in their respective colours which for them represented their affiliation to their teams. The friendly banter and drinking continued amongst this happy group all the way to the ground, while elsewhere belligerent groups chanted obscenities about the Pope and the IRA on one side and the Queen and Brits on the other side. Whilst the Irish police (Gardai) laughed along with the friendly groups, their less lucky counterparts broke up running battles, driving a wedge between the warring factions with bottles, bricks and vitriolic venom flying above their riot helmets.

Honours even at the match with a 1–1 draw, then back to the bar for more drink with the friendly Irish who laid on a taxi for Keith to get back to the airport so that he wouldn't have to run the gauntlet of hatred, fists, bricks and bottles which were flying around outside to the background of wailing police sirens. Back at the airport the mood changed as it became obvious that the people who had been trading insults and blows in the streets for the past five hours would be travelling home on the plane together. The Gardai had one solution: get them on the plane and out of the country. Just as the doors were shut on the plane and it was ready to start taxiing down for take-off the Irish fans at the front of the plane started singing their rebel songs. This was the cue for a renewed outbreak of hostilities, with both sides sitting at the front swapping blows with relish. Keith, resplendent in his England hat and scarf, thought it was funny but hoped it wouldn't delay the opening of the bar, until an Irish guy stuck one on his chin with the remark: 'Take that, you English wanker.' With that Keith was out of his seat and swapping blows with his Irish protagonist.

Just at that moment the captain came out of his door with Keith in full haymaker mode. 'Right, you lot, this plane is not taking off,' shouted the captain. The fighting was stopped by the intervention of the Gardai. The English were put at the back of the plane with the Irish left at the front. For some reason the captain refused to take Keith and his Irish opponent so they were placed under arrest, despite Keith's protestations of innocence.

Back at the station there was absolute pandemonium as warring football fans mixed with IRA sympathisers and other assorted drunks. A senior policeman came into Keith's cell and told him he would be charged with a lesser drunk and disorderly charge if he behaved and would be appearing at 10 o'clock in front of the magistrate. As it was around 7 p.m. he assumed it would be 10 o'clock the next morning so he decided to get his head down. Within 20 minutes Keith was awoken from his brief sleep by a rowdy England fan called Dick from Cheshire wearing his best England shirt. Dick was definitely a 'tattoos keep you warm' sort of guy as they always have their sleeves rolled up whatever the weather, usually to reveal a girl's name whom they hadn't married. As the door slammed behind him he banged on it and chanted 'You can't catch Ronnie Biggs! You can't catch Ronnie Biggs!'

'Wrong country, wrong police force,' said Keith wearily, having been in enough police cells to know that winding up the police was not the best course of action, especially a force as friendly as the Gardai. This only spurred our friend on to greater glory. 'UDA, UDA, Fuck the Pope and the IRA.'

Perhaps if I talk to Dick (head) then he might ease up and settle down, thought Keith, so he engaged him in gentle conversation. What he got was stories which bored him rigid at the time, but made the lads at the local roar when he retold them on a Friday evening.

'Does thou know that the last time I met a commie police force like this lot we was on the train going from Hanover to Berlin in '88 Europeans. Our mate Steve knows a bit about geography and he reckoned that we was in East Germany on that train as it was some sort of corridor and the train couldn't stop yet; when the train stops you are back in West Germany. So when the commie East German ticket collector comes to sell us a ticket we tells him to piss off.

'"Stop the train and throw us off, you wanker," Steve told him.

'"Yeah, throw us off, wanker," added someone.

'You must have a ticket,' continued Dick, and marched around the cell pretending he was an East German ticket collector. 'We gave that commie so much stick that he didn't know what hit. Never got money off us for tickets though. We showed him the value of communism. I bloomin' hate Germans, especially commie Germans.'

'Yeah, good stuff,' said Keith.

Dick continued: 'I smacked this paddy right in the kisser after he said that English soldiers were cowards. I ain't bothered because I have been here before. Got deported from Germany after we done a runner from our hotel and got caught at the railway station. Can you believe it, the train was late in West Germany.' Keith smirked at the irony of that.

'So you reckon you'll get deported?'

'No problem, it's the way it is,' said Dick confidently.

Before he could say any more the cell door opened and the senior policeman entered.

'Okay, lads, there is a special court convened for 10 p.m. tonight. Now, if you play it cool then you should be on for small pocket fines.'

'But I've only got five pounds on me,' said Keith.

'That'll cover it,' replied the policeman, smiling. 'Now lad,' he said to Dick. 'Cover that shirt up and act a bit smarter than you have so far and you will be home to read about yourself by breakfast tomorrow.'

'Piss off and have tea with the IRA, you Irish plonker,' replied Dick.

With that the policeman left, shaking his head.

Upon arrival at court the Irish guy whom Keith had been exchanging blows with on the plane came over. 'My name's Alan, I'm sorry it has all led to this, but you've got a good right hand.' Keith went and joined Alan, leaving Dick on his own, feeling proud that he was wearing his England shirt. They were called into court. As they filed in the senior policeman winked at Keith and said: 'Pocket fine son, don't worry, I've telephoned your wife.'

The first Irish guy went up in front of the magistrate, who was a benign-looking fellow with huge, black, bushy eyebrows, which combined with his world-weary look conveyed an expression of: 'What am I doing here?'

'How do you plead?'

'Guilty.'

'Fined two pounds. Next.'

Keith looked at Alan who was sitting next to him, smiling.

'This is how it is over here,' said Alan.

So the Irish went up one by one to collect their two-pound fines with the magistrate dispensing justice without looking up beyond his eyebrows until he came to Alan.

'How do you plead?'

'Guilty.'

'Fined two pounds.'

'I haven't got two pounds.'

He looked up incredulously, yet somehow one sensed he'd heard it all before. In his proper life I could imagine he was a schoolmaster who heard 'the bus broke down' stories from naughty schoolboys but didn't laugh until he reached the staffroom for his break.

'How much have you got?' asked the magistrate.

'Fifty pence,' replied Alan.

'Fined fifty pence. No time to pay,' stated the magistrate abruptly.

Keith was doing all he could not to laugh when Dick went up. The magistrate looked up to see a sneering Dick glare at him with his England shirt.

'What are you here for?'

'Assault. I smacked some bastard who was insulting England.'

'How do you feel about that?'

'He deserved it, he insulted England,' stated Dick defiantly.

'Mmm,' mused the magistrate. 'Assault at a football match. Five days in gaol should settle you down. Take him away.'

Dick waited for the words deportation immediately, but they never came.

'What about my deportation?' asked Dick.

'Of course we are going to deport you. You don't think we want your type here for any longer than we have to keep you. We have your countrymen here for the rugby without all this punching fuss. You will be deported after you serve five days.'

Keith burst out laughing while they took Dick away, his bemused look telling the whole story.

'At least he didn't cry for his mummy until he gets out of the court,' said the senior police officer, smiling, adding, 'justice one pillocks nil.' Obviously Paddy magistrate had not read the script. Keith's laughter abruptly stopped when he realised that he was next. The magistrate looked up at him.

'What are you in here for?'

'Drunk and disorderly,' replied a sheepish Keith.

'Disgusting behaviour. I bet you 50 English pounds that you don't want to share a cell with that young fool.'

'One hundred per cent correct, sir,' replied Keith.

'Good. Fined two pounds, but I want you out of the country by midnight.'

As Keith left the court the policeman spoke to him.

'Now I realise that you have now missed the last flight and I should lock you up, but if you promise to get the first flight out in the morning then I will take your word that you will be a good boy. There are some B & Bs around the corner which you can stay in.'

'But I've only got £3 left.'

With that Alan chipped in. 'Don't worry, I will lend you the money for tonight. You can pay me back when you get back to England.'

Everyone left the court happy except Dick, but everybody had seen justice done. So Keith went off to stay in a single hotel room costing £50 which was paid for by Alan. The next day Air Fungus flew them back to England for no extra charge and no stamp was put on Keith's passport to say he'd been in trouble and deported. On the plane going home Keith found out that Alan was from Kilburn and the money which had paid for Keith's hotel room was paid for out of funds collected before the match for Sinn Fein, the political wing of the IRA. Keith laughed at the double irony of the IRA paying for Keith to stay in a hotel all the way home from Heathrow airport but never did pay Alan back.

In June 1995, for the first time, a friendly international involving England was abandoned after fighting broke out between the Irish and English fans. The English Football Intelligence Unit stated after the game that they knew there was planned political violence from the ultra-extremist far-right groups who follow England, but the truth of the matter was that all the factors which had been present in 1989 were still there in 1995, with the added antagonism of a cease-fire from the IRA being announced in the preceding week. On top of the usual pre-match hostilities was the jibe from the Irish that the British Army had surrendered to the IRA. With tempers running at frazzle level the Irish scored an early goal and the worst elements started fighting. Images of young, frightened, bemused Irish fans were flashed up all over the world. The police stated it was planned political violence, but as is their way never produced any factual evidence. The media, who love a far-right conspiracy theory, printed the police version word for word. The man from the FA said the fans shouldn't have come. They weren't welcome.

7

1–0 TO THE ARSENAL

Arsenal entered the 1993 European Champions Cup with great hopes. After a creditable 1–1 draw away in Lisbon against Benfica, hopes were high in the return. As it was Arsenal fielded a slightly weakened side and then played all the wrong tactics, finally losing out in extra time after having had enough chances to win two games in 90 minutes. The press wrote glowing orgasmic tributes about the way Benfica destroyed Arsenal, how English football had taken the tactical test to be found wanting. Gorgeous George saw things differently. He had made a fundamental error with the tactics he had used. The shrug which he gave told it all: next time things will be different because I have seen enough to know that Arsenal are good enough.

UEFA ran a league table with points awarded to countries every time their clubs won a match. The countries with the most points got the most places in the UEFA Cup. After the Heysel ban was lifted UEFA decided that English clubs had won fewer matches than Albania so English clubs, who had dominated Europe before the ban, would only have one representative in the UEFA Cup. This didn't stop entry to the Cup Winners' Cup when Manchester United won the FA Cup. Years previously the infamous red army had created havoc wherever they went, but for this campaign fans travelled with or without official backing from the club and conducted themselves in an exemplary manner, as Manchester swept all before them, resulting in a final in Rotterdam against Barcelona. Manchester won 2–0 and the boys partied all night long. A group of them in a hotel partied to excess, their celebration exploits stunning the hotel owner. As they were about to leave the hotel he sombrely told them his opinion. 'I have enjoyed your company but I am sorry to say that you have a drink problem.'

The Manchester lads thought about what he had said for a few moments before one of them replied laconically, 'Drink problem? Not in this city, mate. There's plenty of bars I can still get a drink in.'

Rotterdam also has plenty of places where the lads could get marijuana. On the ferry back to Harwich the Manchester lads were rolling joints as big as cigars and smoked themselves into nirvana. The undercover police who were watching them got high as kites on the smoke. Back at Harwich, half the Suffolk police were employed to search them despite the fact that it had been the quietest return journey the stewards could remember. Nobody got found with any dope.

Two seasons later in the European Cup, Manchester United drew Galatasary, the Turkish champions. After an incident at a hotel a number of Manchester United fans – including innocent holiday-makers, some of whom were elderly – were brutally treated. Upon their return they made complaints at the highest level. The Foreign Office did not want to know and all the complaints fell on deaf ears, despite the Chelsea-supporting MP, David Mellor, asking questions in Parliament. This was the same Foreign Office who had told Jill Morrell that she had a better chance of getting John McCarthy out if she kept quiet. Manchester United fan equals fair game for a beating. Other countries took notice of the fact that the English government were prepared to condone the brutal treatment of travelling English football fans regardless of whether they were badly behaved or not. It all seemed to hinge upon how the fans' personas were perceived.

Arsenal's entry into the Cup Winners' Cup was achieved after a dour FA Cup final struggle against Sheffield Wednesday with a last-gasp goal rescuing the game from a penalty shoot-out. A week later at Wembley stadium the Italians of Parma out-thought, outmanoeuvred and outplayed Royal Antwerp to win the previous year's Cup Winners' Cup by three goals to one. David Lacey in *The Guardian* contrasted the silky skills of the Italians with the dour, prosaic method of Arsenal, stating that Arsenal would struggle should they find themselves on the same pitch as these fluid Italians. I wrote to Mr Lacey to inform him that I would be following Arsenal around Europe next season and I would be speaking to him about the garbage he had written. *Mark my words, Mr Lacey, I will be there when you are forced to eat your words. I hope you are prepared to choke on them!* The last time I had met Mr Lacey in Stockholm he had to go to the dry cleaners to get the brown stuff removed off his pants. When, later, just before the campaign started, Lacey wrote some more derogatory comments about Arsenal, the die was cast. See you, Lacey!

After a workmanlike victory against Odense of Denmark, Arsenal drew Standard Liège of Belgium. I approached Arsenal about buying tickets from them as I had no wish to go on the whistle stop football excursion, bussed in for the match, locked in the ground for two hours afterwards, then whisked home again to arrive in a port or airport at 3 a.m. with mindless jobsworths telling you that it was fun. It's not like they are cheap; after all, the club must maintain its profit margin. Steve Ashford described it as masturbation travel although he doubted there was enough time on these to actually do that. Once again the English mentality surfaced ('if we sell you a ticket then we will have to sell everybody one'). When you get the club to look logically at who they are selling a ticket to, they hide behind other reasons, saying anything to get you off their backs. Offering football clubs the chance to bring people under their umbrella for European matches is too simplistic, especially when this gives them responsibility without profit. A friend of mine procured tickets for the match from Liège, but the tickets were stolen in transit. A local postman has since been arrested in possession of 70,000 letters so they may eventually surface. The four lads who were supposed to be coming with me all started to get whishi fever (I wish I hadn't shouted my mouth off about going somewhere when I'd had a few lagers) so the trip got postponed. Arsenal won 7–0 in Liège which is an unbelievable scoreline for a European match, especially as Belgium produces some marvellously gifted technical players. That is what we are told by the press who, surprise surprise, were still not convinced about Arsenal's pedigree.

Arsenal drew Torino of Italy in the quarter-finals to be played in early March. British Airways and J. Sainsbury plc were running a promotion which meant that you could get half-price air tickets just for buying your groceries. The best deal I ever saw.

Whilst Henry had all the Chelsea fans confused with his tale of the missionary who was actually a mercenary, the sponsors of Torino, Berretta Foods, got confused when a friend of mine told them I wanted four of the best for Turin. Italian is a flowery language so something obviously got lost in the translation when my status as a supermarket meat buyer became director of delicatessen buying, Safeway plc. (Or perhaps I put that in my fax to them.) With Berretta desperate to get an entry into an English supermarket I received a return fax to tell me that myself and three friends were personal guests of the President of Torino FC. I omitted to tell the President that two of the guys I was bringing were two of Croydon's finest: Dibbsy and Dubbsy, numero uno drinkers, known locally as the bright brothers. The other traveller was company director, Charlie Chaplin lookalike, Satchman.

The last time I had been to Turin to watch Arsenal play I had seen a momentous victory but had barely escaped from the stadium with my life. I never thought I would be returning to sit with the Arsenal directors. I even wrote Arsenal's Managing Director, Ken Friar, a tongue-in-cheek letter asking if he would possibly sell me a ticket. 'Sorry . . . due to UEFA regulations we are unable to sell you a ticket, but I'm sure we could fit you in for one of our one-day tours' was the stock reply. I wrote back to Ken saying I would see him in Torino. I might even buy him a drink.

On the aeroplane going over we all tried to imagine Ken's face when we turned up, in between the champagne from the drinks trolley. I looked at Dubbsy, who in his best suit looked like a war refugee who'd trekked 600 miles wearing it. His insistence that the air hostess was mumsy and definitely fancied him brought silent guffaws from the other travelling businessmen. Dubbsy got stopped by the police on the way out and asked if he was going to the football. His reply of 'sponsors' guests' completely threw them. Dibbsy, another young guy with a beer gut caused by frequent kebab suppers after 12 pints, spent most of the flight telling Dubbsy what a sad waster he was. 'Yeah, but my girlfriend loves me and I've got good-looking kids,' was his answer. The look of incredulity on 'Mumsy's' face told us she didn't believe it. Looking at Dubbsy, who made Marty Feldman look sane, it was hard to believe. 'More beer, Mumsy, this champagne is flat.'

The first time I met Dubbsy was at Hamburg airport where, after consuming a bottle of vodka on the flight, he vaulted the barrier into Germany, sprinting past the startled smartly dressed guards with machine guns because he had lost his passport between British customs and the aeroplane. The next time I saw him was as I was leaving Germany and the German police were carrying him drunk on to the plane for deportation. Now I was sitting next to him. Tomorrow evening he would be an honoured guest of Torino FC. At least Satchman and I looked the part with our expensive suits. We had also booked into a classy hotel as we were intending to live the part fully. Upon arrival at our hotel we were given our itinerary for match day. We were being picked up at 7 a.m. for a trip to two factories. One of the factories was four hours' drive so there would be a need to be up at 6 a.m. After lunch in the boardroom we would be dropped at the ground later in the evening.

The intermediary, Serge, who had met us at our hotel, asked if he could have a quiet word with me when he saw Mr Dubbs, as he put it. 'Mr Ward, I hope you understand that I would prefer it if only yourself and Mr Satch were to come on the factory trip. I am not sure your other two friends are quite understanding of the protocol.' I understood fully, especially as Dubbsy had asked our intermediary 'What time are the whores getting here? I've read all about that.' He then started winking at Serge. 'It's okay, Serge, I understand.'

Dubbsy more than understood and moved into a new hotel with Dibbs but was back in our bar before you could say 'my round'. In the bar we met David Platt's father who, it transpired, got free air travel and accommodation in Italy as part of his son's contract to play for Sampdoria.

Around the town we met the usual coterie of Arsenal fans who had travelled out under their own steam. The game was due to be played in the Stadia D'Elia, where England had lost the dramatic semi-final shoot-out to West Germany in Italia 90. The ground held over 70,000 so the stupid cry that tickets would be hard to obtain had an empty ring to it. Serge felt there would be only 30,000 at most. I have a great penchant for good food and jazz so after a superb meal we headed for the Cotton Club. I expected to find a club with some great sax and trombone with the background of light drum. What we found was a seedy club which sold sex to the background good soul music and the sound of AMEX cards being run through the machines as another sad-looking businessman cheated on his wife on his expense account.

I looked around for the press, but couldn't see any I recognised, although we knew where they were staying. I was intending to pop up to their hotel to tell them the facts of life. Besides, watching the suits strutting their stuff on the dance floor before getting their rocks off with stunning imported prostitutes from Eastern Europe and the Dominican Republic was far more entertaining. Plus the music was good, the beer was cold, Dubbsy was well on form and we'd had enough to drink to believe stupidly that we were good-looking enough for the girls to want to try and pull us without us paying. The sounding of the three-minute nuclear warning wouldn't have precipitated that Cotton Club scenario. With the beer and conversation flowing, the impetus to return to the hotel for a good night's sleep departed from me, despite the fact that Satch and I had a reasonably full itinerary tomorrow. We staggered back to our hotel from the Cotton Club at 5.20 a.m. We bumped into the flight crew of the aircraft who had brought the Arsenal team out to Turin, who tried to engage us in conversation.

The 6 a.m. alarm call awoke me, still sitting in the chair. I dragged Satchman out of bed and under the shower.

'Come on, we've got to be down for 7 o'clock breakfast.'

'You're bloody mad,' was his reply. 'I'll get a taxi.'

'Not four hours' drive, you won't.'

I went down for breakfast and walked straight past the two people from Berretta who had arranged to meet us. Later in the car when Satch was fast asleep and I was desperately trying to sound interested about ham processing, they told me that they thought they had seen a ghost when I walked in the room. Upon arrival at the factory we were met by the whole family, led by the eldest son Giorgio who had the biggest diamond Rolex on his wrist I have ever seen in my life. Every time he turned his wrist in the light it looked like he had sparklers going off on his wrist. Walking around a factory trying to be interested in mortadella ham would try the concentration of the Royal family. Attempting to do it on 40 minutes' sleep after a peroni session with Dubbsy that would have put Dean Martin under the table put me in line for a Queens Award for Industry or an MBE (More Beer Eyetie, as Dubbsy put it later).

After what seemed an eternity we adjourned to the boardroom where they had laid on lunch. The sight of them opening up the red wine caused me to start shaking.

'Are you feeling cold, Mr Ward? Perhaps you would like us to turn up the heating?'

Satchman (who was an honorary Safeway director for the day) kept up the conversation and even managed some of the red wine.

'Now, Mr Ward, do you think that these products are what Safeway are looking for?'

'Terrific, I will be putting forward a recommendation when I get back.' (And I did just that.)

We finally left to be taken back to our hotel (loaded with presents from the club including a designer Torino shell-suit, the type the players would be wearing in their pre-match warm-up), where we bumped into the flight crew. The captain spoke to us as if he'd seen us before. Our blank looks prompted him to remind us that he had engaged us in animated conversation the previous evening. I thought he was bonkers. His parting shot to me was: 'What should I say to the Arsenal team on the plane going home?'

'Tell them Colin Ward survived a night out with Dibbsy and Dubbsy, then chant "Ooh, to be a goooner" on the tannoy.' The poor captain thought we were both mad.

Our taxi drive to the ground was an experience in itself. Dressed in our best Armani suits the taxi driver thought we were with the club when we told him we were Arsenal. When the lunatic spotted the Arsenal coach being escorted to the ground he drove in with the escort, pointing out to the motorcycle outriders that he had us as passengers. Off we sped through red lights surrounded by flashing lights. The Turin rush hour evaporated in front of us and a 25-minute journey lasted 15 minutes.

Being first to arrive at the ground gave us a chance to look around. The foyer was sparse yet decorated impressively. Pretty Italian hostesses dressed in red stood around, waiting to escort people to their boxes which were up a flight of open-plan stairs. It was possible to lean over the balcony and see everybody entering. We sufficed with a beer then sat around watching the TV people work. We spotted George Graham and gave him a yell. Two idiots toasting George with cans of Heineken on the VIP terrace 90 minutes from kick-off got us a stranger look than that of the plane captain an hour earlier. People started to roll up, but as of yet no sign of the bright brothers. With 30 minutes to go to kick-off the Arsenal board members arrived. Peter Hill-Wood, Arsenal's Chairman, looked tense. Immediately after him followed Ken Friar, Arsenal's Managing Director, a man I had been writing to for tickets over the past few months. Once, many years previously, one of my ticket-seeking campaigns had resulted in Ken telephoning my father to ask if he knew me. My father denied all knowledge of me. Close on the heels of Ken with an Italian lovely on each arm came Dubbsy, proclaiming to everybody in earshot: 'This is the dog's bollocks, two Mumsys after a serious lager session.' Ken seemed to be accelerating up the stairs to get away from Dubbsy, whose suit was horribly ill fitting as was his tie, although I bet it looked good before he started on the beer session.

Ken was stopped dead in his tracks by myself at the top of the stairs. 'Hello, Ken. I said I'd see you here. How's it going?' Ken looked dumbstruck, more so when I said that we were guests of the Berretta family who were standing just behind us. Giorgio had more gold jewellery on than Joan Collins plus his Rolex. Ken managed to escape just as Dubbsy made his entrance on to the balcony with Dibbsy telling him to 'tone it down'.

Dubbsy looked at Peter Hill-Wood, who fatally made eye contact. 'Oi, Peter, I'm with Mr T here,' said Dubbsy, pointing at Giorgio. 'Official guests. It's all about contacts. You've either got 'em or you ain't. Now are you ordering the beer or am I?'

Peter, a merchant banker in his working life, looked horrified. The Berretta family didn't see anything wrong with his behaviour as they couldn't understand a word he said, as he was littering his sentences with Mumsy, Poopsy, and Shant. Peter Hill-Wood became 'Woody', Ken Friar 'Old Fry Up.' David Dein, Arsenal Vice-Chairman who wasn't present, was Davros. Off we went to our box with the match sponsors which had a fully stocked drinks cabinet. 'Please, mum, can I be in charge of the drinks cabinet?' Dubbsy asked the pretty waitress. 'Behave yourself,' said Dibbsy.

We settled down to watch the football. The English press were constantly telling their readers that English teams can't pass compared to the continentals. Arsenal gave the Italians a lesson in short crisp passing and controlled possession. It was 90 minutes of pure joy. We sat on the balcony opposite a small group of travelling Arsenal fans on comfy armchairs on the balcony. 'If only the lads could see us now. This is the life,' said Dibbsy.

Arsenal were the bosses on the pitch while Dubbsy bossed the drinks cabinet. At half-time Giorgio asked Dubbsy if he wanted a beer. 'Leave it out – I only drink champagne,' was his reply. So we drank champagne. Anybody who tells you that economy is the best way to see a match has never experienced the glamour and comfort of a Turin balcony. If ever there was an incentive to make it in life then this was it. The Italians knew that they had met a good team and were full of praise for Arsenal at the end of the match. We shouted down their comments to the press who didn't hear us. After the match George made his point to the press about passing and movement and which team was the better at it. A point I logged away for a future encounter with the press boys. I fully intended to have an after-match tête-à-tête with Ken Friar but the hurly burly combined with Dubbsy's desire for another lager meant we sped from the ground in a waiting taxi to a watering-hole we had frequented the previous evening. Pre-match drinking is a different ritual from after-match drinking. Before, it's about calming or lowering expectation levels; after is about lowering the tension level or soothing frayed nerve endings. I often need a drink to break the chain which sees my nails in my mouth for the whole of the 90 minutes. My father always used to reckon that had a game gone on long enough then I would have bitten down to my elbow. As the night wore on Arsenal fans returned to the bar or, seeing other Arsenal fans in the bar, joined us.

Billy J. came over and joined us at the table. Billy was a butterfly, flitting from group to group, telling stories and listening, though mostly telling. He had come out here with the main 'firm', containing a number of well-known faces including main face Denton, the coloured Arsenal fan who was now in charge of security for the Pet Shop Boys. Their group had been to Milan because you can't be a young shaker in Islington and come to Italy without visiting Milan. 'Sure, we lifted a few leathers.' Whether or not it was apocryphal was irrelevant as European away matches are awash with the Billies of this world. Fashion, or the need to be seen as in fashion, was as important now as it ever had been, perhaps more so now than ever. With the decline in violence it wasn't how tough you were, but how you were perceived in the pecking order of being recognised. For someone like Billy, being recognised was an important part of his football attendance. His conversation with us was part talk, part about his being known to us next time we saw him at Arsenal. Billy dropped names (names of people who were faces in firms around Arsenal) more regularly than Dubbsy tipped beers down his throat. Billy was popular with the bar owner. He fancied that he was going to pull the bar owner's daughter, but that was a bridge too far, even for a prime mover like Billy.

Later in the evening a group of Arsenal fans came into the bar we were drinking in. They had been locked in the ground for over an hour before being allowed to leave. With them was a girl who needed to go to the toilet outside the ground so had squatted down between two cars. 'Disgusting behaviour,' said Dubbsy. Funny how men peeing up against the wall is seen as acceptable, but a woman doing it is different. We also met some right wasters who were more interested in telling us about their trip to watch AC Milan than the performance they had just seen. They started criticising certain Arsenal players and dared to mock the way we were dressed in suits. It was like listening to a boring tape of the press boys in full garbage-speak mode: Foreign good; English bad. Dubbsy shut them up.

'Look, lads, when you're close to perfection up there with the top dogs drinking champagne you have to look the part. What did you have, warm lager and cold fries? So if your best comment is to slag off Arsenal then my advice is stay home and wank yourself sad and ugly instead of coming out here and frightening the locals.'

When we finally got home I spent the afternoon in bed with my children jumping all over me. 'Daddy, why aren't you playing with us?' The wife stomped around the house because I had been away for three days' holiday and needed to come home for a rest. 'Exhausting work, being a football fan, darling.'

Despite being offered a place in the Berretta box for the return I thought that it might be abusing their hospitality, so the 1–0 victory, after a header from Captain Adams, was observed from economy. So to the semi-finals where Arsenal drew Paris St Germain with the first leg in Paris. Paris in the spring to watch Arsenal. Somebody up there must like me!

Rule number one in travelling away. Never travel with people who are skint, untrustworthy or cliquey. I broke these rules in accepting a lift to Paris from people whom I didn't much care for in return for me obtaining them tickets. Within days of the match the word was that tickets would be rarer than rocking horse dung, so I used my Parisian meat trade contacts to organise nine of the best. Five would be for the car we were travelling in plus four for the Croydon lads who would be going home immediately after the game. The game was due to be played at the Parc des Princes against a team that were streaking away with the French league with a style and panache which Arsenal couldn't hope to match, or so the press said. George, along with the rest of us, knew better. Paris St Germain also had the worst hooligan fans in France, if not Europe. They were called the Boulogne Boys and one of the Paris players said that he would not even take his son to the match because of the violence they caused around the Paris stadium.

I met my travelling companions at 6 a.m. on the Wednesday morning of the match. The game was due to be played that evening so we anticipated to be in Paris by 11 a.m. I had pre-booked a hotel, from where we would collect our tickets and meet with the Croydon lads, including Dibbsy, but no Dubbsy for this one.

As soon as the car turned up late I sensed I had made a mistake. Pisshead Frank was in the front seat, drunk and potless. Whilst Frank makes me laugh in small doses he isn't someone I would want to travel to Paris with. It turned out that he had all of forty pounds which was going to pay for his ticket, hotel, food, drink and petrol money, when even a fool knows that Paris is expensive. As he lay asleep on the front seat I felt like stamping MUMPER across his forehead. Things almost came to a head on the ferry when I informed the four of them that tickets were all laid on but I couldn't guarantee the price.

'How much are you talking about?' asked Frank.

'Forty, fifty pounds face value.'

'I was told that tickets were going to be seventeen pounds.'

'Who by, Frank?'

'The other lads,' he said, pointing to Lawrence, Dave and the driver Steve. The others then all started siding with Frank – especially Dave – so I gave them some home truths.

'Rule number one. Don't travel to Paris without money in your bin. Two. If you think you can do better for tickets without me then I'll take my chances on the train at Calais. So make your mind up what you want to do because there are about 60 guys on here without tickets who will gladly pay face value and give me a drink.'

Before the conversation could deteriorate any further the Croydon lads by chance came into the bar. I went over to join them, seriously disgruntled by some people's attitude. By chance the Croydon lads had booked the same ferry. Once in France we went in convoy to Paris. All Frank did was bitch about the price of beer and how we had to stop in a hypermarket to stock up with cheap beer.

'Frank, I haven't come to Paris to sit on a park bench drinking supermarket takeaways.'

On arrival at the hotel the tickets which were at the desk for collection were sixty-five pounds each, best in the house just above the press-box. The four I had travelled with did not want to pay that much so they decided to wait for the other four tickets which were due for delivery.

I thought they should go and get a hotel and meet me back here in two hours, but they obviously didn't trust me so they waited. It is a curious thing how people are prepared to sponge off the good nature of others. While I sat drinking in the bar, looking forward to the match, four people who wouldn't have had an earthly of getting a ticket if it hadn't been for me bitched about how they were being ripped off. As I pointed out to them: 'There's nothing to stop you walking out and taking your chances on the street.' Out on the streets were hundreds of ticketless Arsenal fans being asked a hundred pounds for match tickets. Around 3 p.m. a large silver Mercedes pulled up and my ticket source came into the bar. One look at the car told me that these would not be cheap. At seventy pounds face value, how right I was. I did not see it as my duty to bail out Frank as I would most probably not see him again. Frank offered me an IOU with the promise that someone else would pay me back the money.

'No money, no tickets,' I told Frank.

'Stuff it, I'll watch it in a bar.'

'Do it, Frank,' I said, putting the ticket back in my pocket. So they all scraped together their money and helped out Frank.

As they left the bar I said to Lawrence, whom I saw as a reasonably sound guy, 'Don't leave me stewing here. If you're not coming back then say so now.'

'No problem, Colin, we'll be back.' Yeah, like Karl Malden went back for Marlon Brando in *One Eyed Jacks*. At least I had my boots and their money from the tickets. (They never did come back.) I saw them disappear around the corner then thought I would give Lawrence the benefit of the doubt and wait for an hour. I could always go down The Frog and Roastbeef (Frog and Rosbif) pub where I knew there would be plenty of Arsenal fans. After about 25 minutes two Arsenal fans staggered into the bar. In full, staggering, English-drunk-football-fan mode they were ticketless, as well as clueless; they had no chance of getting a ticket for the match. Getting a metro ticket looked beyond them. After a little while I suggested we go down the Rue St Denis to meet some other Arsenal fans. Watching these two goons struggle to jump the tube entrance barrier (they don't pay tube fares in frogland) which is no more than three feet high was one of the lighter moments of the day so far.

The Rue St Denis is low rent, or at least the girls who frequent the streets are, in terms of how pretty they are. Fat ones, old ones, dusky African girls with huge bosoms, but exceptionally pretty ones, they mostly frequent other areas. The Parisian authorities were trying to give it a facelift by laying a multi-coloured mosaic of pretty paving stones. Whatever they do, it is only window-dressing, as everybody knows what sort of area it is. In the street is an English pub, The Frog and Roastbeef, which brews its beer in the basement. When we got there the pub was shut, as it had been the focus for the Boulogne Boys the previous evening, who had attacked it with CS gas canisters. We parked ourselves in a bar opposite, while my two drunken friends stood outside chanting 'Arsenal' and calling every other person who walked past 'Frog Face'. After ten minutes of this riveting chanting they left to go up to the ground. I teamed up with two other guys so off to the ground we went a little later. There was still one hour to go to kick-off as we came up the metro steps near the ground. Coming down the steps at speed were a crowd of Arsenal fans. 'Jesus! It's bloody mental out there,' one said to me as he ran past.

I walked out of the metro to be met by a hail of bottles, stones and cans. To my left was a group of around 200 Arsenal fans charging towards a bigger mob of French fans who had retreated but now charged back following their missile attack. A café owner was standing by his door, looking worried about his windows as the stone throwing developed into individual attacks on lone Arsenal fans who were unaware of what was happening. I walked into the café. 'Bonjour,' then walked past and ordered a beer. I saw my two drunken friends stagger past and walk straight into a brutal French assault. Deciding that discretion was better than a beating, I left them to it. They were getting beaten as they ran towards the sanctuary of the Arsenal mob, who launched an attack to rescue them. It was fierce, frantic and frenzied. My drunken friend would sober up later to a split eye that needed at least 12 stitches. Now, all he had was a bloody shirt, as the adrenalin and alcohol blocked out his feelings of pain. Meanwhile the riot police stood around with their tear gas guns. Just after kick-off, when everybody else had gone into the ground, they arrested all the Arsenal fans who were milling around.

I suddenly realised which bar I was in. I was standing in the Boulogne Bar just behind their end. I picked up a copy of *L'Equipe* newspaper and decided to leave as the French would all end up here. I had no wish to end up black and blue or worse.

When I eventually got into the ground, our seats were in the adjacent isle up from the press-box. I could practically lean over and read their articles. I spotted the man I had been looking to have a word with: David Lacey of *The Guardian*. To my right was the Boulogne end with the fanatical Boulogne Boys. Somewhere to my left were the four people I had set out with. I had no worries as I knew what time ferry they were booked on to the next day so I could meet them at Calais. Sitting in the seats around me were the four Croydon guys.

'Bit hairy out there, wasn't it?' said Dibbsy.

'I felt like Custer at Little Big Horn with all those darkies,' one of the others said in reference to the amount of immigrants who were amongst the Boulogne Boys' ranks.

'How did you get on, ginger?'

'No problem. I kept a low profile and they smelt my fear at 20 paces so left me alone.'

The stadium was awash with colour and noise which echoed around the concrete bowl. It was a daunting sight. Paris had a host of star players including two Brazilian internationals and a forward who was rated the best in Europe, the Liberian, George Weah. They also had the French international winger David Ginola, who had been quoted in the press talking about how poor English football was and about how he was going to destroy the English full-back, Lee Dixon. Taunts like this are food and drink to English teams. All Ginola did was ensure the giant was fired up. It was noticeable that the first three rows of the seats at the Boulogne end were not occupied. I was to find out why later in the match.

Once the match got under way the crowd were silenced by Arsenal's brand of power football. The Paris keeper was the one being called into action to make electric saves. Forward Arsenal came like a red sea, pushing the French out of the way as if they were insignificant schoolboys. After 20 minutes Ian Wright scored from a free kick. The stadium was silent save for the 2,000 Arsenal fans to my left, who had earlier seemed inconsequential amongst the sea of French noise and colour. Half-time came with Arsenal in complete control. The most important away goal had been taken in style.

I leant over the back of the press-box and launched into the press.

'What about that, then?' I shouted. 'You lot have got to take your typewriters off the automatic garbage "Arsenal are boring" stories.'

The man from *The Telegraph* was trying to telephone his half-time copy. 'Do you mind, I'm talking,' he said to me indignantly. 'Mind?' I enquired. 'I do mind you writing all that bullshit about English football. Now's your chance to redress the balance.' With that I slapped him on the top of the head. 'Tell it like it is, not how your prejudice is.'

A *Telegraph* man, wearing a Prince of Wales check suit, based in Paris, saw the futility of arguing with me so he agreed that Arsenal had been magnificent, a credit to English football. 'He can't write that – they'll sack him or send him to the nut house,' I taunted. I spotted Lacey who was sporting a beard. 'Oi, fungus face, you've slagged us all year. Now you have just seen 45 minutes of total football. I bet it sticks in your throat to have to write how good we are.'

'Can you do it for 90 minutes? That's the big question,' Lacey replied.

'Fifty quid says we can, and I'll be here at the end to collect.'

In 1979 the Village People released a record called 'Go West', a punchy rhythmic dance-floor filler. Around 14 years later, the Pet Shop Boys re-

vamped the same tune, which for many was better. At half-time the small group of travelling Arsenal supporters sang '1–0 to the Arsenal, 1–0 to the Arsenal' to the tune of 'Go West'. Whilst the song hardly echoed around the ground it was the beginning of an anthem and one the Arsenal fans could relate to and really call their own.

The second half was only two minutes old when Ginola scored with a brilliant flicked header. The noise that greeted that goal nearly blew my eardrums. To my right the Boulogne Boys' whole end moved like a giant wave on Waikiki beach. Forward they surfed across the rows of seats, hitting the fence with a force that made you flinch from 60 yards, up along the length of the wire mesh like swarming ants, cheering, shouting, jumping. Every mouth open, letting out a primeval scream which was part emotion, part energy release, every component piece frightening in its power to ignite the players. I looked at Dibbsy. Neither of us spoke for we thought that the next 40 minutes would need a rearguard action of Dunkirk proportions to hold back the blue French tide.

But it never happened. From the kick-off Arsenal won the first 50:50 tackle and took the battle to the French. Weah never got a kick up front, while in midfield Jensen played like ten men, making crucial interceptions to break up the focal point of the attack. French, as a language, has brilliant words that do not translate into English that well, yet say so much. Jensen in midfield was all *volonté* (will), while up front Wright was all *élan* (dash, flash, speed). At the back the colossal figures of Adams and Bould stood firm. Even the Boulogne Boys saw something special as Arsenal silenced even their brand of guttural synchronised chanting. The human wave crescendo would be no more tonight. At the end of 90 minutes their surge of power would only have the strength to lap the shoreline gently. With a few minutes to go Smith, the Arsenal centre-forward who had led the line like a Trojan, had a one-on-one with the acrobatic Paris keeper who somehow turned the shot around the post. Within seconds the whistle blew for the end of 90 minutes with the Arsenal players ecstatic, fists punching the Paris night air, running over towards the small band of cheering Arsenal fans.

Being as good as my word I went down to the press area to give them some more. 'How about it, Lacey? If that had been a foreign team doing that to an English team you'd have creamed your pants. Your brain would have exploded with superlative overload, but I bet you don't write about what really happened tonight because it's Arsenal.' The French walked past, absorbed by this outburst of passion from an Englishman. The Paris manager told it the way it was. He said he 'never realised an English team could combine such physical presence and technique'. My parting shot to the whole press-box, but aimed especially at Lacey, was: 'I'll be seeing you in Copenhagen when we've won this cup. I'm gonna haunt you. Believe me. I'll be back.'

The Croydon lads returned to their car which had had the back window smashed out. On the windscreen was a card which read, 'WE ARE THE BOULOGNE BOYS!' It was a draughty drive back to Croydon. The metropolitan police stopped them in Eltham at 3 a.m. because their car looked suspicious with their back window missing. The Boulogne Boys' calling card gave the police a belly laugh. For the other Arsenal fans inside the stadium it was time to be locked in for nearly two hours, then straight on to a bus and back to England, probably arriving at 5 a.m. next morning, absolutely exhausted.

I headed for the metro and got lost. I thought I was walking down into the metro but ended up in an underground car-park. I then had to walk back against the crowd, every one of which looked like the Boulogne Boys who had been attacking the Arsenal fans earlier. When I finally did get on the metro there was a gang, about 20 strong, looking at me. I picked up a couple of comments and realised they were talking about whether or not I was English. Suddenly I felt very alone and vulnerable. I opened my *L'Equipe* newspaper and buried my head in it. If this didn't make me look French then nothing would. The whispering Boulogne Boys stayed on the metro when I got off. Had they got off I would have been up the steps and across three streets while they were thinking about their next move. As I made my way back down to the bar in the Rue St Denis where I had arranged to meet my acquaintances from earlier, I felt an inner satisfaction tinged with sadness that I had witnessed a great performance yet I had nobody to share it with. I arrived in the bar, ordered a drink, sat down with my *Guardian,* then waited for some English company. I wanted to talk about the goal, about the tremendous individual performances I had seen. I wanted to relive every kick tonight, but nobody came. Every time I looked up all I saw were scantily clad prostitutes stopping people as they walked past. One came into the bar and gave me a prostitute smile: the lips curl upwards and the face is expressionless save for the all-seeing eyes to see if you have any interest. She looked at me.

'Etes-vous Anglais?'

'Oui. Je suis Arsenal supporter. Arsenal le nombre uno.' Realising she was talking to an idiot football fan whose sole interest was football, she purchased some chewing gum from the machine in the corner of the bar and returned to the street. Later in the evening I swore she gave me a proper smile, but that was probably wishful thinking.

The TV was on in the corner and highlights from the game were being shown. The owner called me over to say how well Arsenal had played. 'Je comprends,' I said, and smiled. Around midnight he put all the chairs on the table then said to me, 'Fermé.' I looked over to the corner where a couple were sitting, drinking champagne.

'Qu'est-ce que fermé pour monsieur et mademoiselle?' I said, pointing to the couple.

In his reply I picked out the words 'engaged' and 'married'. I realised that they were celebrating their engagement. I was supposed to be celebrating so why not invite myself to their party? I walked over.

'Les félicitations sur votre mariage' (Congratulations on your marriage), I stuttered in my best pidgin French.

'Merci,' replied the girl, trying not to laugh. The boyfriend had no such inhibitions and burst out laughing.

'Excellent, monsieur. Apprenez vous le français?'(Are you learning French?)

'Oui, rapidement.' (Quickly.)

Even the owner laughed at that one. He then gabbled something in French which, roughly translated, meant that I was welcome to join them.

'Je suis celebrating Arsenal's magnifique triumph over Paris St Germain. Voudrez-vous une drink avec moi?'

My terrific accent was bringing the house down, as all three of them were falling about.

'Your French is très bad, monsieur,' said the boyfriend, handing me a glass of champagne. 'Vous buvez avec nous.' (Drink with us.)

'Here's to the happy couple, then,' I toasted, with the obligatory 'Prost'.

The champagne really hit the spot so I decided to buy a bottle. After that the owner opened one. Whilst I didn't have any Englishmen to while away the celebrating hours with, I had found some eager listeners. My recreation, including reruns of Ian Wright's goal, temporarily stopped the happy couple from gazing longingly into each other's eyes. The owner babbled on in French while I agreed, throwing in as many Ouis, Nons and Agincourts as was politely possible. Just as long as I didn't antagonise them then I was good for a drink. I've had some great celebrations along with some terrible ones. This was the first one where everybody was celebrating something different around the same table. I knew I'd had enough when I started smiling back at the prostitutes and they started to look half attractive. Once I got outside in the fresh air they looked ugly and mercenary again.

Whoever tells you champagne doesn't give you a headache the morning after hasn't drunk cheap stuff on the Rue St Denis because it does. Only time will tell if that couple's relationship survived my rude introduction or the ramblings of a celebrating Arsenal supporter.

I headed for the station and caught the first train for Calais. On it were a large group of French riot police along with a band of unhappy-looking Arsenal fans. It transpired that they had been held all night and were now being escorted back to Calais. I settled down with a beer and baguette in a compartment with two other Arsenal fans. The train journey seemed interminable with the train travelling slower than the Folkestone to London stopping train; this one seemed to stop every five minutes. At Amiens a guard came down shouting 'allez en avant' along with other words spoken too quickly for me to understand. The guard stood in the carriage, gesturing everyone to the front of the train. 'Bugger off, we're not moving,' was the general consensus. Eventually, it was explained in English. Only the front carriages went to Calais. The Arsenal fans came through the carriages moaning about French railways, the worst insult being 'they're worse than British Rail'.

When the train stopped at Calais town I was off. The riot police were keen to keep everybody on, but on the sound of my 'Excusez moi, s'il vous plaît,' they moved aside. I stopped in the town for a beer and ambled towards the port. I knew that the lads I had set out with would be on the 2 p.m. ferry. If not, then I would cadge a lift from the other Arsenal fans in the car waiting area. As I walked towards the ferry across the railway tracks, the overhead walkway was full of Arsenal fans being escorted back to the ferry by a contingent of riot police. A few of them spotted me walking along eating chunks from a large French loaf with some cheese. (I also had a bottle of French red *appellation contrôllée.* 'Oi, Froggie,' one shouted down. 'You garlic-smelling poof.'

'Qu'est-ce que vous dites, monsieur?' I shouted up.

'Piss off, Froggy, you're shit and so's your football team.'

I had to laugh at the irony of that conversation. Whilst I love France I look as French as John Bull himself. I even had my famous brown leather coat on. At the ferry terminal I went up to the information desk to ask about ferry departure times when I heard someone asking why the ferry to England was delayed. The French woman behind the desk explained in good English: 'The riot police are putting 200 football hooligans on the ferry. They have been smashing up the train and causing havoc in Paris.'

'Pardonnez-moi madame, vous avez le visage d'une grande vache!' (Pardon me, madam, you have the face of a big cow!) That was the best French insult I could relay at speed in anger.) I then went back to full volume English. 'That is absolute garbage. I have just come from Paris on that train. No English football fan has caused any trouble on that train.' (Most of the fans had slept on the journey from Paris to Calais.) 'The only problems on the train were caused by the lack of refreshment. If that ferry is late it isn't the fault of the football fans, who are not hooligans. You don't want to talk about trouble from English fans in Paris, look to your own fans.'

The French woman looked at me shocked, no doubt impressed by my ability to eat French bread and cheese with red wine while calling her a fat-faced cow. Most travelling football fans pride themselves on being able to say 'fuck off' in Italian (vaffanculo), so I had just increased our insult value many times over.

Just then I spotted my travelling companions in the car-park. I got in the car, where they told me that they had called in at my hotel for me this morning. I just shrugged my shoulders. On the ferry going back to England I learnt that they had endured a miserable evening as they had to be back in their guest house at 11.30 p.m. They had drunk in one bar and paid five pounds for a pint of beer. The owner of the hotel wouldn't let Frank in so he stayed in the car, where he couldn't get comfortable.

'Did you have a good time, ginger?' asked Lawrence.

'The way I feel now I must have,' was my reply, which posed more questions than it answered. I informed Lawrence that I felt his inability to return to the bar as agreed lowered him in my estimation. Frank continued to drink on the ferry going home and still had change from his forty pounds when he got back to London. Should he ever sober up long enough then he would be a prime candidate for Chancellor of the Exchequer with his ability to balance someone else's budget. When they dropped me off home I informed them all that I would never attend a European away match with any of them again, adding that I thought them all spineless spongers. A fitting epithet for such wasters.

Ginola had even more to say about how he was going to destroy Arsenal in the second leg because he would have more space. Little did he realise the Parc des Princes had corridors wider than Arsenal's pitch. Better wingers than Ginola had come to Highbury against weaker full-backs and struggled to find space. Arsenal won the return leg at Highbury by the prophetic scoreline 1–0. The Arsenal fans sang their anthem long into the north London night. A Copenhagen version excursion awaited. For those who had attended Brussels 14 years previously it was a chance to exorcise some terrible ghosts. For me it was a chance finally to shut up the stupid Chelsea fan who was for ever telling me that Chelsea had won the Cup Winners' Cup whereas Arsenal had not.

Arsenal were to face the cream of Italian football, Parma, in the final. The omens did not look good. Ian Wright, the goalscoring phenomenon for Arsenal, was suspended, then three weeks before the final Arsenal's dynamic Danish international, John Jensen, was badly injured in a horror tackle playing for his country. The two players who had been outstanding in the cup run would be on the sidelines. Not only that, Parma had been the outstanding team of Italy's premier league in the current season. They were the only team that had beaten AC Milan both home and away and boasted an impressive array of talent. Up front they had the electric Swedish international Thomas Brolin. Alongside him was the Colombian Faustino Asprilla, a leggy striker whose scintillating acceleration and shooting had petrified defenders in Italy since his transfer. Lacey was to write a fawning, sycophantic article on Asprilla just before the final, which made him out to be so good that Arsenal's defence would be better advised to get a gun if they wanted to stop him. Parma also had a brilliant midfield maestro, Gianfranco Zola, with a dazzling change of pace and dynamite in his shooting boots. To top it all Arsenal's international goalkeeper, Seaman, affectionately known as 'Spunky' to the lads, had rib problems.

It was an understatement to say that I was worried about Arsenal's ability to hold the score down to a 2–0 deficit, let alone win. After all, we had replaced great players with honest journeymen, although the players they were alongside were good players.

Lenny White was a wide boy. Not as wide as John Leach but wide all the same. If John was English Channel wide then Lenny would be River Thames at Tilbury width. Lenny loved to organise trips for the lads. Apart from being wide, Lenny loved to chase a pound note. Want to travel, want a ticket, speak to Lenny, he'll get one, but he'll charge you. Lenny wasn't a product of Thatcherism; he was chasing a pound when Harold Wilson stated the pound in your pocket isn't worth any less. Nevertheless, Lenny thrived on the Thatcheristic ethos of profit is good. Boys at football with more money in their pockets. Travel with Lenny, see Europe, meet ugly women and fall over in obscure bars where Lenny always knew someone. Unlike other wide boys who promised the earth yet delivered fresh air, Lenny had sound contacts. Lenny really could get you that ticket for Cats, Phantom of the Opera, *Frank Sinatra or even Copenhagen without queuing. Lenny announced he was moving into the world tour business. Lenny had a trip on for Copenhagen, limited space, first come first served. I was on board with the rest of the Croydon boys, the bright brothers included.*

I had my own contacts in Copenhagen which netted four of the best in the main stand. Lenny appreciated that so much he bought the spare tickets off me to resell with a mark-up. (I finally got paid 48 hours into the trip after threatening to run up a bar bill with Dubbsy.)

I had never been to Copenhagen before. Neither had anyone else on the trip, except SAS Steve, a medium-height, stocky, dark-haired guy who had been to most places. Unusually (as most nicknames don't tend to go with type), Steve had been in the SAS and seemed to have brought most of his muscle confirmation out with him. He spent the whole trip with sleeveless T-shirts which made him look like a miniature Arnie Schwartzenegger. Looking around the departure lounge bar at Gatwick before we embarked upon our adventure, I saw the mottliest crew I have ever travelled with. Part comedy, part drunkard, you wouldn't let your daughters near them but would invite them in for tea if they were delivering your milk. Middle-aged men with their sons. Middle-aged men without sons and with crew-cuts. Young men with baby faces, pot bellies and Dubbsy, a young man with an old man's face and a body made old by lager sessions which started one week and finished the next. If we were to lose then you wouldn't have known it sitting in this bar. Other Arsenal fans were attracted into our company by our *joie de vivre*. Lenny, 5ft 6in tall, late 40s with his balding ginger hair grown long at the sides then pulled back into a pony tail, Armani black dog-tooth check sports blazer, chino slacks and brown loafers, was like a schoolmaster chiding errant boys. Lenny never missed a trick, even if he looked like a rich loser. His eye for spotting an earner extended to spotting people's stupidity, so every misplaced adjective was cue for a dose of abrasive wit which made the other schoolboys roar with laughter. To his right sat SAS Steve like Terry McCann in *Minder*. Lenny, as usual, was carrying a bundle (2K at least) in fifties and twenties, but wasn't buying a round, which caused much ribbing from those who really knew him.

'Are you gonna buy a round, Lenny?' asked Dubbsy.

'What for, you're gonna die of cirrhosis without my contribution. So I'll save my money and donate it to medical research.'

'Or a bleedin' hair transplant.'

That's how the conversation went from the moment we got to Gatwick until we arrived back three days later. Everybody insulted everybody else but nobody said a word about their mums, because everybody loves their mum, apart from Dubbsy, who called every female 'Mumsy' and every male he met 'Little Willy'. Questions about the hotel or Copenhagen were met with Lenny's wit.

'What's the hotel like?'

'Brick building, lobby, beds, room, bath. What do you expect, room service and bloody jacuzzis?'

'What's Copenhagen like?'

'It's Danish, flat, Vikings live there and a football match is being played on Wednesday night.'

Nobody asked Lenny any more questions after that. Lenny gave his tour leader's speech. 'Here's your tickets. The coach will leave for return at 2.30 p.m. on Thursday. Miss the flight and you're on your own.'

'Okay, teach,' shouted Dubbsy, which precipitated a burst of applause from the other fans in the bar. It was Tuesday morning yet already I felt nervous for tomorrow's match. Everybody else was convinced Arsenal could win. I wasn't so sure. I made my prophesy in the bar at Gatwick. 'The best we can do is score an early goal then hang on for grim death: score then shut the shop for business.' The lack of argument said a lot for our collective state of mind.

Arrival at Copenhagen Airport was not met with the usual cold-eyed stares and rows of grim-faced riot police. Instead, smiling police were there to direct people and answer questions. 'I bet they're not like that tomorrow evening,' someone remarked. Outside where the coaches were, souvenirs were being sold. Not the tacky, cheap stuff the hawkers sell outside English grounds, but real quality pennants and scarves for five pounds. Everybody bought a pennant or something. The bus moved off with Lenny sitting at the back making a stupid comment every five yards. Everywhere looked so clean, with people cycling.

Boris, one of the young single guys, had made a special tape up. He went to the front of the coach and on came the music. After the first few bars everybody remembered a long forgotten tune by Danny Kaye: 'Wonderful, Wonderful Copenhagen'. Everybody sang along. Lenny's world tour had turned into a '50s-style Margate day trip. Other world tours via ship, boat and plane would be converging on Copenhagen. None would be singing 'Wonderful, Wonderful Copenhagen' quite so tunelessly. If Copenhagen was worried about 15,000 English football fans descending upon it, it certainly didn't look it as every set of traffic lights saw pretty blonde girls with fresh, clear complexions waving at us. The second song on the tape cut in. Over the past few weeks this had become the Arsenal fans' anthem. The 'Go West' chorus line was replaced by '1–0 to the Arsenal'. Our notoriety was based around us being boring. We were desperate to be boring and lucky just this once. We were owed this. Every man on the bus had been in Brussels 14 years previously. This was an avenger mission. We even had the SAS to lead us.

'I don't believe it. We're in a bleedin' condemned building. You're having us on, Lenny,' shouted the lads. It was true, the building had been condemned, but as there were so many Arsenal fans in town they had opened it early to fit us all in. 'Do not worry,' the hotel manager assured us in perfect English. 'The building is perfectly safe.' Reassured or not, everybody paired up. My decision to have a beer with Dubbsy meant I ended up rooming with him, something I hadn't planned on as Dibbsy said he was 'a nightmare'. As it turned out my nocturnal habits caused him to complain.

The night before a big European final often turns out to be the best night of all, especially if you go on to lose, so everybody went out to party. Lenny, of course, knew someone who owned a bar near the centre called Chez Simon so everybody mustered in there. Win, lose or draw, the next evening Simon was going to lay on the biggest party in town. As it was the evening developed into a big karaoke session with nearly everybody doing their party piece. Some, however, just sat in the corner keeping their thoughts in, the tension already starting to build. The burden of expectation that fans on their travels carry with them is immense. We knew what lay ahead; we just hoped the players did. Every person who entered the bar was scrutinised to pick out some omen which would help allay our fears. Players might think they are superstitious, yet their rabbit's foot or dressing rituals were nothing compared to what every one of 15,000 fans would bring out tomorrow. Scarves from matches played over 20 years previously. Hats which had been accidentally kept in pockets during a cup win. These scenes would all be re-enacted thousands of times over in the belief each fan could tip the balance by his contribution.

Walking back to a city centre taxi rank, we spied our first Parma fans. We said hello. They looked absolutely petrified of us, never letting the mask of fear subside even when they finally cottoned on that our handshakes were genuine. Whatever time we staggered in we knew it was late. We brought back with us a noisy belief in our invincibility. If the players could not see our confidence then they sure as hell would be able to sense it tomorrow.

Woodsy, JB, Divver and a crowd of the other lads from The Tavern knew the best way to get to Copenhagen, that was via Hamburg. Cheap flight, stay a few days just off the Reeperbahn. With the raunchiest clubs this side of Bangkok the boys knew it would be a good time. I first saw Divver early on the Tuesday evening when he told me the story. When I left four hours later he was still telling it. It might have been the 50th time he recounted it but it never lost its humour. 'The first night we went down the Winkelstrasse, the road at the bottom of the Reeperbahn, the same road where The Beatles used to perform in the Star Club. We ended up in Suzie's Show Bar which had a revolving stage with a bath in it. The lovelies were doing a show, like mini synchronised stripping. After the first show a few of the lads stripped off and joined them in the bath. Anyway, the next night we walked down the street and the bouncers started shouting out, "Here are the famous Arsenal Boys." With that all the greeters come out on to the street. Come into our club, boys. Free drink. You are a legend amongst the club owners. After doing a couple of bars we went in the Thai house. We all ended up downstairs in a huge soapy bath with these Thai girls. Old Woodsy wouldn't take his Arsenal shirt off, though. Said it was a bad omen. While everyone else kept their end up, Woodsy upheld the honour of Arsenal.'

'Your waiter today is Eric the Viking,' shouted Lenny in the breakfast room. Eric was also the manager, liaison officer and general dogsbody. On the Wednesday morning Eric was going around the tables opening bottles of Carlsberg for the Arsenal fans who were in the breakfast room in various hungover states. 'I understand that English football fans like to drink beer in the morning,' said Eric, giving a beer to everyone who walked in the room. Someone was going to tell him that whilst the thought was good, not everybody would be drinking them.

'No way, they'll all get drunk,' chipped in someone.

'I love the smell of Carlsberg in the morning,' shouted Dubbsy as he announced himself to the breakfast room. The volume level increased 20 decibels as Dubbsy entered the room, never to let up until he left. Eric became an honorary 'Mumsy' as he was serving beer.

Lenny announced that the world sightseeing tour would be leaving around 10 a.m. to include a visit to the famous mermaid which had recently had the arm broken off by a political extremist. 'Enlightenment; I'll show you lot some fuckin' refinement and culture if it's the last thing I do.'

'Spelt wif a k, Lenny.'

'The only c I'm interested in is Carlsberg,' announced Dubbsy. With that the conversation deteriorated into a game of banter tennis with friendly insults flying back and forward across the room. Eric pronounced that it was good to see everybody enjoying themselves, but he would have to stop the free telephone calls back to England as the meter had clocked up three hours since yesterday. (Eric put the telephone in a cupboard which everybody removed and plugged in, replacing it afterwards, when they wanted a call from that moment onward.)

Lenny's culture tour left at around 10 a.m. to visit the sights. After two hours they adjourned to a bar overlooking the Baltic for some serious culture – testing 8.5 per cent Elephant lager. Dubbsy had long since abandoned the culture shockers and was testing the chilled beers at least an hour before the boys joined him. Later, somehow, Dubbsy ended up in the Baltic. One minute he was in the bar, next minute his mission to save the mermaid resulted in him coming back into the bar soaking wet. The bar owner lent him a pair of track suit bottoms which were two sizes too small for him so it looked like his trousers were retreating up his leg after an argument with his ankles. Dubbsy described his new trousers as real dual purpose strides: punching and pulling pants.

I had made a decision that I would see the match completely sober so I hired a bicycle for the day. With my blue raincoat the others said I looked like Coburn in *The Great Escape*. I joined the other commuters cycling to work dressed in my full Arsenal colours, which got a few funny looks, but mostly smiles and waves. Copenhagen is not a big city. There is a large open square which is the centre point. Named Hans Christian Andersen Square, this was to become the focal point for all Arsenal supporters. Also in the city were the famous Tivoli Gardens. Every Arsenal supporter meant to visit the Tivoli, but most ended up in the bars surrounding the square. On one side of the square was a small cluster of bars opposite a McDonald's. I cycled down to the square at around 9 a.m. Already Arsenal fans were drinking around the bars. Standing around were the ubiquitous smiling policemen. Some of these guys had only just recovered from a savage Tuesday evening lager session. As the day wore on the crowds gathered to sing their anthem: '1–0 to the Arsenal'. I cycled off, getting cheers from Arsenal fans sitting outside bars. As the morning wore on the different behaviour of the two nationalities became apparent. The English wanted to buy beer, find a spot, then sit down and drink to excess. The Italians were just happy to amble around watching the English drink and sing. Everybody caught the smiling sickness from the police.

My decision to remain sober was based upon my Brussels trip when I had drunk too much. I decided to settle for a nice lunch then go back to find a nice bar in the afternoon. I was looking for omens and settled on an Italian restaurant. Inside were some other Arsenal fans. They asked me why I was on my own. 'I'm not on my own, I'm with 15,000 other Arsenal fans. I just need some solitude before the trials and tribulations ahead.' We all drank to that. Outside one of the funniest moments of the trip so far was unfolding. A stunning fashion model was posing for some shots. A group of Italians lined up politely to watch. The young Arsenal fans didn't wait to be asked but invaded the shoot, putting their arms around the girl, going down on one knee to propose, offering full unopened cans of Carlsberg as presents. The Italians, thinking it was some sort of street theatre, started applauding. When a gust of wind blew up the model's dress to reveal white silk knickers, the wolf whistles and gasps could have been heard two miles away. Meanwhile, while we sat in the restaurant the Parma fans walked up to the window, looked, then moved on. One of our party summed it all up. 'They are like sharks in so much as they seem to have to keep moving.'

The meal was great, but we only drank French wine. We saw that as an omen after Paris. Over the meal the level of anxiety was rising. It was reflected in our conversation. I myself felt the first butterflies. Kick-off still six hours away.

Every city has a red-light area and Copenhagen was no exception. However, for a city which is pretty enlightened about sex, the red-light district was nondescript. Also, for a city with the largest amount of beautiful women I have ever seen, the few prostitutes hanging around were butt-ugly. They were also drug addicts with disgusting complexions. Even the really stupid young Arsenal fans who thought about it were stopped by their mates. However, in the centre of the red-light street was the Spunk Bar. Inside were pictures of fully clothed film stars like Humphrey Bogart, Clark Gable and Audrey Hepburn which completely threw all the Arsenal fans who drank in there. Perhaps 'Spunk' was lost in the translation from Danish to English. I ended up in there with some other Arsenal fans drinking Elephant lager. Elsewhere the bars were full with smiling, happy Arsenal fans who were in love after being served by the prettiest barmaids in Europe.

As I left the Spunk Bar I saw Harry emerge from down a side alley with a small legion of nasties. I needed to see Harry like I needed a hole in the head. Somehow he missed me and off he meandered – to look for people to bore with fight stories, no doubt. I eventually returned to Hans Christian Andersen Square around 4 p.m. The small narrow street around the McDonald's was now crowded with singing Arsenal fans. Huge banners had been draped from shops. A café/bar with a balcony was draped with red and white banners. Three guys on the balcony were leading the community singing. Whilst the songs were pretty repetitive, the gusto with which the crowds sang was heart-warming. Nobody could stand here and not be intoxicated with the atmosphere. The smiling police were keeping the roads clear. A senior officer was conducting operations making sure that nobody ventured on to the pavement with a glass. If anybody did another policeman was dispatched with a plastic cup. The glass was removed from the drinker's hand, its contents then poured into the plastic cup with the words 'thank you, now please go and drink some more'.

The event became self-policing with people stopping others from going out into the streets with glass. When one fan dropped a glass bottle in the square a policeman came and swept up the glass with around 20 Arsenal fans apologising. Riot police waited in the streets behind the square, but when you walked past them and smiled they smiled back. All the while the sound of the Arsenal anthem was growing in sound and strength. '1–0, 1–0 to the Arsenal'. The dream was stamped in our subconscious; nothing could deflect from our destination on the victory rostrum. The feeling of comradeship and togetherness was a red and white bond of destiny.

Around 4 p.m. the first of the guys who had been at it since 9 a.m. started keeling over from the effects of too much drink. The laughing senior policeman called up an ambulance who got the poor unfortunate on to a stretcher. After the first one, others followed in rapid succession. Crash, Bang, Oops. Another one bites the dust. Out came the radio. More laughter. 'Another one down.' Ambulance men tipping the stretcher to one side so the poor unfortunate can have a good vomit before they rush him to hospital for a stomach pump.

'Good trip to Copenhagen?'

'Yeah, I spent the entire match with a pretty nurse checking the saline drip in my arm.'

The mass of Arsenal fans outside the bar looked impenetrable, yet as soon as someone went to walk through, it parted like Moses at the Red Sea. A pretty mum saw her baby emerge from the milling throng with more rosettes and kisses than an American political convention.

I left for the ground around 6 p.m. by taxi. Just behind the ground was a park. Around the ground were bars packed with Arsenal fans. I bumped into TC, Tony Madden, Steve Ashford and the rest of the lads in the park. It was my final omen. Now I had joined the ranks. It was like I had attended one of those American evangelical meetings. The constant exposure finally cracked my resolve until I started to march towards the stadium singing '1–0 to the Arsenal'. A committed 'Onward Christian Soldiers' fan. Even though our team was weakened by injuries and suspensions, the force was with us. Italian flair against English stoicism. Everybody was singing the anthem now. Men, women, children and the neutral Danes who had adopted Arsenal as their team for the evening.

Inside the ground I saw Dubbsy, who had the bar owner's track suit bottoms on and had purchased a garish multi-coloured T-shirt outside the ground because the shirt he had set out in this morning stank of beer and the Baltic. So he looked weird, he was having a great time and his Mum loved him. My companion from the Italian restaurant looked at me with absolute disbelief when I expressed the opinion that Dubbsy was all right. 'No, mate. He's lots of things, but all right he is not.' I didn't have the heart to tell him I was sharing a room with Dubbsy.

Beer was being served in plastic cups which you were allowed to take into the seats area. The Danes were more laid-back than the Arsenal fans on the stretcher earlier.

We had tickets in the main stand of the recently built Parken stadium with the Danish neutral fans, so to our left was a huge banked sea of red and white with the Parma fans, who were outnumbered by three to one, to our right. As we assembled in our seats around ten minutes before kick-off a strange thing happened. Ninety-five per cent of the Arsenal fans were in place and the singing was starting. Everybody felt a feeling of oneness, a togetherness which we had forged throughout the day. The DJ was playing music in between announcements. Whether he was an Arsenal fan or whether Arsenal had tipped him off about the anthem I will never know. The first few bars of the song caused a roar to go up which must have shaken the stadium to its foundations. The players would almost certainly have felt it. For a few seconds it was like a Baptist revival meeting with people looking up to the heavens, cheering and shouting 'Hallelujah'. The Danes looked and smiled while every Arsenal fan roared out the first word: 'TOGETHER.' Then everybody sang the wrong words until the chorus.

'1–0 TO THE ARSENAL

'1–0 TO THE ARSENAL'

Then he put it on again, and again. The more he played it the louder the chorus became. Oh no it didn't. Oh yes it did. The players entered the arena to a carnival atmosphere.

The start of the match was almost missed out as an afterthought to the fun everybody was having, but once it started the enormity of Arsenal's task became apparent as Parma scythed through their defence. Seaman, who had had a pain-killing injection before the kick-off, saved at full stretch from Zola. Brolin surged through and hit the inside of the post before the ball was cleared. Adams, Arsenal's captain, a tough, uncompromising centre-half, screamed abuse at his team-mates, telling them in no uncertain terms to buck up their ideas and start believing in themselves. All of our group held their thoughts together. Dibbsy summed it all up: 'If we don't weather this storm pretty quickly then we're going to lose by three or four.'

For five minutes it was tense, white-knuckle stuff, then Arsenal started to play. Tight passing combined with Smith up front, playing like a solid oak tree, holding, laying it back, turning away. The ball moving out wide. A corner, the ball loose, a free header from Campbell, our muscular forward, sheer panic from the Parma defenders. The Arsenal fans responded with the anthem. A miskick from a Parma player, a Smith snap-shot eluded the goalie's lunging dive. The last sound the goalie heard before the huge rush of emotively roared passion from the Arsenal fans was the thwack of the ball against the post and the skid of the ball against the nylon netting. Smith turned and ran, ecstatic, towards the Arsenal bench who were off their seats. For 20 seconds afterwards the sheer bedlam stopped anyone from talking. My own lungs emptied air with a force that could have ruptured a hot water bottle had I been blowing it up.

'YES! YES! YES! GOAAAAAAALAH.'

I jumped, I danced, I went mad while I screamed. I ran on the spot so fast that I almost wore my shoes out. Every Arsenal fan in that stadium did their own manic ritual because this goal had been willed by our power of projection. Now we could dare to believe that our hopes and dreams were happening in front of our eyes.

Then the anthem started. '1–0 to the Arsenal.' This time sung with the force of The Three Tenors multiplied by 15,000. The noise was loud enough to wake the spirits of dead sailors lost in the Baltic. Parma were stunned. They needed the half-time break to collect their thoughts. In the toilets at half-time the laughter was tempered with the thoughts of what lay ahead. It was a mood I have never experienced before, almost as if we were actually masters of the ability to predict. '1–0' we had sung. 1–0 it was. It was 45 minutes until paradise. Forty-five long, pain-filled minutes till the biggest party Copenhagen had ever seen. Everybody sensed that our chance was to hold on to this omen, to keep it at 1–0. The tension in the toilets was manifest in everyone. People around were blowing out air as they urinated because they felt the need to release the tension from inside themselves and this was the only chance they would get until the 90 minutes were up.

The tension was already building in me and I finally cracked about 15 minutes into the second half. For around 20 seconds I couldn't breathe and it felt like an elephant was kneeling on my chest. I went out the back for some fresh air, gulping in breath, trying to clear my head. I sat down on the steps near the exit when the Dane on the gate called a paramedic.

'Are you all right? You look very white.'

'No, I'm fine. I just feel a little light-headed.'

The next thing is he's got me a cup of water and a crash team trying to link me up to a heart monitor. 'Leave me alone, I'm just a bit worked up about the match,' I shouted. The more I shouted the more worried they became. 'We must get you to hospital. We think you have had a mild heart attack.' I imagined myself lying next to those idiots who had drunk themselves stupid, missing out on the celebrations should we hold on. Somehow I stopped the medical Vikings from plundering me into hospital and I retreated to the bar. I ordered a drink and sat listening to the oohs and aahs of the crowd while watching the second hand on my watch go round, seemingly slower than ever. I sat in the bar, a lonely forlorn figure, looking at the clock and wishing the time to be ten minutes later than it was now.

I finally plucked up the courage to go back to my seat, only to see Parma score. However, my second heart attack was prevented by an offside flag. By now the anthem was being sung by weary lungs, their action prevented by the crush of tension from all sides, like a vice was squeezing both of the ribs from either side and restricting the airflow. The last few minutes were absolute hell. Every whistle from the referee was greeted by a cheer. Parma were desperate, but all of a sudden the agony ended. Heaven and hugs at one end. Hell then an outburst of anger as Parma fans started throwing missiles at Seaman. Ian Wright ran on to the pitch, throwing himself around all the players and finally launching himself into the crowd. His minder and fan extraordinaire, Denton, pulled him back on to the pitch as hysteria threatened to drag Wright under.

Two steps up an Arsenal fan sat crying. This was no child. This was a grown man crying, but these were no ordinary tears of joy, these were something more. I sat down next to him and cried as well. We looked at each other. We knew why we were crying. It had taken 14 years to exorcise the ghost of Brussels. The long journey back from hell that had started in 1980 had brought us to this wonderful place. Arsenal might eventually go on to greater things but this was the moment we had waited for. It was fitting that a hospitable people such as the Danes had been here to experience it with us.

Then the DJ played the anthem again. While the Arsenal fans went mad, the Danes realised they had to leave us to let us be here for our moment, rather like the way people leave grieving relatives alone beside a grave. They shook our hands, wished us good luck, then politely left. I just had one more act to complete before I left the stadium. I made my way along to the press enclosure. The friendly Dane guarding the gate refused to let me in. I don't blame him, as I must have looked a mess with red, blotchy eyes and a white face. I spotted Lacey who was on the telephone. I asked the friendly Danish steward to go and inform Mr Lacey that an old friend wanted to give him a message. The steward pointed me out. Lacey looked around, face full of anger as he was working to a very tight copy deadline. I remembered the line Steve McQueen shouted in the film *Papillon* when he jumped up at the bars to mock his gaolers. 'I'm still here, you bastard. Just like I promised. Tell them. You tell them. You tell them how it was.'

He threw his arm up in disgust as if to say 'Clear off'. I had made my point. Now, with no more skeletons, on to the party at Chez Simon. I passed the Croydon lads after miraculously getting a taxi. As I sailed past them I wound the window down. 'Last one at the party picks up the bar tab, Dubbsy.' Dubbsy ran after the cab, caught it at the next red light and jumped in on my lap. 'Take me to Cuba,' he said to the driver, holding an imaginary gun.

Chez Simon was a small bar with a large disco up above. The owner, SAS Steve's mate, had booked a band for the evening. The party was supposed to be private, but the doors were soon opened out on to the street. The noise attracted a large number of pretty Danish girls. The band played a mixture of American rock. Boris had his tape with him. The Sioux Indians say they buried their heart at Wounded Knee. We buried our emotion at Parken. After the tension everybody was drained. The first beers went down without touching the sides. One barman was employed just pouring them.

'Oh, we'll drink, drink together in praise of the AFC.' The Eton boating song had never sounded so good. I went over to the band who were having a break. I asked the leader if he could play a song that meant a lot to me as a football fan. 'Yes, of course. Why don't you sing it with me?' The first few bars of this song never fail to bring out goosebumps on my neck. After what I had just been through I wanted everyone else to know. The Dane played the introduction to the Crowded House song 'Don't Dream It's Over'. Two guitars played, and the keyboards man really bashed the keys, then missing a chord so that I came in one beat early. No one noticed because nobody else in the room knew the lyrics, but as I sang the line about losing battles people took notice. We had travelled a long road together since Brussels and we had never dreamed it was over, not even during the indefinite ban on English clubs in European competition. This wasn't the end, but the journey's end of a collective dream. When I sang the chorus line 'don't dream it's over' it struck a chord with everybody who knew that the words belonged to all football fans – but tonight they were Arsenal's.

While I sang the chorus other Arsenal fans realised what I had said about the poignancy of the words. How it was a song written for us. Together we had dreamed and now, as one, our dreams had come true. When the chorus came again Boris and Slick Steve, the Imran Khan lookalike, joined me on the mike while nearly everbody sang where they were. Even the line in the chorus about building walls between us was true about Arsenal, as the press had tried to do that many times.

In the instrumental interlude lads grabbed pretty Danish girls and danced with them. The musicians extended the instrumental break from a minute to over three. While the lads danced away the last few bars we all sang our own lines for the last time.

Oh Yes We've Won Now
Oh Yes We've Won Now

Once again I saw grown men with tears in their eyes as they realised what they had just experienced or perhaps I was just seeing their tears through my own eyes. I have heard men say the greatest feeling was when their first child was born or others say there is no high like a heroin high. Well, Smith's goal and that final whistle when we sang the anthem is up there for those who were there. After the melancholy rendition, Boris put the tape on and the seaside day trip took over as 'Wonderful, Wonderful Copenhagen' blasted out, followed by the long version of 'Go West'. The throaty roar of '1–0 to the Arsenal' drifted out across the Baltic. Every bar in the city was reverberating to this tune. We all sang like Frank Sinatra with the volume of

Pavarotti. Everybody had their own way of celebrating, but after the stress came the release so it was mostly manic. I suddenly felt very tired; after all, I had been on the go for over 14 hours.

I was woken up face down on the bar by Dibbsy. 'You've had enough, mate. It's time to go.' I was carried out of the bar and put in a taxi. When I woke up back at the hotel I wanted to go back into town. I didn't want the night to end because tonight the moment of victory was still with me. The special feeling that everybody carries with them dissipates after a night's sleep, so I turned the taxi around. Perhaps I would sit by the sea, dreaming and humming our anthem. I needed to celebrate a little more.

Opposite the Tivoli is a large bar. Earlier, the open paved square next to it had been packed with Arsenal fans kicking a football. Now it was empty, save for the tin cans which were being cleaned up by the night cleaning crew. Around midnight John Jensen entered the bar, his leg still in plaster. An hour later he was up on the table singing '1–0' with the rest of the fans. He took off his jacket and left it hanging over the chair. When he went to leave, his wallet was missing. Some chancer had lifted it. John should have realised that while you can take the boy out of Islington, you can't take the Islington out of the boy.

I staggered around and saw the first sign of trouble. A bar had shut at 2 a.m. A young drunken lad was arguing that he wanted another drink. 'Yes, you can have another drink, but not in this bar. It is shutting.' The policeman, who was still smiling, gave him an option. 'You can go and find another bar for a drink or we can take you down to the police station where there is definitely no bar.' Assaulted by this kind of logic delivered with the ever-present smile, the young fan moved away to find his next drink. His mates had long since walked away from him.

I staggered past the Spunk Bar and into a late night burger shop. The next thing I remember was being picked up out of the gutter. I had fallen asleep in my burger and chips while sitting on the kerb eating them. Someone was slapping me in the face. 'Ginger, it's Paul Riley. Are you okay? Christ, you're a mess. I'll call you a taxi.' I hadn't seen Paul since I played against him in a Sunday League match five years previously. I must have had a good game that day for him to remember me.

I woke up in the morning with Dubbsy moaning that I was the noisiest guy he'd ever shared a room with. I had gone out 24 hours earlier with an Arsenal hat, pennant, silk scarf and two rosettes. I looked around and realised I had none of them left. C'est la vie. They had come a long, hard road with me. If I had to lose them somewhere, this was as good a place as any. The superstitious ramifications of their loss wouldn't be realised until our next big final. At breakfast Lenny told me I had two bookings for the London Palladium the following week. 'Was it a good night out?' people were asking each other. Looking around at the sorry faces gulping aspirin and orange juice, it definitely was. Eric came around with the beers for the last time, but only Dubbsy took them.

We went back into Hans Christian Andersen Square and talked all day about the day we had just experienced. After two hours in the pub the general consensus was that Parma wouldn't have scored in a brothel if Arsenal's defence had been in there. The truth was that the last 25 minutes of that match were the longest anyone has ever endured. I bumped into Steve Ashford who was drinking with a young guy around 18. It was his first European away trip.

'Was that good compared to other trips?' he asked Steve.

'That was the best there ever was. In years to come people will talk about Copenhagen as *the* trip of all time. You were fortunate to be a part of it.'

As the coach departed for the airport the tape played 'Wonderful Copenhagen' for the last time while Eric stood waving at us, holding the telephone which we had used to excess. Workmen were waiting to go in to make it habitable for a safety certificate for travelling businessmen. While we sang, Dapper Dave waved at the pretty girls for the last time. The Tivoli disappeared with one last witty aside from Lenny.

'What is the Tivoli?'

'Kew Gardens meets Southend pier.'

'Whoever picked this city for a European final must have known something. The girls, the smiles, the beer, the stadium, the police. It was just perfect.'

'And the result. Don't forget the result,' added Dibbsy.

The comment wasn't necessary. Nobody who was there will ever forget the result.

On the plane Steve hoped that the next time an English team played in Copenhagen, a team with grim troublemaking fans didn't go and spoil it.

The Danish police and City mayor wrote to Arsenal, praising the fans for their behaviour. The people at the FA didn't say anything because they weren't sure if we were welcome or not.

8

WEMBLEY FLOODLIGHTS

Only two seasons previously Arsenal had lost a Wembley semi-final to their bitterest rivals, Spurs. The Spurs fans had nicknamed it St Hotspur's Day (the patron saint of Spurs fans). Today, all Arsenal fans hoped it would be our turn to name it St Gooner's Day (the patron saint of Arsenal fans). The lads had met at King's Cross and were walking through the tunnel towards the underground to get the train to the stadium. Two Spurs fans were abusing every Arsenal fan that walked past, calling them wankers, cowards and shitheads. Mick gave the larger one a short, chopping right to the side of his head and his legs turned to rubber. Down he went, end of story. The other one ran off back towards the station. Nobody kicked him, they just left him there looking stupid, grovelling around the dirty floor.

On the platform the train pulled in and everyone got on. Next thing the police were running down the platform. The train was stopped and the police had got the two Spurs fans going through the packed carriages looking for this guy with a black leather coat. Everybody swapped coats and Mick removed his glasses, then put on a baseball cap. The police had more chance of recognising Martin Boorman than Mick. After ten minutes of this stupid charade the police gave up. As the train pulled out, one of the younger guys noticed the way the two Spurs fans were talking to the senior police officer. 'I reckon they was undercover Old Bill,' he said. Nobody argued with that conclusion because that's what it looked like.

TC had been to a rave club all of Saturday night until 6 a.m. Arsenal were playing Luton in the final of the Littlewoods Cup on the Sunday so he had come straight to the pub for the 9 a.m. meet and started on the brandy. By the time we got to Wembley at 3 p.m. he could hardly stand. A police officer said that he would never get in the stadium for the match. We were loath to leave him but we knew that he would sober up pretty quickly once we got him inside the ground. We went into a chemist and purchased some cheap sunglasses, and then bought a cheap runner bean cane from a Pakistani greengrocer. We held him on each arm, then walked him up to the turnstiles as a blind man, while he tapped his stick on the ground. With his black leather coat and stupid black leather San Francisco (faggots) hat, other Arsenal fans remarked that he looked like a white Stevie Wonder. We sailed past the police, but the impromptu rendition of 'I Just Called to Say I Love You' nearly gave the game away.

Cavan Daines was a West Ham supporter, but he spent all his time playing football so he hardly ever spectated. He was offered four tickets for the Charity Shield, a pre-season friendly between the FA Cup winners and League champions. On this day I attended with Cavan as West Ham lost to Liverpool, but after the match we stayed on to have a beer in the bar. Cavan is a witty guy who works as a plumber and, like most plumbers who spend their life with hands covered in water and boss white, tends to see the funny side of life. During his time as a plumber he had met many scousers and his view of them was that they were sound fellas (which is diametrically opposed to my opinion of them) in all areas except the truth, which they had no conception of. In the bar was a scouser who was wearing rosettes from both teams. He latched on to Cavan, who is a good listener, and he started by mentioning Cilla Black's name. Before he could say another word Cavan shot back at him.

'Do you know something? I've never met a scouser who wasn't at the Cavern Club the first night The Beatles played, wasn't there at the finish line when Red Rum won the National, isn't a personal golfing friend of Jimmy Tarbuck, and didn't get invited around Bill Shankly's house for tea and biscuits every other Sunday. Now tell me. Are you that man as well?'

For the first time in my life I saw a scouse bullshitter speechless. Buoyed up by our moral victory we left and walked around the Wembley pitch where Cavan recreated the run of Geoff Hurst in the 1966 World Cup final, then walked up the steps of the Royal Box to collect the imaginary World Cup, hotly pursued by an irate jobsworth. 'This is out of bounds, I'm gonna have you thrown out.'

We slipped through this door which came out on to the terrace overlooking Wembley Way. Standing there was a visiting Chinese delegation. I walked down the line and asked them: 'Would you like to meet the famous detective C.P. Daines? He smells a scouse bullshitter at 50 yards.' The Chinese, who spoke no English, all smiled as they do on the films and lined up. Cavan walked down the line shaking their hands one by one, every one of them smiling, laughing and nodding their heads as Cavan said ridiculous comments like: 'I love your food. I recognise you, don't I? You served me a dodgy special fried lice the other Friday.' All of the comments were delivered in a Benny Hill-style mock Chinese accent. As he got to the end of the line Ted Croker (the late General Secretary of the Football Association and predecessor of Graham Kelly) walked out of the VIP lounge. Ted was immediately pressing flesh with Cavan, who struck up an immediate conversation as though he had known Ted all of his life. 'Now, Ted, about these restaurateurs getting the best seats in the house. Are you getting plenty of spring rolls provided at the Lancaster Gate?' Poor Ted was as speechless as the scouser in the bar.

The Chelsea crowd behind the goal were growling. Chelsea had just gone 2–0 down to Manchester United in the 1994 FA Cup final. Suddenly, the third went in. A middle-aged Manchester fan who had his 12-year-old son with him jumped up to celebrate the goal in the middle of the beer belly tattoo brigade. The first blow hit him sickeningly on the back of the head, the second came from the other side and caused blood to squirt everywhere. Other people in the surrounding seats were raining blows in on him while his son watched in horror and cried. By the time the police and stewards arrived the man was lying in a crumpled heap in the passageway, covered in blood with his son sobbing by his side. Other Chelsea fans looked at the ground, shocked by the savagery of the attack on a man with a young boy by other fathers.

Jock Hyland, like all Scots, lived for two things: New Year and the England v Scotland match at Wembley. It was a two-yearly pilgrimage which had to be saved up for. Every other day of the year he loved English people, but on this day he used to put on his kilt (we used to call it a skirt) and go up to Baker Street to meet his other Scotch friend who used to travel down. Win or lose, he used to have a day out celebrating a long-distant battle called Bannockburn. Jock used to punch at least one Englishman during the after-match Saturday evening celebration in the West End. He used to show them his hand which had once shaken the hand of Henry Cooper.

'This is the hand that shook the hand of the hand that shook the world. [A reference to the night Henry put Muhammed Ali on the seat of his pants.] In the words of Shirley Bassey, the party's over.' Wallop, absolute mayhem, guys going over tables, girls screaming. Quite how this fearsome army of lunatics came to be seen as friendly by people who reported football spectators is beyond me. Seeing these nutters walk along swigging gulps from whisky bottles never failed to freak me out totally. To get alcohol into the stadium they used to get a hypodermic syringe and inject vodka into the centre of oranges. Seeing this drunken caterpillar meander up Olympic Way is one of the more frightening sights in football spectating. The fixture was eventually banned, the reason cited: the bad behaviour of the England fans.

England were due to play Holland in a friendly international. All the tabloids had been saying was how fearsome the Dutch hooligans were. England were due to play the Dutch in a few months' time in Germany for the European Championships, so this was seen as a hooligan dress rehearsal. The Dutch 'top boys' were quoted as saying they were coming *en masse* to put on a show. All day long the England fans arrived at Baker Street and waited for the Dutch hoolies. By 5 p.m. there were so many England fans milling around Baker Street that they started to spill out on to the main road along with assorted camera crews from most European countries. This is one of the busiest thoroughfares in London and evening rush-hour traffic was brought to a standstill as the fans decided to walk along the road towards Wembley. Camera crews did impromptu interviews with fans who didn't know what they were doing, let alone saying. 'What is this all about?' the journalist asked. 'Bottle. This is all about bottle. We've got to show the Dutch we've got it, haven't we?' replied the fan. That was about as illuminating as it got, as the Dutch never showed because they never were going to show. The tabloids had manufactured another phoney war.

Another end-of-season friendly, this time against Russia. A nothing match with the people who owned Wembley Stadium taking their cut from another overpriced match. Nothing else to do but go dressed as Cossacks complete with silly Russian hats. All morning in the pub drinking vodka then getting all the other drunken silly England fans to do the Russian dancing. We show them how to do it with the aid of a discreetly positioned bar stool which created the illusion that we were actually able to do the dancing. Then the drunken silly has a go and falls over onto the lager carpet. 'The cockney legend grows,' shouted Soccer. 'Best looking and now best dancers.' With that some northern dancer gets up and gives us a real lesson in movement including Russian, tap and any other type of dancing you care to name. Soccer was a lot quieter for at least ten minutes after that. During the game we had a slight argument with some England fans who started calling us commie bastards. Why bother enlightening such planks? We just kept saying 'Prostitye Mickhail' and they eventually went away. After the game, which Russia won quite easily, three other fans who had also come dressed up as Cossacks for a laugh got beaten up at Baker Street.

Yugoslavia was in the midst of a brutal civil war when the FA organised a friendly against Croatia at Wembley. On the day the date of the friendly was fixed, the Croatian military were committing abominable atrocities against civilians just the same way the Turks and Saudi Arabians were ignoring human rights when England played them at football. Politics and sport don't mix, do they, so why not play football against Croatia? (These are the successors to the same FA people who made England players do Nazi salutes when England played in front of Adolf Hitler in Berlin.) However, when the English public, who hadn't heard of the newly formed state of Croatia despite them being one of the top teams in Europe, only purchased 1,600 tickets seven days in advance of the match, the FA suddenly stated that they would have to call the friendly off because some civilians had been massacred. All the media printed the FA reasons verbatim. No paper looked below the paper-thin veneer excuse. The same media who called themselves 'The Voice of Truth' or 'Gives it to You Straight' mercilessly mocked people who gave their all for their love of football – a proud man like Graham Taylor, the England manager who had a turnip superimposed on his face, or like Tony Adams (Arsenal and England centre-half) who had donkey ears painted next to his picture after some cruel fans had barracked him with the word 'donkey' when he had made an error during a match. These honourable gentlemen of the media passed no comment on this pusillanimous sop to mammon.

There wasn't long to go in the semi-final against the Spurs. Tension filled the air as one mistake would settle it either way. It was evenly balanced at 0–0. Arsenal had a free kick. For what seemed like an eternity it was delayed as an Arsenal player received treatment. Finally the kick was taken. Into the box came the kick and Adams met it with a firm header downwards. The ball was in the net and half the stadium went wild as the other half sat in complete silence, apart from those who hurled abuse at a delighted Tony Adams. The Arsenal fans knew their reposte would hit the spot: 'Donkey won the Derby! Donkey won the Derby!' sang the Arsenal fans to the tune of the conga. At the end of the match Paul Merson walked over to the Arsenal fans and intimated by hand gestures that he too was going to have a few drinks after the match.

The Chelsea boys had been on an all-day bender ready for the match against Middlesbrough in the Zenith Data Systems Cup, a worthless trophy which featured a final at Wembley for teams who would not otherwise be able to get there for a final. A group of about ten lads had been putting them back for a few hours. As it got near time to leave, Mugsy Eastman, who loved to get his shirt off to show off his muscles after a skinful, got up and made the challenge. 'I bet twenty pounds that nobody can knock me out with one punch.'

Quick as a flash Richard, who was part of the same group, took up the bet. Outside they went with Mark holding the money. Dick took two paces back and gave Mugsy a real belter on the chin, but Mugsy bounced off the car still upstanding, barely conscious, although it was a close run thing. 'See, I told you so,' said Mugsy groggily.

'Double or quits,' shouted Dick, connecting Mugsy with an overarm right that would have downed a horse. Mugsy went down and everyone went back inside the pub. Mark had the job of borrowing the slops tray to throw on Mugsy's face to bring him round. When he came back in to cheers he asked Mark as referee to ensure that Dick bought him a drink for cheating.

'Piss off, Mugsy, you've got no chance. I don't buy weak chins a drink, plus I think I've busted my hand.'

9

BARMAN BUBBLEHEAD

Beesty loved Chelsea so much he used to train at the boxing gym with a 1970 royal blue FA Cup final shirt. He used to fight at welterweight, but could really bang with both hands. I don't know whether he started boxing because he felt it was a prerequisite of being a Chelsea fan to be hard; nevertheless, he took both banter and opponents' right-handers on the chin. With his jet black hair and baby face he never looked more than 17, even when he reached 24. Beesty was like all football fans: they idolised footballers and loved to meet them. I have lost count of the number of times people have told me they met footballer so-and-so, then added afterwards, 'he was a nice bloke'. Perhaps it was because they had become tainted. Love of money is the root of all evil and there is no doubt that it would be hard for footballers not to love money with the amount that was being thrown at them in the years following the entry of satellite TV.

Jimmy Hill started the ball rolling when he got the players freedom of contract, but there is no crime in demanding what your value is. Salaries for players went from just around the average wage to supertax bracket. Their contractual negotiations spawned an army of advisers: sharp-suited, fast-talking businessmen calling themselves agents who signed players on to their books, then took a percentage cut of everything. Agents didn't need to quote the axiom that their players had a short life; they knew the money was lapping over the edge of the barrel and they only needed to catch some of it. All the agent needed was the ability to impress young lads who were more brown ale than champagne, which was easier than doing a real job for a living. The rules, drafted before money became god, stated that agents weren't allowed to be involved in transfers, yet after the freedom-of-contract rule no player moved without his agent's nod of agreement.

It wasn't 25 years since Ray Kennedy (a player who won more medals than any other footballer) travelled home with my father and me in the tube train carriage after Arsenal had drawn their semi-final with Stoke at Hillsborough. Now footballers travel home in Porsches and Mercedes Sports, the drink-driving convictions telling everybody that while their incomes have risen, boys will always be boys.

Beesty's first encounter with a top professional footballer came in the Chelsea executive lounge after a long, enjoyable evening with his friend Pat, drinking the contents of the executive box free bar. After a great evening entering the cosy world of executive hospitality, where people called them sir and ran around opening more drink, when it was obvious they had consumed too much, the duo spied Kerry Dixon, Chelsea's top goalscorer, standing at the bar. Tall and blond, like most footballers he was vain and in love with himself. It was difficult for Kerry (and most footballers) not to love himself, because apart from when he was having a lean spell he was being told how good he was more often than Saddam Hussein. Tonight Beesty and his mate Pat were talking to Kerry, or trying to, as Kerry was looking bored by the whole 'player meets the fans' ritual. Beesty's mate Pat spoke to Kerry.

'Do you know that Beesty here travelled all the way up to Barnsley to see you last Wednesday?'

'So what?' replied Kerry, yawning.

'Who do you think pays for the flash suits you're wearing?'

'Cunts like you and him, that's who,' replied Kerry.

With that Beesty launched himself at Kerry, who was knocked backwards. Kerry could see that Pat and Beesty were going to have a go and despite being over 6ft he was off, using his striker's speed to put distance between himself and Beesty, who gave up the chase after 30 yards.

Despite this brutal awakening to the harsh reality of footballers' lack of admiration for their fans, Beesty loved to meet footballers. When he was offered the chance to meet every footballer in the Premier League by working as barman in the Chelsea players' bar he jumped at the chance. Beesty became a regular feature behind the bar and smuggled in his mates, who revelled in the chance to meet their heroes. One of the players nicknamed Beesty Barman Bubblehead. Quite why nobody knew, but the name stuck.

The players' bar is 'the' place to be seen at a football ground. All players' bars have a mindless jobsworth on the door and Chelsea was no exception. Gary, with his crippled hand, used to guard the door like a hungry rottweiler, his sole aim in life seemingly to make everyone as bitter as he seemed to be. Woe betide anybody who tried to get past Gary into the players' bar without a pass. Football is all about players. Psychologists call the way people react to attractive people 'the halo effect'. Footballers have a sort of halo effect on rich, older businessmen and young, beautiful women. People with money, and especially night-club owners, love to have fit young athletes around them. Money can buy many things, but it can't buy the glow of fitness which sparkles from athletes' eyes.

Simon Stainrod was sipping lager with his friend in a plush café/bar. His friend introduced him to our group who were noisily celebrating a good away win at a real Croydon kickers' team. (We had just paid two pounds in subs to have absolute Neanderthals threaten to kill us because we dared to run past them.) At this time QPR were top of the Second Division under the astute management of Terry Venables, who was to lead them to the FA Cup final. Here was a man who was living my dream: a fit young athlete given the chance to play against the greatest in the land, the chance to play in one of the greatest leagues in the world. 'It must be very exciting to be going into the First Division,' I said. 'No, but it should mean more money,' was his indifferent reply.

The first time Kerry returned to Chelsea after his transfer from them, he came into the bar. Beesty smiled at him and said 'Hello, Kerry' but was met with a blank look. Kerry wanted to buy all his old mates a drink so off he went. 'Steve, Den, Mal, Tricia. Get 'em all one, barman.' Beesty served the drinks, added £6.00 to the bill for badness, then asked Kerry: 'One for myself?'

'Sure, have a large one.'

Later, when Beesty was laughing and Kerry had pennies in change from twenty-five pounds, he gave Beesty a quizzical look.

'Do I know you from somewhere?'

'Everybody knows me. I'm Beesty by name and beastly by nature.'

The same evening Beesty had smuggled in scouse John. Although born in Shepherd's Bush, John had moved to scouseland and had inherited the scouse love of a chat. John thought he had died and gone to heaven because he was in the bar getting drinks bought for him by his heroes. It all turned sour when a young cocky reserve who had just broken into the first team started sending up John, who offered to introduce him to his friend 'Stanley'. The young reserve shook like a leaf all night, while John left saddened.

Being a football fan means that you get to feel bad when the opposition trounce your team. When Manchester United came to Chelsea and trounced them, Beesty was having a bad bar day. Four of Manchester's finest, Peter Schmeichel, Mark Hughes, Steve Bruce and Gary Pallister strolled into the bar. Perching themselves in a corner, Schmeichel shouted at Beesty in his loud Danish accent.

'Boy, get some drinks over here for the men.' Beesty hated being called 'boy' even more than he hated seeing Chelsea lose, and he hated the cockiness of them, so he ignored them, serving other players. Schmeichel continued to shout, thinking he was clever. 'Boy, I'm talking to you, boy,' like Elmer Fudpucker shouting at Daffy Duck.

'I'm busy serving other men,' replied Beesty tersely. With that Mark Hughes took the money and waited patiently. When Beesty finally went over to serve them, Hughes's face was like thunder. 'Give us four lagers.' When the four were put on the counter Hughes thought he was being clever. 'Four more, boy.'

Beesty took the money and started to pour the next four, with Schmeichel going 'cheers, boy'. Beesty had just finished pouring the next four lagers but hadn't put them on the counter just as the coach driver walked in the bar. 'Gaffer wants to leave now.' ('Gaffer' was Alex Ferguson, Manchester United's no-nonsense Scottish manager.) The four players had to leave their beers as 'Gaffer won't have beer on the coach,' as the driver put it. Beesty gave Mark Hughes a cheeky look which said 'see what happens when you mess with Chelsea'. As they walked away after taking two gulps at most of their first beer, Beesty gave them the full verbals. 'Thanks for the drinks, boys. Bon voyage. Cheers, boy,' he said to Schmeichel, in a mock Danish accent, holding up two of the beers and drinking from one of them.

I was playing alongside Jeff Bryant, Wimbledon captain, the only player who played for them in the semi-professional leagues as well as the Fourth Division of the Football League. He had played a big part in their famous FA Cup run when they had drawn 0–0 at Leeds in front of 40,000 people.

'I bet that was fantastic. What did the Leeds players say to you?'

'They told us we were nothing, and Alan Clarke (who had played for England on numerous occasions), who I was marking in the match, spent 90 minutes telling me I was crap, a donkey.' I thought that those Leeds players must have operated in a sad world. My illusions about honour and sportsmanship were shattered for ever by that conversation. Now my boyhood dream of playing professional football didn't seem so sad now that I'd grown too old without realising it.

Everybody knows the person who serves them beer and Beesty was no exception with the Chelsea players. Once Beesty got over the hero worship bit he started talking to the Chelsea players at their own level and they liked that. They also told Beesty things that they would never have told anybody else. Beesty realised that they were really him playing on a bigger stage. Beesty also observed the cliques and hierarchies that existed at all football clubs. When Glenn Hoddle, a born-again Christian, came to the club, Gavin Peacock, another Christian, along with other players, became part of Glenn's inner circle.

One evening the larger-than-life agent Eric Hall walked into the players' bar. Eric had started life as a record plugger but had seen the main chance to earn a good percentage from low-wattage athletes and now had a number of footballers on his books. Eric had a slight lisp and used the word 'monster' to describe everything, as well as calling everybody 'my man' as if he owned them. (In the case of some people, I'm sure he did.) Whenever Eric walked into the bar he was surrounded by fawning players, because Eric could open doors at all levels and players want to be asked to big events. The players' bar was non-smoking, but Eric used to love to light up a monster cigar. One evening Beesty went over and told him to put it out.

'I will later, my man.' Beesty pulled the cigar from his mouth, reminding Eric he was his own man. Beesty gained a lot of kudos from that act, especially with the players who weren't considered good enough to get taken on by Eric.

Chelsea reached the FA Cup final. Beesty was told he was okay for tickets, but one by one the players all reneged on their promises. Two senior players within the club were the talk of the players in the bar as they had collected the junior players' tickets for their agent's contacts. With three Saturdays to go he was getting nowhere. After one match one player, who knew Beesty was desperate for a ticket, made great merriment by waving two tickets at him. 'Got any tickets, Bubblehead? How much will you offer me?' Beesty had met Matthew Harding, the new Chelsea director, and had been impressed by his honesty. Matthew had offered him his business card with the words, 'Anytime I can help you, then give me a ring.'

On the following Monday Beesty rang Matthew Harding, who left his important weekly management meeting. Matthew said he'd do what he could, but never came up with the ticket. Beesty got his Cup final ticket by sleeping on the pavement overnight outside Stamford Bridge. Ken Bates, Chelsea Chairman, had thought up a great wheeze to earn Chelsea some more money. Chelsea had some spare ticket allocation, so he offered fans the chance to buy a piece of the pitch for two hundred pounds in return for the one-off chance to buy a Cup final ticket. It was a cheap way to squeeze some more money from fans, but Ken didn't always treat the boys this way.

Chelsea played Le Havre in the Cross-Channel Cup. It was a worthless game but that didn't stop 500 Chelsea fans travelling and drinking themselves into oblivion. At the ground at least 300 slept through the game. Before the match Beesty and some of the other lads turned up at the players' hotel and started drinking. Ken Bates came into the bar and promised to buy them a drink after the game if Chelsea won. When Ken left, the lads used the fact that Ken had offered them a drink as a reason to run up a huge bar bill on Ken's account. After the match, around 150 Chelsea lads turned up in the team's hotel bar for a victory celebration. Ken walked in and ordered the drinks for the lads, then swept his arm around the bar and bought all 150 a drink. Beesty saw the look in his eye and realised that this was Ken's family. He was proud of all his boys and just for a few seconds he was one of them. Ken hadn't bought Chelsea for money but because he loved it every bit as much as those boys loved their team. The next morning Beesty was invited to jump on the players' coach by the players he was friendly with. When Ken got on he looked the worse for celebration and, spotting Beesty and a couple of others, started asking how many freeloaders they had on board, although he never asked them to get off.

Footballers operate in a world where the merciless baiting of each other reflects their roots. Whilst their income has risen, their intelligence level hasn't. Vinnie Jones came to Chelsea as a big media name. His demeanour in the players' bar reflected this. His ordering of drinks, to be collected a few minutes later, some of which he forgot to pay for, reflected the way people were supposed to view him as a hard man. As the players paid for the bar, he was actually stealing off himself and his team-mates. Mal Donaghy was signed by Chelsea after he had passed his 33rd birthday, an age when most players are looking to pack it in. His age was to be the cruel butt of Jones's humour which reflected where he had come from. Vinnie entered the bar one evening after Donaghy had played poorly.

'Oi, Den, what did you get when you signed for Chelsea, a car, right?' shouted Vinnie.

'And what did you get when you signed, Nigel, a car, right?'

'Yeah, Vinnie.'

'Well. See Mal over there. He got a house. A bloody house.'

'Really, Vinnie.'

'Yeah, a fuckin' room in an old people's home.'

Vinnie roared along with his cronies, while nobody else laughed. Life was tough enough already, what with the season drawing to a close and new contract negotiations being sought, without this. Jones was an honest journeyman, but someone who added physical presence to a team, so he had been bought by three managers for fees in excess of half a million pounds. The signing-on fees and subsequent wages had made Jones richer than he had ever imagined when he was working as a hod carrier in south London. Jones the hod was like one of the nutters who used to threaten to kill us when we dared to dribble past them in local football, only Jones was getting paid a king's ransom to do it professionally. Now he was earning a small fortune and being paid to espouse his views on satellite TV and in *The Sun* newspaper. Jones, a man who had earned his 15 minutes of fame by grabbing Gazza's testicles. Jones, a man the fans loved because they saw someone doing things that they did in their Sunday leagues: tackling late, shouting abuse at referees and getting fired up. He'd become famous which gave him the right not to buy his round; footballers never have to buy a drink because that's the way it always was, only now they can afford to buy the pub they frequent.

'What's your vice – booze, gambling or women?' was a question asked to footballers by Peter Taylor, Brian Clough's right-hand man, before he signed a footballer. Were he still alive today he could add drugs to that list. As footballers' money rose so did the number of positive drug tests. With the cash comes the temptation. Harrys with money was how the fans saw it.

Chelsea signed David Rocastle from Manchester City. At 17 Rocky was predicted to be a future England star. Now he was struggling to get into Chelsea's first team which was no great shakes. Only a few seasons earlier Don Howe and Bobby Robson thought he looked unfit when playing for Arsenal. Now, with his habit of popping in the players' bar before the match, his weight had increased; consequently, his speed had deteriorated to the level where he definitely wasn't Premier League-fit. Reduced to the ignominy of reserve-team football, a once-proud athlete in his prime, who once drew the admirers and hangers-on like a magnet, was fast becoming a has-been.

Players were always being asked to sign footballs or do other such trivialities for charity. Most did it even if it was done grudgingly. For the Liverpool players at Chelsea it seemed above them ever to do it. One year when Liverpool were visiting, Beesty had a football he needed signed for a local charity, although he doubted he could get it signed by the Liverpool players. However, this day Razor Ruddock, Liverpool's uncompromising centre-half, needed two extra tickets for his family so Beesty offered an exchange. He would go and purchase him two tickets outside if Razor got his football signed. Beesty took the money, then heard Razor go into the dressing-room and ask his team-mates to sign it. The ones who ignored him were told in no uncertain terms: 'Sign it or else.'

Arsenal played Chelsea with five senior players suspended or injured. While their team-mates got beaten out on the park, the players sat in the bar while one of them tried to pull the barmaid with the big tits. As one of them remarked to Beesty: 'Why bother watching us play crap when you can watch some real entertainment.'

Two Chrises, Waddle and Woods, were always good customers for Beesty. Successive bottles of Budweiser gulped down and a crate for each of them to drink on the coach. One of the other Sheffield Wednesday players was at the bar one day.

'Good drink for the lads on the way back, eh?' said Beesty.

'That's not for us, that's all theirs.'

The contractual negotiations for the new player were being held in the office of the Chairman, Ken Bates. After long negotiations the player had more or less settled his wage demands.

'Now, Mr Bates, about my appearance money.'

'Appearance money? I've just paid a small fortune for you. Of course I expect you to appear for us. What do you think I have just spent all that time negotiating your wages for? So you can sit in the stand?'

Arsenal signed a new foreign player. His first wage demands made grown men weep. When it had all been settled, player and agent left. Within 24 hours all the senior players knew his salary payments, as did the tabloid press. As each senior player went in they discovered their worth to the new regime by what the club was prepared to offer them in relation to their new foreign star.

Beesty and Pat met Vinnie at the Chelsea supporters' club dance. Beesty bumped into Vinnie as he and Pat were leaving. Vinnie, who was with a friend, recognised Beesty and thought he was in for a spot of hero worship. All he got was a sharp retort from Beesty.

'Vinnie, bought any drinks tonight or have you been nicking them?'

'What do you mean?'

'It's Barman Bubblehead. I know your game.'

With that Vinnie turned on Pat, knowing it was Beesty who had made the remark.

'What did you say?' said Vinnie aggressively.

'Nothing,' replied Pat.

'Good. Watch your mouth.' Then Vinnie disappeared into a taxi, leaving Beesty laughing and Pat perplexed.

It was during this evening that Beesty learnt the facts about athletes' magnetism. Fans attending the supporters' club dance could pay a basic fee or a bigger fee to have a player sit at their table. Beesty had no need to take up the player-on-the-table option as he knew all the players. During the evening Beesty flitted from table to table with Pat, talking to the players who acknowledged him like a mate. After all, Beesty had only recently accidentally thrown a dart into one of the star player's feet, this having boosted his standing among the players. Two girls noticed Beesty and the way he carried himself, so they invited themselves into Beesty's company. These girls were real page three glamour types and Beesty started well when he won a ten-pound bet off one jealous player who bet he couldn't get a slow dance. One of the girls had a thing about athletes and had just finished with Gary Stretch, pro-boxer turned male model. Beesty, with his boyish good looks and amateur boxing fitness, looked the part.

Club owners need celebrities to give their club credibility and footballers with their abundance of energy and desire to drink around pretty girls are great for a club owner. This evening there was one in particular who inhabited the players' bar regularly who was inviting his friends among the players to his club party, including Beesty. The two girls drove Beesty and Pat, who couldn't believe what was happening. Just before they arrived at the club they pulled up at a set of lights alongside a taxi containing four of the Chelsea players, one of whom had lost the ten-pound bet earlier. The players started waving at the girls, only to receive two fingers from Beesty and Pat. Once inside the club the owner sat down with Beesty, Pat and the two girls and kept free champagne flowing like it was going out of fashion. Unfortunately, the lads couldn't keep up the pretence with their off-the-peg poorly fitting suits and bricklayer wallets so the girls drifted away, but just for a brief moment they experienced the world of footballer celebrity.

Beesty no longer works at the bar. A new franchise means that there is no room for the likes of Beesty, who no longer has much time for footballers because they are corrupted by money and power. However, Beesty still has a soft spot for Matthew Harding, who was totally uncorrupted by absolute wealth.

10

CUP WINNERS' CUP REVISITED

Chelsea qualified for the 1994–95 Cup Winners' Cup by losing the FA Cup final 4–0 to Manchester United who, as they had won the league, opted for the European Champions' Cup. The profile of Chelsea's fans was THUG. Police forces throughout Europe waited for the moronic blue army to descend upon them. Whether or not their image was strictly justified didn't matter once the mind set was cast.

Chelsea drew Vittoria Zizkov, the small city club of Prague, in the first round. The match was due to be played on the Thursday evening. When the Chelsea fans arrived they realised what Eastern European travel was all about. All the taxis were Ladas, the hotel was like Wormwood Scrubs and the food was grim. It wasn't like that at all, but there was no Rose and Crown or takeaway kebab houses, so that was how it seemed to the low-wattage, English-breakfast-please-mate travellers. The lads who arrived on the Wednesday attracted a few funny looks, but for the main it was cheap and fun. John Rake was with them, tall, stocky and trendy because he wanted to be, not because he was a travelling Chelsea fan. He looked like Robbie from Take That. John, like most of the other Chelsea lads, had not been two years old the last time Chelsea played in Europe.

On the day of the game Wenceslas Square looked like a scene from the 1968 Russian invasion with Czech paratroopers patrolling. Quite what the papers had written which caused their finest shock troops to be placed on duty was hard to comprehend. The Chelsea fans who had turned up in Prague under their own steam found out that the match had been transferred to a provincial ground close to the Polish border, about two hours' drive from Prague. The designated stadium was falling to bits so the crumbling terraces were thought to provide too much temptation for the fans if they decided to throw missiles.

John made his way down to the bus station along with a small group of other Chelsea fans. At the bus station was a small party of Sparta Prague fans, among them a girl, who wanted to see Chelsea. Not the team, but their fans. All the way on the trip the girl kept asking John: 'When are Chelsea going to fight?'

'Who's to fight?'

'Our army.'

At the ground the group walked round to join the one-day travellers who had adorned every square inch of fencing with flags. Most of the flags had a home town, pub name or silly message on them. On the running track stood rows of Czech paratroopers. Behind the terrace were enough police vans to fit three times the amount of fans that had travelled. John noticed that as he walked around the ground with the girl no guy gave her any verbal stick, which contrasted with the amount of verbal she would have received back in England had she done the same. This girl was like a known face amongst the Sparta Prague fans. All the Chelsea lads nicknamed her 'Butch Olga'.

While the Chelsea fans cheered every kick by the team who played the Czechs off the park, John was at the back of the terrace regaling the girl with stories about heroic battles with West Ham and Arsenal. John, who by this time saw himself as a cross between Warren Beatty and thug of the year, skipped the final whistle and caught a taxi back to Prague for an evening of cheap vodka and Eastern European sex with 'Butch', the Czechoslovakian shot-putter. On the flight going home the boys wanted to know why he had missed the battle of Wenceslas Square when the lads got attacked by the Czech mob and got shot at with rubber bullets for their trouble. The lads who got hit while they were running had bruises as big as footballs. The unlucky ones who got caught ended up paying a one hundred pound spot cash fine-cum-bribe. His answer? 'I had a dicky tummy so I went to bed early. It must have been the Czech Budweiser playing me up.'

Next stop Vienna. With the game being played on the Thursday the only way to get a cheap return air ticket was to travel out on the Thursday and stay the Saturday night. Whilst the majority didn't want the whistle-stop tour, the thought of three nights in Vienna didn't thrill any of the lads, who saw sightseeing on a par with a home defeat by Spurs.

John travelled out to Vienna on his own, but the maxim of a football traveller that you're not on your own for long came true for John the first night. There were two places to be in Vienna, either The George and Dragon English pub or the three streets of bars which became known as the Bermuda Triangle. The atmospheric charm of Vienna epitomised in *The Third Man* didn't exist to the travelling Chelsea fans. Foreign cities for English football fans are all about finding the place that most resembles The

Rose and Crown. Sightseeing is for wimps who can't drink all day. One of the Chelsea fans declared Vienna to be 'rustic'. He must have heard it somewhere. He certainly didn't read that in *The Sun* or *The Mirror*. His friends were unimpressed by his attempt to describe Vienna and thought he meant plastic.

The Thursday evening when Chelsea beat the Austrians became known as the night Chelsea drank The George and Dragon dry. By Saturday evening everybody had seen enough of the inside of the bars of this city to last them a lifetime. It's one thing to drink all day, another thing to drink all day for three days. A crowd of around 60 Chelsea fans sat around the bar with yet another cold lager. It was getting late but the owner had kindly offered to let some of the lads stay in the bar all night as they had checked out of their hotels to save money and were all desperate to get home in the morning.

Around midnight a group of six Nazis walked in. Outside were at least another 40 of them. They were dressed in uniforms with swastika armbands on. A couple of the lads got up to shake hands with them. This spurred on the Austrians who were Rapid Vienna fans to walk around the bar, attempting to shake hands with everyone. John along with nearly everyone else ignored them.

'We would like to invite Chelsea to join us in attacking a punk rock club.' The two Chelsea fans who had joined them said 'come on, lads', but nobody was interested. The Austrian spokesman continued. 'We have heard all about the famous Chelsea Nazis and how you like to fight.'

'We fight for Chelsea, we fight for England, but we've got no argument with these punks. What harm are they doing?'

'They are punks.'

Everybody waited for more but that was it. The Rapid Vienna Nazis left the bar with the two Chelsea fans, completely baffled by the behaviour of the remaining Chelsea fans. His parting shot of 'I thought we were all Nazis together' caused many to shake their heads. The entry of the Nazis caused the owner of The George and Dragon to shut the pub, so groups drifted to different bars in the Bermuda Triangle. 'Christ, it's bad enough being labelled as Nazis. When a group of them get us thrown out of a bar for no reason it adds insult to injury.'

A group of eight lads had travelled out on the train leaving on the Monday, stopping for a day in Germany. Some of the lads had bought CS gas canisters in Germany and were planning to take them home. On the Friday the lads were sitting in their hotel room drinking cheap Polish vodka. One of them thought it would be a great laugh to let off his CS gas canister as a practical joke. He was unaware what CS gas would do to one of their group who was a chronic asthmatic. When they left on Friday the lad was still under observation in hospital in Vienna.

John walked into a largish bar, ordered his beer and settled down. Just over from him were the bad news boys. Four guys talking about Combat 18, proper Nazis the likes of whom had been responsible for a savage attack on a Chelsea fan back in London after he had criticised their far-right views. They were a shady group who travel to all the matches and are the main reason why Chelsea had so far been the object of unhealthy interest from police forces which was disproportionate to their ability to cause trouble. The loudest of their group was a Scots guy called Davie who was wearing the red hand badge. He was originally a Rangers fan but hadn't attended a Rangers game since they had signed the Catholic player Mo Johnston. With him was a black guy and two shifty-looking friends. Davie spoke to John, who struggled to understand a word of his Glasgow accent. Not that it made any difference. 'The lights are on but no one is home' was made to describe people like Davie. His conversation with John summed it all up.

'Adolf was born here.'

John knew he meant Hitler, but thought if he professed ignorance it would make him go away. Unfortunately, Davie was in full Scotsman I've-been-drinking-so-I'm-gonna-talk-you-to-death mode.

'Really, what in Vienna?'

'No, not in Vienna, in Linz. A few of us went up there, but there's no memorial. When we spoke to the locals they didn't like us asking questions about him. Basically they're wankers. Adolf was a great man with a vision.'

'A lot of people aren't of the same opinion,' replied John.

'What the fuck do they know, anyway?'

John managed to strike up another conversation with other people in the bar who professed that Davie was making everybody nervous. 'He's so paranoid he thinks most people without a red hand badge are either undercover police or communists.'

When Davie went to the loo another friendly Austrian had attempted to talk to him which resulted in Davie punching him, breaking the glasses he was wearing. This caused the confrontation with these 'fuckin' German-speaking communists who surrendered to the Russians' (as Davie put it) that the Combat 18 lads were looking for. When one of the Austrians in the bar walked over to ask who had broken his friend's glasses, he was met with a brutal head-butt to the face from Davie. As he went down among the smashed bottles and glasses the boots went in. Nobody else was interested in joining in and stood back, aghast at the behaviour. The police were expecting trouble and were on the scene within 30 seconds. They moved in and arrested the four nasties, but the damage had been done. The English weren't welcome anywhere in the Bermuda Triangle after that. The Thursday camaraderie had been replaced by suspicious whispers from people and sad, sorry shakes of the head. A chance for the Chelsea fans to adjust the balance of trust in their favour had been lost by Davie and the three tag-along nutters.

The quarter-final draw made in December saw Chelsea pitched against Bruges. With the game due to be played the following March there was still plenty of time for the authorities to get themselves worked up into a frenzy. So far the Chelsea fans had been neither violent nor troublesome. This would be the big test as it was the first time Chelsea's day-tripper army had access to a match.

Holland v England in Rotterdam was the big qualifying match for the 1994 World Cup. Whichever team won would take the second slot in their qualifying group. For the first time travelling fans seeking tickets were subject to arrest and deportation without argument. Just wearing an England shirt and congregating in a bar was considered enough to get you arrested. Mass arrest and deportation had returned to Holland for the first time in 50 years. Parliament cheered as the English Prime Minister praised the preventative actions of the Dutch riot police. The Belgians just across the border took note.

The Bruges v Chelsea game was set for the Tuesday evening. John set out for Bruges via the Dover–Ostend hydrofoil. On the boat he teamed up with a couple of lads from Fulham. There were about 150 Chelsea fans on board, and only a few of them had tickets. Also on board were a number of day-trippers. Upon arrival in Ostend there was an announcement in Flemish and French. One of the guys on the boat who spoke French realised the relevance of it. 'Would all Belgian nationals please make their way over to the right-hand side of the immigration control and separate themselves from the English people attempting to enter Belgium.'

Just in front of the immigration desk stern-looking police stood with dogs on a short leash who were barking loudly, making the atmosphere even more tense. The returning faces from the desk told the whole story. English people were being turned away from Belgium unless they were in possession of a match ticket. Not just young football fans but elderly day-trippers who were on their way to Bruges. A couple who were about 55 years old with their children who were in their late 20s were also turned away when they said that they were on their way to Bruges and that they liked football. When the youngest daughter admitted that she had been to see Chelsea play, all four were turned away. Whilst Chelsea do play criminal football sometimes, it must be the first time someone has been labelled a criminal just for admitting they had seen them play.

All the while the immigration officers kept stern, unsmiling faces. The young Chelsea fans at the front of the queue had no chance as they were caught completely unawares, but as used to be the way when bluffing the English police when trying to get into a different part of the ground, the lads were all going straight through to Amsterdam. By the time John got to the desk the exchange had become almost comical.

'Passport.'

'S'il vous plaît est une langue internationale,' said John as he handed the grim Belgian officer his passport. John smiled at the officer who smiled back. John's French words attracted the attention of another senior officer who walked across to see who had spoken French.

'Where are you travelling to?'

'Amsterdam.'

'Are you stopping long in Belgium?'

'Long enough to get the train to Amsterdam.'

As he handed the passport back and John walked past him, he muttered the word 'Gestapo' just loud enough for the senior officer to hear. As John and the three other lads walked out of the station they passed a group of about 50 lads coming the other way. They were in plastic handcuffs and were having them removed as they were being brought back into the ferry terminal. An English news team was filming for the news. The journalist was giving his spiel for the camera: 'Here at Ostend the first Chelsea fans are being put back on the ferry after a fight broke out in a local bar and some glasses were smashed.' As one of the lads stopped in front of him he asked him a question.

'What were you doing that got you deported?'

'Just being English,' was the reply which answered a thousand questions to those who knew but left those who would watch this item on the news later totally clueless.

Carl Denman got off the ferry late on Sunday afternoon. He'd already done a serious lager session on the ferry and he walked out of Ostend Port straight across the road into the first bar he found. It was run by an Englishman and he drank another six pints. Straight into a Chinese 25 yards down the road. When the Chinese owner gave Carl the bill he thumped him and proceeded to trash the restaurant. When the police turned up he thumped the first one, but got knocked to the floor by the butt of the pistol. He had got 50 yards and five hours into Belgium before he was arrested. On the ferry home the next day one of the lads who had been turned around at Ostend asked him the reason for his behaviour. 'We're in Europe now. It's a European thing. I act this way every Friday after a skinful so I was just being respectful to Europe by acting the same way when I crossed the channel.'

John walked out of the port and perched himself in a bar with his three mates. Police were everywhere so it didn't look safe to try and get the train into Bruges. As there were four of them they decided to split a taxi into Bruges. Bruges is a beautiful medieval city with hundreds of bars and restaurants. It is a city which throngs with tourists and thousands of English people visit it every year. For the next two days it looked like a good place not to be English. Upon arrival in Bruges the lads looked for a hotel. At every hotel they tried, the polite smiles of 'hello' were met with frightened looks and shakes of the head. Finally they found a hotel where the owner spoke English. 'You must understand that there is a Mardi Gras jazz festival going on so there will be a shortage of beds in the city, but I do know that there is hotel about 15 minutes' walk down the road which has some spare rooms.'

So off they set for the umpteenth time, looking for somewhere to get rid of their bags so they could get on with the serious side of obtaining tickets. After 20 minutes' walk they arrived at the hotel. One of the lads nicknamed it Billy Butlin's as it had an orange plastic frontage. The reception was clean yet spartan. The room keys hanging on the board at the back of the reception gave the four lads hope that here was at last somewhere they could stop. John rang the bell and the owner appeared – middle-aged man with a beer belly and a gruff manner.

'Christ, he's even more unsmiling than the Port Stasi earlier.'

'Have you got any rooms?'

He shook his head. 'No, fully booked.'

'Typical. Do you know anywhere?'

The owner showed them a map and told them where to catch a bus so John, who was bursting for the toilet, used the wait to go. When he came out the owner was ranting and raving in Flemish. 'Piss off, you miserable git.' The owner picked up the telephone while John walked outside to wait for the bus. In the distance they saw a small bus arriving. As it got closer they noticed it was a police van. 'Look away, lads, they'll just drive on past.'

The van stopped just in front of the bus stop and an officer got out of the front passenger seat along with two helmeted officers armed with rifles.

'Expecting an invasion are we?'

'Where are you from?'

'England.'

'What are you doing?'

'Waiting for a bus.'

'Please get into the van. You must come with us to the station to fill in some forms,' said the senior officer.

'You're having a laugh, aren't you?'

'No, you must come with us to the station.'

By now the two armed guards were fingering their rifles rather uneasily. It was like a scene from *Midnight Express*. John didn't like the look of it. The owner walked out of the hotel and crossed the road, speaking to the senior officer and pointing to John.

'What's that goon saying? I used his toilet and forgot to scrub it afterwards?'

The other three got into the van but John had something to say to the hotel owner. 'Oi, tubby.' The owner looked at John. 'I know how your father got enough money to buy this hotel. He was a fucking collaborator. He got rewarded by the Gestapo when he grassed up Jews and they got transported to the gas chamber.'

The owner replied in Flemish. John walked up and put his face two inches from his. 'Fuckin' collaborator. I hope you feel good about this.' He then got brutally manhandled into the van by the police. 'Collaborator,' he shouted angrily one more time from inside the van, pointing his finger at the scowling Belgian as the van sped away. Further down the road they met half the Belgian army. After an animated conversation the mood changed and the van back door was slammed and locked. 'It doesn't look good,' said one of the group.

At the police station the desk sergeant asked them any number of questions. 'Why have you come to Belgium?' John completely threw them when he said he'd come to see the Mardi Gras. After 20 minutes of banal questioning they were put in cells. An hour later it was obvious that they were not going to be let out when the Special Patrol Group Morons came into their cell with some more Chelsea fans. 'English pigs. You will not be seeing any football in Belgium.' The door was then slammed shut. 'I want to see the British Consul,' shouted John. This was met with the Belgian police outside banging their riot sticks against the door.

About an hour after that the door was opened and two more fans came through the door. One of them was shouting, 'I've got a ticket in my bag.' Five minutes later the door was flung open and one of the sneering riot police ripped the ticket into hundreds of little pieces, sprinkling the tiny pieces across the cell like confetti.

All the stories were the same. They had been picked up and brought here for being English. It was 24 hours to kick-off. After three hours they were allowed a toilet break. A request to see the British Consul was met with a truncheon across the back. Their numbers were swelling now. The unluckiest guy was the English guy who had been in Australia for the past three years, but was coming home for a visit. His brother had got him a ticket. The Australian had arranged a flight stop-over from Bangkok at Brussels and had arranged to meet his brother near the ground. The Aussie made them all laugh with his comment that only 18 hours previously he had been with the most beautiful people on earth (Thais) and now he was with the ugliest, although nobody ever quite knew whether he meant his fellow Chelsea fans or the Belgian riot police.

It didn't matter who you were; the police were not listening to reason. At the toilet break one guy was saying that he had come over by car. He was later to be deported on the ferry and had to return to Belgium to get his car later. Any request for food or even water was met with verbal and physical abuse if the request was made again. After the first toilet break every cell was given a bucket for people to go to the toilet in. John was in a cell with five other guys. In the next cell there was a commotion as English guys were shouting for help. After five minutes of the Belgian police shouting abuse and banging their sticks on the door they opened the door. One of the Chelsea fans who had been arrested was an asthmatic. The police had confiscated his inhaler. The combination of stress and lack of water had caused an attack. The police ignored his friends' cries for help for five minutes. When they eventually saw him they called a doctor, but just dragged him out of the cell like a rag doll. One of the police shouted at the other Chelsea fans: 'He deserves this, you hooligan shit.'

This went on for another four hours. No food, no water and no telephone calls to the British Consul. Eventually a German Chelsea fan was brought in. He listened to the Flemish insults then gave some back, adding a bit of spice with some German and English thrown in. After ten minutes of this the door was banged open for the German to receive a beating. The German was a lot quieter after that.

'I never expected to sit in a police cell playing I Spy.'

This went on for 15 hours, during which time nobody was given any food or water. The irrepressible humour of the lads was to be shown up as they got back on the ferry, when one of the lads called it the P (for police) plan diet. Finally, they were let out to be informed that they had been found to have committed a serious offence and were being removed from Belgian soil. They had to sign papers admitting their guilt and would be put back on the ferry and escorted back to England. The last 15 hours had been the longest of their lives and nobody was about to argue, especially as the goon squad were waiting in the wings, ready to dish out another beating.

As everybody signed they were handcuffed with plastic tape which was pulled so tight around John's wrists it cut into his flesh. 'Right, collect your bags and get on the bus.' One by one they marched out with their deportation papers, like the Jews in *Schindler's List*.

Back at the port they met another huge group of Chelsea fans who had been pulled in, but had been held in a disused aircraft hangar. They had been given food and drink while they waited. One of these looked at John's group.

'Christ, mate, you must have really caused some aggro.'

'Yeah. John forgot to flush the loo.'

As they got to the steps of the boat the handcuffs were removed. The boat, which was Belgian, had a Belgian crew. The purser stood at the end of the gangplank, looking at the Chelsea fans as they walked up the gangway. With the deprivation over, some of the lads were laughing at their ordeal.

'I slept on the pavement overnight to get a Cup final ticket. That was no worse.'

'I bunked the train fare all the way to Darlington by hiding in the toilet, then I stood in the pissing rain while we played absolute crap, missed the train home, got a slap off the locals and got the sack for missing work the next day. Compared to that this was a picnic.'

One of the lads waited till his handcuffs came off, then gave his verdict to the Belgian riot police. 'You lot. Your fathers surrendered to the krauts after two days and your mothers spent the next four years sleeping with them. Even the French think you're thick. No pop stars and your capital city is a vegetable. You're sad, that's what you are.' The Belgians looked on impassively. Later, on the boat, the same guy gave them the same soliloquy after he had consumed some more beer, adding that they were 'whore sons of Hun'.

On the boat going home the bars were open and all the Chelsea fans celebrated as if they had achieved a great victory, all except for the poor guys whose cars were still in Belgium. The Australian stood at the bar holding court. 'Shit, I was down the Patpong Road the night before last up to my ears in birds and I had a choice of staying an extra night there or coming back 24 hours early to see this match. When they pulled me in they said to me, "Where are you from?" So I said for a laugh "Little Australia". When they looked at me real funny I said Earls Court, near Chelsea, just for a laugh. They pulled me in then wouldn't listen to reason.' Everybody fell about while the Aussie looked puzzled as to what he had said that was so funny. 'Well, with that accent you are a criminal anyway,' said John.

Like the Monty Python sketch where the four Yorkshire guys exaggerate their childhood memories in reminiscing, so did the lads. Every beer that went down diluted the memory of the deprivation of the past 15 hours. Everybody remembered a moment worse than that which they had just endured. The Belgian riot police who were escorting them back were regaled with a drunken rendition of 'Throw the bastards overboard,' to the tune of 'Bless Them All'.

Only football fans could be so phlegmatic about their treatment.

Back at Dover, 'proper' passengers were allowed off through the foot passengers' exit while the Chelsea fans were kept together on one of the car decks. As they emerged on English soil they were met by a contingent of Kent police and yet another film crew asking silly questions.

John, after arriving home just in time to see the second half of the match on TV, decided to write to the Belgian Embassy to complain about his treatment.

Belgian Embassy
103 Eaton Square
London SW1 9AB

2nd March 1995

Dear Sirs,

With reference to my recent visit to Belgium, I feel I have to make an official complaint to yourselves and the Belgian Government.

The brief time I spent in Belgium was the most harrowing and exhausting experience I have ever encountered. My colleague and myself arrived in Bruges at approximately 2 p.m. on Monday 27 February, with intentions to find suitable accommodation in the surrounding areas.

At 4 p.m. again my colleague and myself were standing at a bus stop with four other people when a van load of police officers pulled up at the bus stop and bundled six of us into the van.

We were then escorted to the cells where we endured 15 hours of:

1. No food or drink allowed – even after asking on numerous occasions to be supplied with a glass of water.
2. No regular visits to the toilet, only at three-hourly intervals.
3. Constant abuse shouted at all six of us by the police officers on duty.
4. Refused the use of a telephone to contact the United Kingdom or even the British Embassy in Belgium.

My colleague, myself and the four other people detained in the prison cells were then issued with deportation papers and told never to enter Belgium again. Please find copy enclosed.

After the 15-hour ordeal, we were handcuffed again, and taken by police escort to the ferry where we boarded and were sent home.

I hope that you will note this complaint and take action.

Yours faithfully

John Rake

The Belgian Ambassador replied, but his reply was arrogant to the extreme. He didn't even bother to address John by his name; after all, he was only writing back to a football fan. The reply made John think about how the Heysel stadium tragedy came about under their jurisdiction.

EMBASSY OF BELGIUM
103 Eaton Square
London SW1 9AB

Dear Sir,

I thank you for your letter concerning the Chelsea–Bruges football match on February 28 last. I wish to make the following comments about it.

Like in any other country the Belgian authorities are responsible for maintaining law and order on their territory. In this case they had been forewarned by their British counterparts of the possible presence among the Chelsea supporters of a number of hard-core extremists bent on creating trouble.

They had to take every precaution to avoid a repetition of the incidents at the Heysel stadium in 1985 where 47 people lost their lives. Nothing of this sort took place in Bruges, where only one Belgian fan was stabbed. Three Belgian policemen were wounded.

While it cannot be excluded that in some instances and in the circumstances described, some actions by the police were more radical than necessary, this, however regrettable, was preferable to laxism.

It is strongly felt in Belgium that, thanks to the security measures in place, major incidents and especially serious bloodshed were avoided. Practically all legitimate supporters were able to enjoy a peaceful match. A certain number of would-be troublemakers were expelled, in some cases after identification by the British police, for whose help we are thankful. Nobody was permanently detained. Few will dispute the right of every government to remove from its territory any person who has come from abroad, it is reasonably believed, to disturb the peace and break law and order. The Embassy has received numerous calls from the British public that were supportive of the Belgian police.

It would appear, however, that a number of incidents took place where

British citizens whose conduct was peaceful were either not allowed into Belgium or locked up and deported. The Belgian Embassy regrets any inconvenience suffered but wants to remind the special circumstances prevailing on that day, when literally thousands of people were converging on a relatively small and usually peaceful city.

Finally it should be noted that there had been ample warning, including by the British authorities and in the press, that trouble was possible and that it would be wiser to stay away from Bruges on that particular day, especially when not in possession of a valid entrance ticket, and maybe watch the game on TV.

In conclusion, it should be appreciated that in these kind of events FOOTBALL HOOLIGANISM IS THE BASIC PROBLEM, as has been recently demonstrated by the incidents in Dublin and at other places.
Yours sincerely

P Thuysbaert
Ambassador

So there it was. No apology. Just written in black and white that being a football fan in another country was now an offence. Just being English in Belgium the same day Chelsea played there was reason enough to get deported. Had the Belgian authorities kept animals in a cage for 15 hours without food and water they could have been prosecuted by the European Court.

Once more the shady role of the British authorities was exposed. Who were these people warning the Belgians about this hard-core element? What warnings were given and if the undercover police knew the so called hard-core hooligans, how come they just arrested everybody? For the status quo to survive, innocent fans had to suffer. When John spoke to me later I remarked that it sounded like the American general in Vietnam. After he had bombed a village flat, destroying everything, he stated: 'We had to destroy them to save them.'

While John and a number of others were suffering, other Chelsea fans spent the whole day in Bruges having the time of their life. John's crime was not to be clued up and walk around with his bag. The others were just guilty of the desire to see their team play football in the flesh.

In another quarter-final Arsenal were playing Auxerre in Chablis country and were the recipients of French hospitality which was second to none. The lady who owned the local bar/restaurant spent all evening with Lenny's world tourists. When Dubbsy retold the story she was regaling them with 'La Marseillaise', but the truth of the matter is that it was Dubbsy serenading Mumsy with the words to 'Je t'aime' (a '60s pop hit which was banned by the BBC for its explicit lyrics about sex). At the end of the evening she laid on fleets of cars to run them back to their accommodation.

In the semi-final Chelsea drew Real Sociedad and once more the Chelsea fans were attacked by the police. This time, even the local Spaniards (who are Basques and have no time for the Madrid Specials who were policing the match) were shocked as the Madrid police meted out an unjustified brutal beating to Chelsea fans. Chelsea went out at the semi-final stage, whereas Arsenal, in the other semi, fought their way to the final after a heart-stopping penalty shoot-out against the Italians of Sampdoria.

11

PARIS IN THE SPRING

Paris in the spring for a European Cup Winners' Cup final. Pretty girls, jazz clubs, great food and the chance to sit in the same café where Hemingway and Clive James have sipped coffee, gained inspiration to write and watched the world go by. Somebody must really love Arsenal fans. After Copenhagen, this was the next best thing to heaven. Halfway through the season Arsenal had dismissed their manager, Gorgeous George Graham, for taking a £500,000 gratuity from a Norwegian agent. Despite paying back the money in full plus interest, Arsenal felt they could no longer employ George so he went without compensation. When George came to Arsenal they were over £1 million in the red. Together with George we had experienced a roller-coaster success ride with six trophies in seven seasons. Arsenal were now firmly back at the top, yet their results in the past two seasons domestically had been atrocious. George departed, leaving his assistant manager to hold the reigns until the end of the season.

The dismissal of George Graham exposed the shady world of cash bungs which had been going on in football for as long as the game had been in existence. It's a cash business. Louis Edwards, Ray Bloye and others, including the taxman, who had been investigating football for some time, understood that, as did the members of the Premier League panel who were conducting an inquiry. I remember my father telling me stories about the financial shenanigans at Leyton Orient just after the war. I have played in Sunday leagues where the opposing team's star players were on appearance money plus cash incentives. It was nothing new. It was just that the progression to the new marketing age couldn't afford the stigma of people being on the take. It wasn't moral issues they were concerned with, but the perceptions of their new customers, as a scandal might hit the bottom line. Anything that decreases marketing efficiency and profit margins must be eliminated. Would the fans still desperately search for tickets if they thought their money was financing dirty deals? The old fans who stood in the rain didn't care. The new wave designer pretzel type might, so the new marketing men couldn't take a risk.

Cash bungs didn't stop the Arsenal fans stampeding for tickets for the Parc des Princes. Both Arsenal and Real Sociedad were given 12,000 each for the final with the other 24,000 going on sale in Paris. After protestation both clubs were given another 4,000 tickets each. Arsenal could have sold another 5,000 at least. UEFA, the governing body of European football, were well versed in the administrators' maxim that football fans don't count, based upon the equation that being stupid increases their net worth. Why put a final with at least 60,000 people clamouring for tickets in a stadium that holds 75,000, when Buggins turn decrees that it must be Paris with a capacity of 48,000. Years previously they had allocated a European Cup final between Bayern Munich and Leeds to this stadium holding 50,000 when the fixture would have sold out a stadium holding twice as many.

I had no problems getting tickets from Paris and as the final coincided with the 50th anniversary of VE day, I decided to cycle to Paris. I also promised my wife that if she let me cycle to Paris I would never attend another European away match again (Okay, so I'm a lousy liar!). I placed an advert in the programme offering other fans the chance to cycle 190 miles and experience the beauty of northern France. For some reason nobody replied, preferring the tried and trusted methods of ferry, aeroplane, train and car. Lenny's world tour was going via the recently opened channel tunnel. Lenny had become a consummate professional at the travel game and had produced a one-page home computer flyer offering Arsenal fans the trip of a lifetime with as much lager as they could consume plus the option of a trip to a seedy horhouse (*sic*). After our semi-final win in Italy against the odds, our feelings of superiority were overwhelming. I was due to meet Tony Madden's version excursion beer festival outing at 6 p.m. on Tuesday evening in a hotel located right at the end of the metro in the south of the city.

I set out from Folkestone on the 12.00 Jetfoil which takes one hour to get to Boulogne. The other Arsenal fans on the ferry looked at me as if I was bonkers. When they realised that I was the nutter who had advertised in the programme looking for people to accompany me, they shook their heads. 'Look at it this way, lads. Imagine how great I'm going to feel when I cycle into Paris tomorrow evening.' This didn't convince them at all. 'Allez Le Tour', as we say when cycling to Paris. With the hour time difference I was due to arrive in France at 2 p.m. I had set my first day's target at 90 miles, aiming to get to Aumale by around 8 p.m. I saw no problems as I knew the first 30 miles from previous cycling trips.

The first doubts in my mind appeared when the two customs officials at the gates started laughing when I told them I was cycling to Paris to see Arsenal play. They laughed and shouted comments of 'Allez! Allez!' They obviously didn't believe me as I had nothing with me except a puncture repair outfit and a toothbrush. Travel light, travel far was a motto my father had given me many years earlier when I set off on one of my foreign trips. My luggage was being transported by Damien, although should he have had a bad evening previously at three-card brag, I could see some of my better belongings being sold off to pay sundry creditors. However, I did not share the misgivings of the customs officials, because at the end of the road was the City of Light and a victory in the Cup Winners' Cup.

I hadn't bothered doing any training so the steep climb out of Boulogne took its toll, but with cars full of Arsenal fans tooting their horns giving me a fillip, I set about my route with gusto. Unfortunately I hadn't allowed for the village street parties which seemed to be going on at every village and meant I had to dismount. Nor had I anticipated the problems of reading a map doing 22mph, so by 6 p.m. I was an hour behind schedule. Putting my head down for the next two hours meant that by 8 p.m. I was almost in Aumale. I decided to stop in a small rural bar for a swift well-earned lager, but I wished I hadn't when my Arsenal pennant attached to the back of my bike attracted the unwelcome (welcome under any other circumstances, yet tiresome with a strict deadline to meet) attention of a local retired French football fan who wanted to talk about the magnifique Arsenal football team in pidgin English.

I entered Aumale around 8.45 p.m. Whilst there were no cheering crowds, I pretended that I had just triumphed in a stage of the Tour de France. I had figured that it would be big enough to have a hotel, so I stopped in a small bar for a celebratory drink.

The locals thought it funny that I had stopped off the beaten track, and when I finished my first beer and asked where the 'hôtel centre ville' was, everybody started saying 'fermé'. The owner informed me that everywhere was shut for VE day. It was nearly dark, I had no lights on my bike and the nearest town was 30 miles away. Only one thing for it. Order another beer and prey on the French sympathy factor and hope they will let me stay in the bar. I put on my best hangdog look. 'Avez-vous une chambre pour moi ce soir?'

The owner's wife, realising I was desperate, got straight on the telephone and organised me a night in a little farmhouse about three miles away. As I left the bar, all the locals came out to toast the Arsenal. I finally found the farmhouse before pitch blackness descended. I walked into the dining room to be met by 30 people having a huge party. Around 12 of them were French

Canadians having a VE day reunion. They had just started their first course so my appearance at the table five minutes later in Arsenal shirt and baseball cap went down a storm. The first bottle that was drunk was a Chablis, the second a dry Bordeaux. With the cheese was a particularly fine Claret followed by a liqueur. After that the rest of the evening became a blur, although my half-hearted attempts to tell stories about my previous trip to Paris in French caused hysterical laughter amongst the French-speaking hosts. Whether they were laughing about my pronunciation, the fact that I had to cycle 100 miles the next day, or my midnight rendition of 'And it's Arsenal, Arsenal FC; le premier team Anglais le monde has ever voyez', I will never know.

Getting the Canadian veterans to join in was one of the funnier moments. Waking up the next morning at 6.45 and not remembering how I got to bed, with the worst hangover imaginable, took the humour out of the situation. It felt as if someone was drilling a hole from the inside of my head. I hit the road at 7 a.m. with 100 miles in front of me. Back in England the lads would be just sitting down to bacon, eggs and the first beer of the day. One day, no doubt, I would tell this story and remember it with great affection. Right now I would have swapped my bicycle for a train ticket and two aspirins.

All I had for company on the lonely road were the French lorries who thundered past me around six inches from my helmet. I looked at my map and decided to take a short cut across country. Forty-five minutes later, after a number of oblique turns, I cycled back into the town of Aumale which I had left earlier in a drunken haze. I hated my bike, I hated France, VE day and Arsenal for forcing me to do such stupid things.

Nothing else to do except get my head down and grind away the miles. Around 12 o'clock I looked at my watch. Lenny's channel tunnel experience would be sampling the delights of *le shuttle* along with their first beer and friendly insult of the day. Those unlucky bastards didn't know what fun they were missing!

For four hours I pedalled away the hangover while my mind drifted back to Copenhagen. Armed with the knowledge that by four o'clock I would be able to smell the sewers of Paris, I could almost taste my first beer on the Champs-Elysées. Even a broken spoke and a buckled wheel couldn't stop me, as around 4 p.m. I surged on to the Place d'Italie amongst the mad Parisian drivers. Every English car I encountered at traffic lights got a shout of 'Gooners' and a celebratory bang on the roof. 'Sacré Bleu.' Who is that mad Arsenal fan on the bicycle sweeping along the Paris streets at 25mph?

Even two drunken Arsenal fans in full 'Hop Off Froggie' mode, staggering across the road insulting the French, couldn't believe it when I insulted them in rhyming slang with a mock French accent. 'Excusez-moi, qu'est-ce qu'une Jodrell Banker (wanker)?' Their 'fuck off, you French shitbag' was diluted by the fact that I had used a very London slang term plus the fact I had Arsenal colours on, but our intrepid ambassadors were too thick to notice. I spotted a bar with some Arsenal fans in, but they seemed to think I was slightly mad, almost backing away from me in case they should catch a disease which forces them to cycle 200 miles to watch a football match.

After a quick shower I waited for the arrival of Tony's coach which arrived around an hour late. Some of the lads were much the worse for a day's drinking and retired to bed. I was ready to meet Dibbsy, Dubbsy and the rest of the Croydon Mafia on the low rent, dirty Rue St Denis. The Frog and Roastbeef was bound to be the focal point, and so it proved, with the café opposite providing the first entertainment of the evening.

Mingling with the odd assortment of Arsenal fans, pickpockets, pimps and prostitutes was a small contingent of plain-clothes policemen. They stood around trying to look like everybody else, yet stuck out like sore thumbs. Only the thick twins who swore at me earlier would have missed them, but there must have been one or two more English goons in the vicinity as a couple of them tried to rob the till when the owner wasn't looking. As they sprinted out the door they were pounced on by four police. One of the fans was pushed to the floor and was cuffed immediately. The other was rolling around the floor with the two other policemen. As the two got the cuffs on the other fan they roughly led them away.

A shout went up. 'Do the Frog Bill!' A couple of Arsenal fans ran over and set about two of the police who let go of one of the fans, who just stood there perplexed. 'Run, you pratt,' shouted one of the Croydon lads. With that a shout went up. 'Christ, he's pulled a shooter!' I looked over and, sure enough, one of the other policemen was pointing a gun at a group of Arsenal fans outside the bar who were advancing at him. The Arsenal fans stopped dead in their tracks. A large black guy sprang out from a doorway and ran towards the gun-toting police officer, catching him with a beautiful right hook and knocking him to the floor. The gun fell from his hand. The other plain-clothes policeman ran forward and was punched to the floor. Shouts went up in English and French. 'Do the Frogs!' 'Get the shooter!' 'Run for your life!' The poor guys who were handcuffed stood there looking bemused as the two French plain-clothes officers crawled around the floor trying to get the gun back. While they crawled they were taking a good kicking around their ribs. The sound of sirens filled the air. The French had called up the cavalry.

The black guy who had punched the policeman grabbed one of the cuffed fans and together they ran up the road. The cuffed fan's knees were high into the air, like he was training for the Olympic high hurdles. The other fan ran after them, but his running technique was not as good which caused everybody to burst out laughing. By now, half the French riot police had descended on the bar and they were walking around, grim-faced, with their batons drawn. The riot police wanted everybody back inside the pub so I walked over the road to watch proceedings from outside another bar.

The two escapees were off up the road with half the Paris riot squad in hot pursuit, along with the two bruised policemen. Two other plain-clothes officers ran with them. They had been there all along, but had not stepped in to help their fellow officers when they were on the floor. The cheers from other Arsenal fans further up the road signified that the lads were progressing with their great escape. Quite what they were going to do with a pair of handcuffs on was beyond me. Where one can buy a pair of bolt croppers at 10 p.m. on the Rue St Denis was a mystery, although the question never arose as the boos and jeers from the distance told me the escape committee had failed. As the plain-clothes officers led our Franco Ronnie Biggs to the awaiting police van, he endured the taunts of all the Arsenal fans outside our bar. Red weals on his face along with a pained expression told the whole story.

'Took a slap, did you froggie?' along with 'your mates will be giving you a ribbing back at the station,' echoed out to the sound of raucous laughter. Okay, so they had their man but after coming in like the French SAS they had been forced to pull a shooter, then had the ignominy of being forced to crawl around the gutter while the lads kicked the arrogance out of them. The fate of the two Arsenal fans was forgotten with the 'it's his problem – shouldn't have got caught' shrug.

It was Tuesday 11 p.m., and the warm evening meant we were sitting outside the bar where I had spent a memorable evening the previous year. The owner constantly asked us to stop singing as the police had expressly forbidden it. Every time he came out to remonstrate with us after a chant of 'Arsenal' or some witty ditty aimed at yet more passing Arsenal fans, we assured him we would keep it down, only to erupt into song 20 seconds later. It was like a scene from a farcical comedy or children's pantomime. Dibbsy, Dubbsy, young Dave, myself and some of the other lads felt relaxed and confident about the result tomorrow. Andy from Bristol was especially enjoying it as he had missed the night before's drink in Copenhagen the previous year and, like many Arsenal fans after the match, had been too exhausted to celebrate the victory.

Arsenal fans were walking past along with a selection of prostitutes. An Arsenal fan emerged from an alleyway with one of particularly fat and ugly extraction who was in her 40s at least. 'What did she pay you, mate?'

shouted Dubbsy. The fan looked over and saw me laughing. He marched over to me.

'Are you taking the piss?'

'No, but she is the ugliest or second ugliest prostitute in Paris,' I replied. He then pointed out another prostitute (who definitely was the ugliest prostitute in Paris), whom he said he had been with earlier. 'She's on ugly pills,' stated Dubbsy matter-of-factly, which caused me to laugh even more. I thought the guy was having a laugh so when I informed him that they were 'quality sorts' in a mock French accent he went berserk. He pulled out a wad of notes, at least a hundred and fifty pounds in large denomination francs. He thrust it in my face.

'Go on, mouthy. Here's a free one on me. Go with her,' he said, pointing out an elegant blonde woman who had been turning heads all evening.

'Leave it out, you must have been given too much money as a child if you can afford to offer me that.'

'You haven't got the bottle. What's the matter, are you frightened she will laugh at the size of your willy?'

Young Dave, single, and rather keen to take on his offer, pushed his way to the front, telling my accuser that he also thought the two women were ugly, old, fat. The guy's reply stunned us into silence. 'Sure, I know they're ugly, but I just wanted to call old choppsy's bluff here' (pointing to me). He then called me a sad wanker and marched off. As he walked away to find some really fat ones (his words), Dubbsy made the statement which sent the whole bar into serious laughter convulsions. 'That geezer's got a serious mumsy fetish, but you really are a sad, cowardly wanker for not taking the offer of a freebie with Sharon Stone over there.'

'It's moments like that which make it so worthwhile paying for an extra night in the hotel before the big match,' said Andy. After my pathetic performance I was fined one round of Kronenbourg for everyone, including two other fans who had joined our laughter party.

At the top end of the Rue St Denis is a narrow street with the scruffiest dingiest bar in Paris, if not Europe. Inhabited by pimps, thieves and prostitutes on a break it became our watering-hole. The bar of last refuge for chattering Arsenal fans. By the end of the evening our destiny as the first club to retain the Cup Winners' Cup was absolute. We knew how many beers we had by the girl on the corner who had been up the stairs 14 times. Every customer she had meant another round. In fact the biggest worry wasn't the Spanish team we would be playing later today (by now it was early Wednesday morning), but the crap exchange rate which meant that getting drunk was costing a king's ransom.

Wednesday morning, match day, the breakfast room was full of sad-looking middle-aged souls who had drunk too much, dressed up to the nines in Arsenal shirts. One guy came down with most of what he had the previous evening on the front of his shirt. Whereas last year we had hoped, against expectation, to win, this year it was our preordained destiny. Real Zaragoza, our opponents, had recently faded in the Spanish league which, as every English fan knows, isn't a patch on the English league.

I walked around the streets of Paris, having arranged to meet Dubbsy and Dibbsy at Lenny's hotel after lunch. The looks on the faces of the riot police told me that it wouldn't be the same as Copenhagen. I was stopped and asked for ID. When I couldn't produce any I was told that it was illegal not to carry ID in France. My suspicions about the riot police were confirmed when a group of Arsenal fans assembling at the Eiffel Tower were attacked by a stone-throwing mob of Zaragoza fans. The Arsenal fans were stunned by this and backed off. The riot police knew who were to blame and waded into the English hooligans, clubbing them as they ran.

Apart from this it became apparent that there was a lack of the togetherness which had characterised the previous year's final. Paris, unlike Copenhagen, had no central focal point which would bring everybody together to create one huge positive mass, which could create the tidal wave which we would surge through on.

It was epitomised by the aimless gathering of Lenny's world tourists in the hotel. Everybody sat around waiting. Making our way to the ground, the pre-match drinking ritual that was Paris became unfocused, resulting in confusion amongst the Arsenal fans. Stand at the bar, cheapest. Sit inside the bar next price. Sit or stand outside the bar most expensive. It is difficult to focus on the forthcoming match when the price of beer changes with each round! To make matters more complicated some of the lads went into a supermarket and sat outside the bar with takeaways.

Amongst all this confusion we met our first Zaragoza fans and their confidence really took us aback. These guys were supposed to be sacrificial lambs here for the slaughter, but every point we made was countered with a reason why we were wrong. Statistically, they knew everything and slaughtered us. Their knowledge of English football was second to none, as was their excellent English grammar. The cakewalk scenario we had cocooned ourselves in had cracks appearing in the icing.

The French riot police started shutting the bars near the ground around an hour before kick-off, so you had the unusual spectacle of Arsenal fans walking away from the ground looking for a drink. The atmosphere was not the same as the previous year. It was the Spaniards who were setting the scene with their colourful flags and singing. They were also drinking far more than us. No one in our group was drunk. A Spaniard lurched into the bar we were drinking in and fell flat on his face. We left the bar and went to the ground. All around us the Spaniards seemed to have the spring in their step. We were blasé, like we were on a Calais day trip. Turn up, win the match and get stocked up with duty-frees on the way home.

I walked across the concourse through the massed lines of French riot police towards the stadium. The Parc des Princes is a wonderful stadium which generates a special atmosphere all of its own. Although it holds only 48,000, the sound reverberates around inside making it louder than Wembley stadium. The design of the stadium looks so simple I am surprised it hasn't been copied elsewhere. I took my position in the stadium. To my left I had the huge mass of Zaragoza fans. Whilst I hadn't seen many during the day and none the previous evening (only English fans deem it necessary to drink the town dry the night before a match), they had now organised themselves into a solid mass of green and yellow. When they started to sing as one the whole end moved up and down. It was frighteningly impressive, like watching surf waves swell on Bondi Beach, only this was a human mass of colour moving and singing as one. Last year, we made the foundations shake with our 'Go West' 1–0 theme. Now in Paris the Spaniards had stolen a march on us with their punchy rhythmic singing.

The Arsenal fans' reply of holding up red and yellow cards whilst chanting 'Come on You Reds' was admirable but paled into insignificance against the Spaniards. Oh, for the days of organised singing when every football fan worth his salt knew at least 20 songs. The chant of 'Maybe It's Because I'm a Londoner', 'Knees up Mother Brown', 'When You're Smiling' or 'My Old Man' would have united us, but this sort of singing had died with the birth of mass marketing and designer away shirts.

As the match progressed and the synchronised singing from the Spaniards got more vibrant and enthusiastic it became obvious that a throaty, tuneless roar of 'Good Old Arsenal' was needed to get the fans moving. Spectators brought up on electronic scoreboard messages with little men clapping to the sign of 'G O A L' didn't know how to sing a song which was plagiarised from 'Rule Britannia' over 25 years previously when Arsenal had played Liverpool in an FA Cup final. Then it was felt that Arsenal fans would be outsung by the illustrious Liverpool Kop who were renowned at the time for singing. Any chant would have done, but the monotonous 'Come on You Reds' prevailed. Even a few abusive songs about fat prostitutes from my sad friend would release some passion, but nothing came out. A soporific torpor settled over the Arsenal fans, and was made worse by Arsenal's most effective player, Keown, going off injured.

When the inevitable happened and the Spaniards scored first, a sense of gloom settled over the Arsenal fans. I walked out of the stand and down on to the concourse and over to the gates where around 100 ticketless Arsenal fans were holding on to the metal, hanging on every cheer from inside the ground. Suddenly a roar from the Arsenal fans. A brilliant equaliser. Yeah, back in I went at full speed. But something was missing. Whilst Arsenal didn't look like getting beaten, they just didn't seem to have that extra push to get the winner. We had been this way before, but then we had our lucky manager in charge. If only Gorgeous George Graham were still here instead of watching on the TV then he would have seen a tactical edge to help us. He would have pulled out a master stroke, like he did when we first started down the road together back at Wembley when he pulled on Perry Groves to run at a tiring defence. The game went into extra-time. Arsenal fans felt confident we could win if it went to penalties, as we had been down that route in the semi-final against the Italians of Sampdoria. Then, our brilliant England goalkeeper Seaman had saved three penalties to get us to Paris. I couldn't face penalties so with minutes remaining I went down to the concourse below to buy a Coke. A couple of other fans had the same idea. Standing next to the bar were two undercover policemen. When two of the other Arsenal fans spoke to them they pretended to be Arsenal fans, denying they were undercover. The retort of 'Bollocks, you're Starsky and Hutch' made one of the other fans laugh so much he blew Coke out of his nostrils on to the undercovers. When I asked them the only insulting question in French I knew, they didn't understand. 'Pardonnez-moi, monsieur, avez-vous le visage d'une grande vache?' Only the English police would send undercovers out to a foreign country who didn't speak the native language.

With a couple of the Arsenal fans giving the undercovers some stick they walked away. Now with nobody to take my mind off the drama being played out beyond my vision the terrible reality of penalties dawned on me. My chest felt tight. My mind drifted back to Brussels 15 years previously. I didn't think I could face them but events pre-empted my worry.

With the last kick of the game a Zaragoza player latched on to a bouncing ball. He aimed a kick into the Paris sky towards the Arsenal goal. As it left his boot Tony Madden prophetically said, 'That's trouble.' As the ball went forward the linesman on our side signalled that Esneider, scorer of the Zaragoza goal, was offside. However, the referee did not blow. Seaman, the Arsenal goalkeeper, was slightly off his line to counter the threat of Esneider, suddenly realised the ball was heading goalwards and started back-pedalling furiously. In a second Seaman and the ball were in the back of the net. The referee blew his whistle, the game was over. Real Zaragoza had won with the last kick of the match. It was the most dramatic end to a football match in the history of the game. Only football can do this. This was high drama which makes football the greatest world game, but its effect on the losers is impossible to gauge. Why? Why me? Why Arsenal? Why do I like football when it gives me such terrible lows?

I walked straight out of the ground, absolutely numb. The riot police were stunned as well for they didn't know what to do. Arsenal players and fans alike started crying but most just shook their heads, unable to comprehend what they had just seen. Arsenal fans started to file out silently, but the French riot police were not to be denied their action and locked the gates. People just wanted to get out and the people at the back didn't know what was going on at the front where people were being pressed against the locked gates. The French riot police then sprayed CS gas into the tunnel area where women and children were stuck in the tunnel. Quite what terror those parents and children went through for those next couple of minutes is hard to imagine. It was a brutal and unnecessary awakening for many people to the realities of being an English football fan. The French riot police still had the 1985 'English fan equals thug' script. They had no idea that this lot would only riot if the scoreboard told them to. Plenty of tears on the designer shirt now, some caused by the defeat, but mostly chemically induced.

I wandered around aimlessly, hoping that I had been mistaken in what I had witnessed. This had to be a nightmare which I would wake up from to find out it wasn't true. I ended up in the bar of last refuge. The grim inhabitants of this dingy twilight world were blissfully unaware of the catastrophe that had just taken place at the Parc des Broken Dreams. I had arranged to meet Dibbsy and Dubbsy in here, but unbeknown to me they had been locked in for an hour, so they would not get here until 1 a.m. I looked around this bar and suddenly realised how dirty it was. I went into the toilet and the stench of ammonia made me retch. I felt dirty and the beer was warm so I walked out and headed back to my hotel. On every street corner were the sad, sorry, defeated faces of Arsenal fans.

Tony Madden and a large group were in a corner bar having a serious drink so I joined them. Around 1 a.m. the defeatist mood changed and we turned our defeat into an Irish wake, remembering all the good times we'd had along the way. Eight years ago we started along this road together by walking up the Caledonian Road. During this period we had ridden the switchback of success as friends while the face of football had changed. Our Clock End and Northbank had gone, the new development paid for by Gorgeous George's relentless march for trophies. We felt privileged to have been a part of it, so why feel miserable that it had ended? 'Nothing is for ever in football' isn't a cliché; it's a fact which only greedy directors can't understand. We talked about the worst times we had endured against the romantic backdrop of the Seine.

So we drank our toasts to our greatest absent friend, George Graham, and we thanked him. I expressed the opinion that our defeat was retribution for the shabby way Arsenal had treated George and nobody argued. One of the group impersonated our goalkeeper (Able) Seaman by falling backwards into a pile of wicker furniture, a feat that raised a laugh from everybody except the bar owner whose furniture it was.

We reminisced like old codgers because we had lived something special together. It might be a long way before we come down this road again.

Around 1.30 a.m. a group of six Spaniards walked in. They looked nervous and almost left before ordering a drink, but we raised our glasses to them in salute.

'No trouble, lads,' shouted Tony Madden, so a couple walked over and joined us. Whilst we were happy to spend a small fortune on beer they wanted no part of it, but had a cheaper way to celebrate. In perfect English they told us that it was a waste of money buying beer and that they would meet us outside in the square in five minutes for a party. Off they went and duly appeared with bottles of whisky, bacardi, rum and cola for mixers. I stayed in the bar to have more beer while the party got going in the square. I looked outside and saw the looks on the faces of the Spaniards. I realised that this was their Copenhagen, whereas this would never have been that for us even if we had won. Our party had never started, whilst theirs hadn't stopped from the moment they had left home 24 hours earlier.

After the bar owner physically threw me out (in the movies they let the sad people sit in the bars all night and they watch the sun come up over the Seine) so he could go home for some sleep, I joined the party, to be given a large measure of rum and Coke in a plastic glass. Two of them and I was singing 'New York' in my best Frank Sinatra voice along with 'Je ne regrette rien' in my worst Piaf.

Around 3.30 a.m. four vans full of riot police turned up with all of us in full voice while the worst were flamenco dancing with the Spaniards. The senior policeman walked over to our group. 'Does anybody here speak English?' he asked, as he didn't speak Spanish. 'Well, we used to, but now the only language we can speak is you lucky Spanish bastards,' replied Tony, quick as a flash. The senior French police officer was dumbstruck. The look on his face told the whole story. I could see his mind trying to comprehend the fact that we were English who had just lost an important football match, yet here we were partying with the Spaniards instead of trying to punch out their lights. Tony caught the drift. 'New era, guv, you've got to get with the beat baggy,' he said, jokingly copying the line from *The Jungle Book*.

The senior officer turned to his men and explained what was happening in French. A couple started to laugh, a few more said they didn't believe it whilst a couple looked disappointed they weren't going to be able to bust English heads. 'Whilst I understand that you are wishing to have a party it is nearly 4 a.m. and all the local residents are complaining about the noise of your singing, so we must ask you to return to your hotels. We will run you back in our vans should you wish that.' His logic was impeccable even if we all felt our singing acceptable, so after one final toast we walked back along the road. We said our goodbyes to the Spaniards and headed for our hotel. The senior officer came back along the road, tooting the horn of his van which must have woken up everybody who wasn't already awake. Some of the riot police waved at us and gave us the thumbs up.

'Funny old world, isn't it?' said Tony Madden. 'They came to bury Caesar, but ended up praising him.' I smiled, as did the others with us. Down in the gutter was a discarded Arsenal scarf. I remembered how I had lost my scarves to the gutter the previous year and blamed myself for the defeat. The loss of my scarves in Copenhagen had jinxed Arsenal. I considered picking up this scarf to end the jinx but thought better of it in case I interrupted someone else's ritual and brought more bad luck in the future. The albatross of Coleridge would not hang around my neck. The scarf would stay there as a present for the Moroccan street cleaners who were the only other people out so late. I looked back up the dark, cobblestone road which 24 hours previously had looked so romantic. The drink was suddenly having a down effect on me. The City of Light had taken on a foreboding look and turned an ominous black colour. Now it was just another city I wanted to get out of.

The next morning breakfast at our hotel was eaten in silence as the full extent of what had happened sank in. The end of an era it most certainly was. As the coach departed I decided that Paris was a smelly, expensive, horrible place that I hated. The pretty girls of yesterday now looked bleak, ugly and grasping like the rest of France. The romance of the cobbles and the Seine had been washed away by our tears. Paris had joined Brussels as a city I would not visit again for a long time.

12

EURO 96

UEFA rewarded England for its new all-seater development by awarding it the Euro 96 tournament. Right from the start the focus was on the hooligan problem, although the police had ample intelligence to know that the main protagonists would not be causing trouble. This, combined with a press which had long since got bored with blowing up boorish behaviour into riotous assembly, meant that the focus became fixed on the football. What the press should have been focusing on was a ticket sales operation which would baffle Hercule Poirot. It wasn't possible to purchase a ticket for the one game you wanted to see, but only possible to buy in advance all three group match tickets.

As no major competition had been played in England for 30 years (since the 1966 World Cup), interest was intense. Everybody knew that England were hosting a tournament when a tuneless singalong came out and promptly went to the top of the pop charts. 'Football's Coming Home' sang everybody, and dared to dream that Johnny Foreigner could be vanquished on the football field after he had taken our beautiful game and made it better. The press poured scorn on England's chances. The fans knew better and even adopted the flag of St George, something the silly 'disgusted of Tunbridge Wells' had been invoking in *The Daily Telegraph* letter pages over past decades.

As the tournament grew closer it became obvious that something was awry with the FA ticket sales hotline. With the line engaged at 3 a.m. it became difficult for anybody, let alone a committed hooligan, to purchase a ticket. The simple fact of the hooligan matter was that Germany and Holland don't export their hooligan problem unless they play each other in mainland Europe. The Rotterdam pre-Euro 96 friendly between Germany and Holland was accompanied by thousands of ripped-out seats and a number of fights and stabbings.

Much as the press tried to play up the threat of hooliganism, the police felt confident. The police even approved the licence extensions to bars and pubs in cities on match-day evenings. Not that the police didn't go in for a little showboating to cover their backsides and justify their expenditure on video surveillance and mass photography of football fans. After Newcastle lost the 1996 Premier League Championship, their fans reacted in the traditional fashion and went on the rampage in their home town, smashing windows and throwing bottles at the police. It was something they used to do regularly in the 1980s. Three weeks before Euro 96 kicked off the police issued photographs of fans they wanted to interview about the disturbances, adding the rider that this proved that there would be no hiding-place for hooligans in Euro 96. Whether or not innocent fans were in the pictures cut no ice with these new police control methods.

Much the same could be said of the dawn raids on Arsenal fans who, eight weeks previously, had indulged in their annual pastime of ripping out seats to throw at each other after the north London derby. The police raiders, who turned up with TV camera teams to arrest the fans, stated that three Euro 96 tickets paraded in front of the cameras were proof that fans were planning to cause trouble. All it actually showed was that fans who had got angry at their most-hated local rivals had purchased tickets for the three England group games as they were required to do so in order to be guaranteed a seat at Wembley. In some countries local derbies are so fierce they keep a seat replacement financial budget.

But the police had procured a massive budget to eliminate hooliganism, so to be seen to admit that it had gone away would cause political questioning of the existence of the whole hooligan undercover structure. Much better and easier to play to the camera and state that a return to violence was only being prevented by dawn raids with TV crews. Journalists also got sound bites from half-wits who stated that they were going to attack visiting fans when they visited their cities. The truth of the matter was that any hooligan who was going to do anything wasn't going to talk to a journalist. The hard-core Chelsea lads had already realised that trouble at Wembley would be a futile exercise, so resolved to drink in the Fulham Road before the England v Scotland match, hoping to meet an unsupervised mob of jocks on the tube. Plus everybody knew that the Dutch fans would be the Amsterdam day-tripper families, so the two potential flashpoint areas which the press kept going on about were always going to be non-events. Attacking foreign visitors in a city before a match isn't football hooliganism any more than smashing up an Indian restaurant on the Friday during a Lord's Test match is a cricket problem.

The FA had a major event on and the public wanted to buy tickets. Now that ticket reselling had been outlawed by Parliament, the FA could designate whom they could sell tickets to and what would then happen to them. Every aspect of ticket sales would be controlled by the FA, including hospitality. A few weeks before Euro 96, police raided premises of companies offering hospitality packages, arresting people whose only crime was to try and make an honest pound. Lenny White was proud of them, but the police were straight out of a George Orwell novel. It later came out that these companies had authorisation from the FA's own commercial department. Writs flew, along with denials and accusation. Manchester United plc, whose Old Trafford stadium was a host for some matches, had sold match-day packages which were not allowed under the FA terms. Trevor Phillips, the FA Commercial Director, resigned when it came out that his understanding of exclusivity didn't match that of the FA or the companies who had paid a lot of money to fill those ubiquitous executive boxes. The drunken posturing of the National Front morons looked insignificant compared to the squabbling over who could have the biggest share of the Euro 96 money cake.

Paul Scarrot died a lonely death in Spain just before Euro 96 after a bizarre drinking binge. The Spanish police identified him by a tattoo in his mouth. This was the man who had the reputation as the hooligan superthug: hooligan incarnate. For the Italia 90 World Cup he was identified as hooligan supreme and was declared persona non grata *by European police forces, yet despite two police forces along with battalions of undercovers searching for him, he got as far as Rome before another drinking binge left him penniless and incoherent. The subsequent deportation and publicity was Scarrot's finest hour. His obituary before Euro 96 was really that of the hooligan as a group.*

The biggest hooliganism before Euro 96 was caused by the England players who were pictured in a bar in Hong Kong ripping each other's shirts off and squirting tequila down each other's throats while strapped in a dentists chair. On the plane home, five thousand pounds' worth of damage was allegedly done to a Cathay Pacific jumbo jet. The tabloid press were off and running, making a bit of laddish horseplay into the biggest circus this side of Las Vegas. Paul Gascoigne was blamed. The *Daily Mirror* quoted the airline: 'The worst incident ever on one of our aeroplanes.' The FA described it as Gazza being himself. Politicians demanded heads, the way they used to demand that fans be stopped from leaving the country and Maggie wanted to ban the World Cup when the press went over the top in Stockholm.

Gazza threatened to sue but it was all smoothed over when all the players took collective responsibility and the FA condoned the cover-up. Travelling fans have been ostracised for singing in public, but the FA decided that the pursuit of money was better than the pursuit of the truth. The tabloid press were denied their culprit and the news hounds, in the shape of George Jackson, lampooned them for missing the story whilst being on the same flight. The story, which ran for the week leading into the championships, turned into a McCarthy-style witch-hunt with every paragraph mentioning Gazza.

Headlines got worse when England drew their first match at home to Switzerland and tired badly in the second half. With no hooligans to write about, the press turned their vitriol on the England players and especially Gazza. The press even started eulogising about how bad English players' diet was compared to the scientific continentals. England bad, foreigner good. It was only the Old Enemy battle looming which stopped the hysteria.

Scotland came to Wembley in their usual tartan-wearing singing mode and proceeded to drink most of London dry. England triumphed and although there were 100 arrests, mostly for drunkenness and ticket-touting, and a number of scuffles in London's West End later in the evening, the match passed off without problems. Scotsmen sporting mock ginger wigs and kilts, a mixture of Scotland the brave and Scotland the silly, sat next to Englishmen wearing detergent white shirts during the game without trouble.

Suddenly the police started to act like their Copenhagen counterparts and the policing became a smiling face. Stories of policemen doing karaoke turns at campsites, along with the turning of blind eyes to the Turkish *amigo* who chanted through a loud-hailer to rouse his fellow Turks into a mad frenzy, filtered through, along with ones about police giving touts' confiscated tickets to fans despite it being against the law.

While the police smiled the nation sat transfixed as England progressed. England players and fans alike sang the national anthem with a frenzy which would earlier have been called xenophobic, but was now patriotism. When the boneheads did it a few years ago and held their arms up it was fascism and frightening; now it was great and the Conservative political spin doctors talked about riding the feel-good factor and calling an election. John Major, beleaguered Prime Minister, eulogised about bidding for the 2006 World Cup, enlisting the help of Lennart Johansson, the friendly Swedish UEFA president.

Suddenly the press baiters became fawning sycophants, eager to heap praise upon England. Journalists whom Terry Venables called traitors one day miraculously fell over themselves to give him plaudits. The chief England/Gazza/Terry Venables baiter, Harry Harris of *The Daily Mirror,* was lampooned by his own editor who superimposed a picture of Harris in the stocks having rotten vegetables thrown at him. Harris, who had spent all his journalistic life criticising successive England managers and had run a tabloid campaign against Terry Venables, was supposedly livid with the boot being on the other foot and considered legal action against his own newspaper. The fans who didn't think England were ever as bad as the press made them out laughed at the change of heart as much as they had laughed at the rubbish they had previously written.

Meanwhile, the FA just saw Euro 96 as a giant marketing exercise. Vast rows of empty seats at early matches were criticised by football supporters who argued that they were being priced out of attending. Quick as a flash the off-pat answer came back in the form of a statistic: '90 per cent of seats have been sold, with the percentage increasing as the tournament progressed.' Meaningless comparisons with Grand Prix racing and other big sporting events were trotted out in monosyllabic marketing speak to show that the fans were getting a good deal. The empty seats told everybody that they didn't agree, but as the budget was 20 per cent ahead of financial targets, a few empty seats were not considered a problem. The FA even trotted out statistical comparisons with the 1966 World Cup. They were obviously expecting criticism as they had their smarmy answers ready before the fans complained. When England beat Spain the fans slept out all night for a chance to buy a semi-final seat, only to be told by the FA the next morning that they were only being sold by telephone, on a line which nobody could get through on.

Comparisons to stormtroopers were levelled at the FA commercial department as they employed a team of miked and earpieced spotters to ensure that no unlicensed sponsors got any publicity at Euro 96. They were even briefed to look out for any punters holding up names during matches. The fan who wrote 'Hello Mum' on his flag of St George only just made it past the steely-eyed guardians of exclusivity who looked like they had auditioned for a bit part in a film about General Pinochet's Chilean nightmare. It was rumoured that during the Holland v Scotland game a steward was asked to get the attention of Andy Goram, Scotland goalkeeper, and ask him to remove a sweet wrapper from his goalmouth as it wasn't a Snickers (official snack food of Euro 96). With 8,000 mad Scotsmen behind the goal and no-teeth Goram guarding his goal against the relentless Dutch attack, the steward politely refused.

The Polish triumvirate, Clemmo, Harold and Jerry, attended the Spanish game and left afterwards intoxicated by the atmosphere. England had triumphed on penalties after being outplayed by the Spaniards who must have felt hard done by to be beaten.

In the toilets at half-time below the jolly atmosphere upstairs three Spaniards started to get very macho, insulting England and their manhood. Whilst the mood was predominantly happy, it didn't take much for fans to revert to type, so the Spaniards very quickly felt the urine on their backs as they hit the floor under a barrage of punches and kicks.

Victory over Spain was the cue for the whole country to have a celebration. The result was even relayed to the most British of institutions, Lord's Cricket Ground, where play was stopped in the match between England and India for everybody to cheer. The trio made their way to Trafalgar Square where they observed the traditional invasion of the fountains. The police looked on benignly, half smiling, half wary. Sure enough, a few idiots couldn't stop themselves and later in the evening started throwing bottles at the police and passing cars. It was started when the police moved in to arrest some thugs who had started punching two Portuguese fans who thought they would be welcome to join the party. Clemmo and the lads went home sad that a few idiots spoilt the party.

The showdown that most teams eventually have to face – to win the European Football Championship most teams have to beat Germany – came about in the semi-final of Euro 96. The previous round the tabloids had insulted the Spanish by calling them paella-eaters and a nation of waiters. Of course the contribution the Spanish have made to modern history was conveniently forgotten. Nobody mentioned this, but when the tabloids started using insults about the war to describe the Germans there was uproar. It was tacky and illegal, but the police didn't arrest anybody. The German press actually pointed out a few home truths about football matches (since 1966 Germany had won every important match between us while we had won two inconsequential friendlies), while *The Sun* and *The Mirror* were reliving the Battle of Britain. German fans interviewed felt sorry for England. 'God save the Queen from her subjects.' It was easy to see why when one tabloid newspaper turned up at a hotel full of German fans and draped St George flags over the seats (in reference to the German holiday-makers who reserve poolside chairs by draping their towels over them). 'We'll fight them on the beaches,' said *The Daily Mirror*. 'Ho, ho, ho,' went the people who thrive on such xenophobia. 'Ha, ha, ha,' went the Germans who had a sense of humour but were laughing at our stupidity.

The only problem was that Germany had not missed a penalty shoot-out kick since 1990, whereas England didn't have Biggles shooting for them. The last time the two countries met at football Germany had won on penalties. The constant references to the war only served to point out that the German mentality was stronger than ours because they had rebuilt their country from ruins to lead Europe. After all, what sort of nation has to remind their friends that they once sent their finest young men to kill their young counterparts? The only reason we had gone to war with Germany was to defend Poland, yet Clemmo had seen how much we had done for them . . .

On the day of the showdown with Germany a fact was unearthed by one newspaper. Within the 80,000 capacity stadium, 14,000 people would be seeing the match free. Many of these would probably never have attended a match in their life, such was the new hold of corporate hospitality on the game now. The biggest match in England for 30 years was being used as a corporate junket, with suits using football to garner favours to be tucked away for future use. Whilst the fans would be physically sick or emotionally uplifted by the result, the corporate entertainers used the prestige of this event for business relationship building.

When the game of football finally got under way (yes, that's what it was: 11 against 11 on grass with one ball, just as it always was), the nation sat gripped as the best game of the tournament unfolded. England scored after two minutes, then the Germans fought back in their indefatigable fashion, equalising after 16 minutes. Nobody who was at the game or watching in the thousands of pubs around the country could fail to be gripped by the drama. UEFA, who had tried to stop the stalemate of extra-time, had introduced a sudden-death 'golden goal' rule, so that the first team to score in extra-time would win the game.

With less than a cigarette paper's width between them, England and Germany went into this extra-time agony, one mistake meaning sudden cruel elimination. England had the better of the period and the better chances. At the end of an exhausting two hours the teams lined up for penalties, as nothing could separate them. England had now played two stamina-sapping two-hour matches in the space of five days. The same press who had talked about physical conditioning only 14 days earlier were made to look silly, as is their wont. Gazza, who had been described as an overweight disgrace, made surging runs up until the last seconds, finishing one of the strongest players.

With the game going to penalties the TV cameras flashed into the stands. Sitting there was Bobby Robson, a picture of concentration, his facial expressions telling us he wanted England to win so much, his hair now white. This was the man who was the manager the last time England had battled to a standstill with Germany, only to lose on penalties. A man who had endured more malevolence, misrepresentation and outright dishonesty from the press than any other person in the public eye. Yet his presence only served to remind football fans that since his departure we had not played the Germans in any meaningful match, because the Football Association suits who never could work out whether or not travelling fans were welcome had sacked Bobby and then appointed a man who was big on PR yet small on tactics. PR was important to the Football Association, who were consistently guilty of acting like the donkeys of 1914 who led the lions to the slaughter then. (At the end of Euro 96 Terry Venables, who had developed a continental playing formation, would be leaving because some FA Committee members were unhappy about events surrounding Terry Venables's business dealings.)

Small wonder that the Germans took a winning mental toughness into the shoot-out. After both teams had scored with five great penalties each it went to sudden death. A young Englishman, Gareth Southgate, who had played a great tournament, missed. The nation held its breath to see if Seaman, who had already saved two penalties in the tournament, could stop the German Moeller. When the ball hit the roof of the net the dream was over for England. All the pent-up emotion spilled into the streets as people's expectations were dashed by the Germans again.

At the end of Brighton pier six guys threw themselves off the end into the sea, necessitating the coastguard being called out to rescue them. (I know how they felt because I thought about doing the same in Ostend 16 years previously.) A Russian visitor was also stabbed in Brighton after his accent was mistaken for that of a German. In Trafalgar Square the mood turned surly and riot police waded in to restore order. One paper reported that the violence was planned. That is why the police waded in indiscriminately to crack heads and why violence spontaneously broke out all over England. Where did the paper get this planning theory from? No doubt the police put out a conspiracy theory to ensure that their budget requests weren't scrutinised more thoroughly after a trouble-free tournament.

The violence was not allowed to overshadow the genuine warmth that had existed inside the grounds and the remarkable atmosphere that had been generated amongst unsegregated fans. But the eruption of drunken violence after the defeat came as no surprise in a country which teaches its population a biased view of their role in a war which happened nearly six decades ago, and continues to breed insularity which dictates that puerile tabloid rantings are met with increased sales from the low-wattage masses.

The press boys wrote in glowing terms about England because that's what their editors realised the country wanted to hear, as hype replaced rationale. The same press boys who only a few days earlier had mocked Terry Venables's stupid Christmas-tree tactics now contrived to extract a tactical triumph which they had really known about all along. Alan Shearer, whom the tabloids had urged Terry to drop because he had previously struggled to score goals at international level, finished the top goalscorer in the tournament. Had the press been operating in any other business they would have all been picking up their P45s. As it was they went away for an expense-funded drink to think up more future vitriolic abuse for Terry Venables's successor, God Squad graduate, Glenn Hoddle.

The irrefutable fact that Euro 96 threw up was that violence inside the grounds had long since passed away. The new era that Frank Partridge had talked about back in Stockholm over seven years previously really had come home with football in a big way, notwithstanding that English macho drinking is an inbred trait which is taught as part of our national psyche and breaks out at many diverse events throughout the year. Whenever England fans travel abroad their behaviour won't really change much. Eight lagers and they start singing 'God Save the Queen' with a frightening passion, yet most couldn't tell the difference between the Houses of Lords and Commons and have no idea of the constitutional meaning of this song. Deep down the people who condemn their behaviour and tut-tut are the same people who really know that this drunken yobbo posturing means that the status quo in England will always remain the same. By the same token every time England fans travel they will come up against foreign police forces who will have their own mind set about England fans. If they are open-minded like the Copenhagen chief then it's fun, fun, fun. However, if, as in the case of the Belgians' ambassador with Chelsea, they have been briefed by the shady, mysterious Englishman who spends most of his pleasure time in sado-masochistic clubs, then our future travelling boys are in for one hell of a beating!

13

GOODNIGHT SWEETHEART

In May 1996 Rupert Murdoch's BSkyB won the biggest sports rights battle ever seen in Britain when he purchased the four-year rights to televise Premiership football for £670 million. Only ten years previously, top-flight football was earning £2.5 million per year from TV. But, as with everything touched by someone as powerful as Rupert Murdoch, the deal would have ramifications for those souls who want to watch the game live. Paying that sort of money meant that the paying punters would need to be able to watch football at times which may not necessarily be when they desired it. No longer will games be settled in time-honoured fashion on a Saturday but at times which the suit – with a schedule to fill – designated. The days when the punters' cash through the turnstiles was much greater than that of TV were not that long ago, yet it seemed as far back as George Best in full flight and swaying terraces.

The old man stood on the corner of Gillespie Road. He was old, codger old, at least 80, with a lived-in, gnarled face that looked like it had seen the Boer War. Arsenal had just lost at home for the third time that season. He was berating some young guys who had dared to call him old. He called them cheeky bastards, reminding them that he had seen real crowds, he had seen 80,000 at Highbury when snotty brats like them used to get passed over the heads of real men down to the front. Plus he'd seen real teams with proper stars: Boy Bastin, Alex James, the Comptons, Jimmy Logie, Duncan Edwards, Eddie Coleman and the Double Side. He shouted that he'd queue in the rain to see that lot. This lot, he said, weren't fit to lace their boots. Football's now played by a group of overpaid nancies with plimsolls for boots and footballs with no laces in them. The Northbank was still standing then. He used to turn up at 2.45 on a Saturday and gain entry via the OAP reduced-rate entrance. Young footballers were still travelling on the train to matches and the only agents in England were being played by Sean Connery and other actors. Codgers don't stand on the corner of Gillespie Road (or any other grounds) any more, because they haven't got plastic money and can't turn up at 2.45 and just go in so they don't go at all.

No sooner had the ink dried on the new TV contract than the satellite TV people were mooting the idea of pay per view. Players' agents were quickly looking at clauses in contracts, as was the Professional Footballers' Association. They all wanted a larger slice of the cake which had now become so big it resembled a bakery. Rick Parry, Chief Executive of the Premier League, said: 'Football on TV is entering a new era both in terms of technology and level of consumer interest.' That was it. He summed it all up. Football was no longer about fans and passion for the game. It was all about consuming. To the old codger who used to stand on the corner of Gillespie Road, consumption meant the dreaded disease tuberculosis. While Sky licked its lips and prepared to use football as part of its global sports strategy, fans nodded at the satellite dish and consumed as never before. They had no choice, with players strutting around as walking adverts. In between adverts a series of pontificating has-beens showed us action from ten different angles.

Even the referees were given fancy-coloured shirts. Now the man in black we loved to hate was no more. No more the words sung at the dreaded referee:

> Man in Black
> No one knew his name
> It was the devil himself
> Reffing that game.

Now he would be in fancy stripes, still a figure of ridicule, but his every move scrutinised by ex-professional footballers who once played the game yet didn't know the laws. Somehow it just didn't seem the same. The pantomime shouts at the referee became sheer hatred as the consequence of failure became too horrible to contemplate. Nobody could afford the fiscal fallout.

In 1996 George Best reached 50. Best the footballer, a man who could make a football talk, but lost his career to the bottom of a vodka bottle. Young people brought up on a diet of media superstars ask how good Best was, unable to comprehend his effect on football and society. He was so good that 25 years after he kicked a sober ball, taxi drivers in any city in Europe could talk you through one of his goals. George opened the doors that the young, rich superstars of the modern era have benefited from. George earned more in 1996 doing one advert than he ever earned in a full year playing football, when defenders wouldn't have sex one week before facing him, yet still weren't good enough to kick him. Seeing footage of Ron 'Chopper' Harris of Chelsea run 30 yards to try and scythe Best at the knees, yet seeing Best go away from him and a packed Stretford End terrace gasp in air as one lung while flinching together was not that distant, yet it seemed so long gone that it made me feel old. It wouldn't be long before the youngest lad asks his dad: 'What were the terraces really like?'

In the background an ever-decreasing minority refused to conform, unable to grow out of their terrace upbringing, still attached to the old way of violent conflict like old cowboys who wouldn't accept that the frontier days of Indians, posses and gunfights had passed them by. Being low wattage, their thought processes could not comprehend the realisation that the culture of hooliganism was old hat, ready to be consigned to the history books. The night before the 1995 Coca-Cola Cup final between Leeds and Aston Villa, a group of Leeds fans attacked the Jazz Café in London. Aston Villa hooligans in their semi-final of the same cup had ambushed an Arsenal pub. The shocked looks on the drinkers' faces who witnessed the antics of these dinosaurs told the whole story. This sort of thing just didn't happen any more. The police continued to make statements like: 'There is a small minority who want confrontation but there is a growing group of people who, given the opportunity, will join in. The violence is perhaps increasing but it is away from the ground.' It was tasteless and stupid. An empty delivery which even the cheap-jibe, birch-brigade politican could see through. To the politician the terrace bums with lager cans who were once a disgusting alien culture had become a designer, lager-bellied, posterior-on-seat, vote-winning opportunity.

In March 1996, the FA managed to do something nobody else had ever managed before, not even the hooligans with their pitch-invading, punch-first, ask-questions-later mentality. Never, even in the darkest days, when pimply malevolents hunted in packs, had empty spaces ever been seen at an FA Cup semi-final. And it was not just one or two empty seats, but huge banks of them. When one of the many strategically located cameras panned across the emptiness, the gleaming plastic rows almost grinned back at the armchair experts. The fact that the spaces were amongst the fans of the two best-supported clubs in England made the fact even more alarming. Manchester United and Liverpool supporters had balked at being asked to pay huge prices for their respective semi-finals. It should have set alarm bells ringing in the FA marketing citadel which doubled as the administration centre for English football. It certainly made some club chairmen sit up and publicly ask if they weren't treating the fans as a sponge, a sponge only absorbing so much before it stops absorbing. The ultimate irony of seeing empty seats left by Liverpool fans was not lost on many who follow football, because it was the original disaster at a semi-final in which Liverpool were participating that had caused the game to go all-seater.

The FA had their marketing spiel ready and put out their press releases which explained why tickets had cost so much. They had to charge higher prices because so many seats were deemed grade one, and the FA were obligated to charge a premium for them. But of course they cared about the fans. However, this caring didn't go as far as implementing a sensible pricing policy. The fans' complaints fell on deaf ears, just as the cries of 'foul' from the Brighton fans fell on deaf ears when they asked the doddering FA to step in to stop their beloved Goldstone Ground being sold from under them to become a supermarket.

So the Brighton fans took their grievance on to the pitch and, with nothing left to lose, smashed up their ground to make their final protest. Just one more pitch invasion which showed that people cared and wanted still to watch their team because it meant something to them. Whilst the marketing men had hijacked the beautiful game, the fans still sang their songs with a passion the suits would never appreciate. When the Brighton boys charged across the pitch one last time it signalled the end. One last pitch invasion flashed across in front of me as the bulldozers waited to turn the terrace turnstiles into a checkout. The spot where only 17 years previously men danced with other men while crying tears of joy after Brighton had gained entry into the then First Division in front of over 30,000 fans, would now be a fruit and vegetable gondola where plastic people shopped till they dropped, and passion would consist of talk about the price of Granny Smith apples and how exciting the latest TV soap opera was.

And I looked along the lines of faceless robots lining up with their supermarket shopping, and the faces of the fans queuing up outside the Manchester United superstore waiting to get the words CANTONA printed on the back of their Japanese corporate advert. As the colours of the aisles and new shirt designs merged into a nondescript blur, I suddenly realised their faces were all the same. They were the same people.

When suits can make that happen there is only thing left for me to say. The Kop, Shed, Stretford End, Kippax, Shelf and Northbank, Highbury: we've all stood on the terraces.